DATE DUE

DEMCO 38-296

SEXED WORK

SEXED WORK

Gender, Race, and Resistance in a Brooklyn Drug Market

Lisa Maher

CLARENDON PRESS · OXFORD
1997

n Street, Oxford OX2 6DP
rk
ogota Bombay
wn Dar es Salaam
Delhi Florence Hong Kong Istanbul Karachi
Kuala Lumpur Madras Madrid Melbourne
Mexico City Nairobi Paris Singapore
Taipei Tokyo Toronto Warsaw
and associated companies in
Berlin Ibadan

Oxford is a trade mark of Oxford University Press

Published in the United States
by Oxford University Press Inc., New York

British Library Cataloguing in Publication Data
Data available

Library of Congress Cataloging in Publication Data
ISBN 0–19–826495–X

1 3 5 7 9 10 8 6 4 2

Typeset by Hope Services (Abingdon) Ltd.
Printed in Great Britain
on acid-free paper by
Biddles Ltd., Guildford and King's Lynn

for Christie Lee Kable

General Editor's Introduction

Clarendon Studies in Criminology, the successor to *Cambridge Studies in Criminology*, which was founded by Leon Radzinowicz and J. W. C. Turner more than fifty years ago, aims to provide a forum for outstanding work in criminology, criminal justice, penology and the wider field of deviant behaviour. It is edited under the auspices of three criminological centres: the Cambridge Institute of Criminology, the Mannheim Centre for Criminology and Criminal Justice at the London School of Economics, and the Oxford Centre for Criminological Research.

Lisa Maher's outstanding ethnography of the lives of homeless—mostly ethnic minority—women crack cocaine users and sexworkers on the streets of a run-down area of New York is the first book of its kind to appear in the *Series*. *Sexed Work* combines a rich 'appreciative' account of the relationships forged, and the survival strategies employed, by these impoverished women, with a convincing analysis of the structures—economic and social—which constrain the choices open to them. It skilfully reveals and analyses the symbiotic relationship between the attractions of drug use to women on the margins of society, the limitations imposed by gender and racial disadvantage on their ability to successfully compete in the street-level crack market, and the consequent pressure to seek income through one of the few alternative opportunities available—sexwork on the 'stroll'.

This is a remarkable piece of work to emerge from a doctoral dissertation. Dr Maher deserves congratulations for the extraordinary social skills—combined with not a little courage—which enabled her to produce an authentic account of an area of social life which has been tainted by speculation and prejudice. She challenges many assumptions about the impact of crack-cocaine on the sexuality, criminality, and the economic position of these women. They are shown to be far from passive and pathetic victims of a pharmacologically induced lifestyle. The story is one of creative resistant actors: of supportive female networks mediated by racial and ethnic alliances; of sharing drugs to overcome sickness; of searching for safe shelter; of 'viccing' (stealing from) dates; of adopting an aggressive 'bad' or 'mad' pesona as a means of self-defence. But there is no vestige of romanticism in this account. The picture is bleak: dire poverty, exploitation, insecurity, harassment, victimization, aggressive competition, racial discrimination and economic marginalisation.

Dr Maher reveals that involvement in the street drug economy has not, as some have claimed, provided economic emancipation in an equal opportunity market. Far from it. Women, especially African-American women, were at the bottom of the socio-economic hierarchy in the illegal drug market, for similar reasons, Dr Maher argues, that poor ethnic minority women suffer from gender and racial inequality in the formal economy. Dominated and marginalised by men in the drug economy, they have become reliant on sexwork. And here too Lisa Maher's market analysis is revealing. As competition grew from other marginalised female drug users prices for sex fell, cheaper 'rougher dates' were attracted to the area, and the dangers facing these women increased yet further.

As can be gathered from this brief introduction, *Sexed Work* illuminates many subjects. It will be read not only by criminologists and sociologists of deviance interested in the impact of illegal drugs, but by those concerned with issues of gender, race, social inequality, the economy of the workplace, sexual mores, and ethnographic methods.

The editors welcome Lisa Maher's innovative and stimulating study to the *Series*.

Roger Hood
March 1997

Preface and Acknowledgements

I first met Rosa during the summer of 1990. It was not a particularly remarkable day. She did not appear to be a particularly remarkable woman. Central Brooklyn in midsummer. There are better places to be I thought as I watched the emaciated figure scouring the recesses of cracked and buckled concrete. She straightened, revealing a tell-tale swollen belly. Her eyes caught mine—a flash of hostility and an instant warning: Don't mess with me. I hesitated. Moment of truth stuff. Smile or turn away? Grimacing, I gestured to the blunt and blood-stained syringe at my feet. In return, a long quizzical stare as a lifetime of suspicion told her not to yield to a flicker of curiosity. Finally, a verdict: Wassup white girl? We worked together that day— Rosa and I—silent accomplices collecting spent syringes on the streets of Bushwick.

I went home that night with a million questions. What kind of a country was this where bloodied syringes had a commodity value? How had such a task come to be defined as a primary source of income for this woman? Was it only women who did such things? Why didn't she do something else? What were her options? Or was this the lot of women like Rosa—outcast by their drug use and criminalized by their survival—eking out a living on the margins of the drug economy. I wanted to ask her so many things. As the research progressed and I continued to probe the spaces in which Rosa and women like her lived their lives, I became increasingly obsessed with documenting the strategies they used to generate income and began to focus in detail on the street-level drug economy as a site of production, earnings, and expenditure.

My initial interest in women drug users did not stem from any a priori interest in either drug use or economic activity. It was stimulated by the 'monster stories' about women crack users that began to appear in the media during 1988. As a feminist, I was distressed by the way in which these women's lives were represented. As a graduate student, I was curious about the kinds of cultural and socio-legal assumptions that underpinned these moral narratives. I wanted to explore the connections between these 'monster stories' and the 'lived realities' of women drug users, and, in particular, women who smoked crack cocaine. This project, then, was conceived out of a desire to interrogate the cultural templates which organize the way society views women drug users.

My encounters with Rosa, and women like her, produced a quest to understand the gendered and raced nature of survival on the streets. The end result is this book. As it turns out, the women I studied were remarkable in many ways, but perhaps most of all for their resilience, their capacity for the hardest of labours, and the sheer tenacity of their struggles to survive. As Rosa, who has been drug free for almost five years now, wrote in a recent letter: 'I am still working in same place. I don't know, is so much to do and the money is so low you would not believe it. Is so hard. I just doing it to keep my mind occupied from you know what—just doing the right thing and take-caring-business.' For Rosa, who is now (legally) employed taking care of business in an office in Queens, the words in the title of this book continue to have resonance in the context of her 'straight' life and formal sector employment. Indeed, Rosa's life and her ongoing experiences bring the theoretical arguments contained in this book full circle.

The street-level drug economy is not an anomaly. It cannot be understood as a peculiar bastion of racism and male domination; a product of cultural values unique to a particular group, system, or way of life. It does not stand alone, independent of, and isolated from, broader systems of social stratification. The production of inequality within the street-level drug economy mirrors the production of inequality within the labour and income-transfer markets of the formal economy. The division of labour within the drug economy and broader systems of social stratification external to the (illegal) workplace work together to produce and maintain the disadvantaged status of poor and minority women. It is in this sense that the drug economy, no less than the family, the state, and the formal workplace, serves as a site of social and cultural reproduction.

This book has two main aims. First, I want to present the accounts of a group of women we hear much about but little from, and, secondly, I want to use these accounts to develop a theoretical framework for understanding the ways in which gendered and raced cultural narratives structure the organization of illegal work. In doing so, I leave many issues untouched. However, I would be derelict in my obligations to the women who participated in this research were I to remain silent in relation to the continuing epidemic of HIV/AIDS among injecting drug users in the north-eastern United States. I have been forced to confront these issues both in the course of my research and in light of my extra-curricular involvement in needle and syringe exchange programs in Australia and the United States—both legal and illegal. I continue to ask myself, what kind of society condemns its drug users to play microbiological roulette with such lethal equipment? What kind of government jeopardizes the public health of a nation by refusing to act to stop thousands of preventable infections, untold human suffering, and ultimately death on a scale unheard of in the so-called first world?

In New York City, between 40 and 60 per cent of injecting drug users are infected with the HIV virus. In Bushwick, the principal site for this research, one in every 36 people is HIV positive. Most of those infected are injecting drug users, the majority are Latino, and many are women. By 1995 almost 2,000 people had died from AIDS in this neighbourhood alone (Brooklyn AIDS Task Force, 1996). People are dying and they will continue to die. Try telling the families and friends of the now deceased women who were part of this study that they died slow, painful, and needless deaths because needle exchange programs send the 'wrong message'.

The debts incurred in the production of this particular ethnographic text are numerous. Because it is time-consuming and labour-intensive, ethnography requires financial support. The ethnographic research was supported by the award of a Dissertation Fellowship from the Harry Frank Guggenheim Foundation. Preparation of the book manuscript was supported in part by the National Institute on Drug Abuse research grant for the 'Natural History of Crack Distribution/Abuse' (5 RO1 DA05126-09) and by an AIDS-Fogerty International Research Collaborative Award from the National Institutes of Health for 'Heroin Smoking and Injecting and HIV in Brooklyn and Sydney' (5 RO3 DA00562-02). I am particularly grateful to Bruce Johnson at the National Development and Research Institutes in New York and to Karen Colvard at the Guggenheim Foundation for their support of the research. I remain especially indebted to Ernest Drucker and the Department of Epidemiology and Social Medicine at Montefiore Hospital for providing me with a job when I needed it most.

By definition, ethnography makes considerable impositions on the personal and professional worlds of others. I want to thank my parents for loving me wherever I went and whatever I did. I want also to thank Christie Kable who has been an important part of my life for two decades now. As a daughter, she has given more than I expected and much more than I deserved. Many friends and colleagues responded with interest, criticism, and encouragement at various stages of the project. I am grateful to them all and especially to Jenny Bargen, David Brown, Anne Campbell, Jason Ditton, Eloise Dunlap, Jeffrey Fagan, Judy Greene, David Greenhill, Sam Friedman, Anne Healey, Frances Heidensohn, Sally Hillsman, Drew Humphries, Judy Johnston, Bill Kable, Elizabeth Mackay, Alan Neaigus, Nicole Rafter, Dorothy Roberts, Elizabeth Stanko, and David Weisburd. My homegirls in New York deserve a special rap: Marie Adrine lived with me for the bulk of this research, putting up with my hopes, fears and myriad vices; Vanessa Hamid gave generously of herself and allowed her family to become mine; and Dory Dickman, Linda Kelly, and Trini Ross provided me with a reservoir of love, laughter, and great gossip.

Several people have influenced my intellectual development in critical ways. Throughout this research, I was guided by the work of Maureen Cain, whose question 'How is gender constituted in these sites?' (1990: 10) provided a central frame of reference. Andrew von Hirsch supervised this project from its inception, believing in both the project and my ability to do it. As a mentor and dear friend, he has provided wisdom and intellectual guidance, balancing subtle and acute criticism with generous encouragement. I owe a deep and sincere debt to Richard Curtis without whom the research would not have been possible. In addition to serving as a teacher, collaborator, and co-author, Ric provided me with a source of inspiration and example. I have also leaned upon, and borrowed heavily from the thinking of Ansley Hamid, whose intellectual production and critical insight infuses the analysis presented here and the way in which I experience and reflect upon the world more generally. Special thanks are also due to Kathleen Daly who has given unstintingly of her time and energy throughout the course of this project. Her unwavering support, incisive critique, and truly gendered imagination exemplify feminist scholarship and practice.

Transforming a thesis into a book is never easy. I especially want to thank Richard Hart, who saw the potential for a book back in 1991 when I was still writing fieldnotes. I am grateful to my editors at Oxford University Press, Timothy Barton and Elissa Soave, for helping to realize this potential. The demands of productive labour have also meant reconciling the primacy of new ethnographic encounters over old. I wish to thank Wayne Hall at the National Drug and Alcohol Research Centre for providing me with a supportive research environment and the young heroin users I currently work with for providing me with a new set of questions and new challenges. Most importantly, I will always be grateful to my partner David Dixon, for whom 'doing ethnography' remains an excuse for smoking cigarettes, having a mobile phone, and not being able to get out of bed in the morning. Within our household, ethnography also provides a rationale for unexplained loyalties to mysterious others, staying out all night, and gross inequalities in the division of domestic labour. While I was 'taking care of business', David took care of our children. As a colleague, he has always found time to help me and his sense of history, attention to detail, and critical reading of the final draft have strengthened more than this manuscript.

Ultimately however, a 'good' ethnography is dependent both on the skill of its author and the quality of the materials provided by ethnographic informants. I have been truly fortunate concerning the latter and, if this is not always apparent, then fault must be located in relation to the former. I especially want to thank Rosa for her lasting friendship and for allowing me to be part of a most remarkable life; Latisha for being herself and strong enough for all of us; Candy for the times—good and bad—and the best one-liners in the world; Boy for setting me straight even when I didn't get her straight; Rachel for her sharp, sassy, and insightful commentary; Slim for never failing to let me know what time it was; and Esmeralda for sharing her beautiful daughters. These women allowed me into their lives and found a place in mine. It is my sincere hope that the window on their lives opened here endows them with agency, humanity, and grace.

Lisa Maher
New York City
November 1996

Contents

1

Readings of Victimization and Volition

The linkages between contemporary criminological literature on women's involvement in 'crime' and 'deviance' and current research and theory in relation to women drug users are rarely made explicit. There are, however, a number of ways in which these discourses both intersect and overlap. In particular, two distinct readings or interpretations appear to inform the literature. These readings tend to dichotomize agency. The first practically denies women any agency and the second over-endows them with it. In the first, women are portrayed as the passive victims of oppressive social structures, relations and substances, or some combination thereof. Women are cast as submissive objects, serving as mere automata for the reproduction of determining structures. Constituted by and through their status as victims, they are devoid of choice, responsibility, or accountability; fragments of social debris floundering in a theoretical tide of victimage. In the second, women are viewed as active subjects—rational volitional agents seeking to maximize 'deviant' or 'criminal' opportunities in a brave new world devoid of structure, power, and domination. These are the new generation 'new female criminals'; the 90's style 'gangsta bitches' and corporate criminals pushing the boys aside as they carve out a space for themselves in the ''hood', and in the office. Both readings are guilty of over-simplification and both ignore the relationships between broader social, economic, and cultural formations and immediate, specific, and local contexts in structuring the conditions by which women's agency is enacted. This book seeks to problematize these readings by describing and analyzing how structures and relations of gender, race, and class are articulated by, and within, divisions of labour in the street-level drug economy.

Readings of Victimization

Myths about women's passivity and submissiveness—whether 'natural' or socially induced—continue to condition the production of knowledge concerning the motivations for, and nature of, women's involvement in lawbreaking and other 'deviant' conduct. According to Steffensmeier (1983), the 'homosocial reproduction of the criminal underworld' works to exclude women, except from certain limited roles. If women are involved in male crime groups or dyads they generally act as accomplices to males and are usually confined to 'sexual-media' or 'cover' roles. 'The observed dependence of females on males in the underworld stems not only from the socialization of females toward dependence, but from women's lack of strength and muscle to survive or go it alone on the streets' (Steffensmeier, 1983:1015). Although such a reading is far from inevitable, here too women are presented as 'dependent'.

While there is a dearth of research on the gendered dimensions of the drugs/crime nexus,[1] within the general literature on drug use the stereotype of women as passive and dependent clearly persists. Women drug users have been characterized as 'pathetic, passive, psychologically or socially inadequate' (Perry, 1979:1). They are perceived to be 'out of control of their own lives and unfit to be in charge of anyone else's' (Perry, 1987:6). In particular, the literature on initiation is replete with studies which suggest that women are rarely active agents in this process (e.g. Freeland and Campbell, 1973; Waldorf, 1973; Eldred and Washington, 1976; File, 1976; Rosenbaum, 1981a; Hser, Anglin and McGlothlin, 1987; Parker et al., 1988; Blom and van den Berg, 1989). For the most part, women are portrayed as the hapless victims of stronger, more experienced, and, in some cases, 'evil' males.[2] Post initiation, women drug users—and heroin users in particular—have been persistently characterized as unable to support their consumption without a man (e.g. Sutter, 1966; File et al, 1974;

---

[1] This is not to say that there has not been research on the drugs/crime connection which utilizes female samples. However, much of this research has been preoccupied with establishing the temporal sequencing of drug use and crime (e.g. Chambers, 1974; Eldred and Washington, 1976; James, 1976; James et al., 1979; Inciardi et al., 1982; Datesman, 1981; Anglin and Hser, 1987).

[2] The theme of the evil doper seducing women into drug use was a recurrent feature of historical attempts to explain female participation in prostitution (e.g. see Dai, 1937; Lemert, 1951).

Fiddle, 1976; File, 1976; Smithberg and Westermeyer, 1985; Hser et al., 1987; Morningstar and Chitwood, 1987).[3]

Similarly, what we know about drug-related lawbreaking tends to suggest that women are likely to be 'led' (astray) into crime by men. In a study of heroin users in treatment, Covington concluded that 'females passively acquiesce and follow males into crime rather than launching their careers independently in female-dominated peer groups . . . there is no female subculture that supports and reinforces crime among women in a manner parallel to male cultures' (1985:348). Covington also reports that the most 'traditional' women in her study experienced the most arrests, suggesting that women addicts' chances of upward mobility in the underworld are restricted to those that arise out of personal rather than professional relationships (1985:349). Similarly, research by Pettiway draws on a sample of women drug users in New York and Miami to suggest that '[b]eing married or living with a boyfriend or husband is clearly one of the more important elements in establishing the probability of crime group participation' (1987:761).

While there is a paucity of research in relation to women and cocaine, a recent 'popular' book on women and cocaine provides excerpts from interviews with a number of prominent 'experts' in the field of drug research and treatment (Greenleaf, 1989). These quotations[4] suggest that many clinicians, researchers, and treatment professionals continue to view women cocaine users in 'traditional' terms. For the most part, women are seen as victims of a 'dual dependency'—drugs and men. To date there have been few published studies which focus specifically on the lawbreaking activities of women cocaine users. Those that do exist tend to characterize such lawbreaking as either generalist and ungendered insofar as women crack users appear to engage in a wide variety of offence types (Inciardi et al., 1993), or specialist and gendered insofar as opportunities for income generation appear to occur within sex-segmented labour markets (Maher and Curtis, 1992). Not surprisingly, there have been no studies which specifically examine the aetiology of women's crack use

---

[3] Recent research indicates that women drug users may be more independent in providing for their drug use than has previously been thought (e.g. Anglin and Hser, 1987; Taylor, 1993; Maher, 1995b). Some studies also suggest that Black women are less likely to be passive partners in either heroin use or criminal activity and less likely than white women to be taken care of by male partners (e.g. Rosenbaum, 1981; Pettiway, 1987).

[4] See for example the quotations on pages 7, 21, and 22 in Greenleaf (1989).

and current lawbreaking within the context of childhood experiences of victimization.

However, a growing body of literature confirms the existence of a strong correlation between abuse and neglect in childhood and adult lawbreaking (e.g. Widom, 1989; 1990). Widom's research found significant gender differences in patterns of adult lawbreaking with abused and neglected males evidencing substantially higher rates of arrest for violent crimes than a matched group of controls, while women were at increased risk of committing property and drug offences (Widom, 1989). Research also suggests that survivors of sexual violence are over-represented among populations of incarcerated women.[5] The observation of a correlation between women's early experiences of victimization and lawbreaking, including drug use, has led some researchers to posit a causal relationship. In a study of 50 Black women imprisoned in New York City, Arnold proposes a trajectory from gender victimization to imprisonment in accounting for Black women's criminalization. Drug use plays a prominent role in this process whereby young Black women respond to or resist their victimization, both in terms of 'dulling the pain' and in providing a 'pseudo-family' (Arnold, 1990). Similarly, Miller's study of Milwaukee 'street women' suggests that,

[sexual abuse] is a much more important factor in patterns of running away and drug use and, thus, in recruitment to deviant street networks than is generally acknowledged. It is also my belief that the experience of emotional distancing during sexual contact that incest victims often describe is too like the psychological state described by prostitutes when they are servicing a trick for one not to be a sort of rehearsal for the other. In those cases, sexual exploitation on the street seems but an extension of sexual exploitation in the family (1986:115).

---

[5] Recent statistics indicate that 41 per cent of women in prison in the United States have been either physically or sexually abused, with an estimated 22 per cent sexually abused before the age of 18. Women convicted of violent offences were more likely than other women to report prior physical or sexual abuse (49 per cent) and more likely to be serving a sentence for violence committed against a relative or intimate (37 per cent). Thirty per cent of women convicted of drug offences reported prior physical or sexual abuse (Bureau of Justice Statistics, 1991). Qualitative research indicates that physical and sexual abuse may be even more common among this population. Gilfus (1988) reports that 88 per cent of her sample of women in prison had experienced at least one of the following: childhood physical abuse, childhood sexual abuse, adult rape, and domestic violence (see also Chesney-Lind and Rodriguez, 1983; Gilfus, 1992; Easteal, 1994).

However, feminist accounts often lean towards an uncritical acceptance of this linkage as direct and unmediated. This is evident in unreflexive claims such as, '[s]ubstance abuse has repeatedly been found to be one of the major long term psychological effects of childhood sexual abuse' (Gilfus, 1992:80). Here, the unfortunate use of 'effect' is compounded by the use of the adjective 'psychological'. Drug use—a social process which encompasses a range of diverse patterns and activities, including consumer behaviour for example—cannot simply be reduced to the status of a 'psychological effect' (cf. Zinberg, 1984; Hamid, forthcoming).

While, within criminology, feminists have focused on the role of victimization in precipitating women's lawbreaking or 'criminalizing survival' (Chesney-Lind and Rodriguez, 1983; Miller, 1986; Arnold, 1990; Chesney-Lind and Sheldon, 1992),[6] drug researchers have typically sought to draw attention to the role of victimization, and, in particular, childhood sexual abuse, in the context of dual diagnosis (drug abuse and psychiatric disorders), treatment, and the cessation of use (Hussey and Petchers, 1989; Young, 1990; Hurley, 1991). For the most part, drug studies have ignored the role of victimization in the aetiology of women's drug use and drug-related lawbreaking. A powerful exception, of course, has been the drug use as 'self-medication' hypothesis which basically asserts that women use drugs as a coping mechanism in order to deal with situational and/or psychological problems and stresses (e.g. Suffet and Brotman, 1976; Hser, Anglin, and Booth, 1987; Mondanaro, 1989; Reed, 1991).[7] Feminist interpretations of this thesis have sought to draw attention to the way in which these factors relate to the general lot of women in society.

The legacy of growing up female in a society that undervalues and denigrates the role of women is a low sense of self-esteem, high levels of depression and anxiety, and a sense of powerlessness. Learned helplessness is another result of the daily confrontation with the dominant culture . . . All these

[6] According to Chesney-Lind and Rodriguez, 'young girls faced with violence and/or sexual abuse at home . . . become criminalized by their efforts to save themselves (by running away) from the abuse' (1983:62).

[7] Moreover, as Inciardi et al. (1993) have noted, if women are attracted to drug use as a means of self-medication, (especially those seeking to escape painful realities such as victimization), then (given its pharmacological properties and psycho-social effects) cocaine is an unlikely candidate as the drug of choice. Indeed, the 'blocking' or relieving qualities attributed to heroin would appear to render it eminently more suitable (A. Taylor, 1993).

characteristics act in concert to immobilize many chemically dependent women (Mondanaro, 1989:2-3).

In its more extreme variants, this thesis insists that '[d]ependency is an integral part of women's daily lives, use of substances is only the outward sign of it' (Merfert-Diete and Soltai, 1984, cited in Oppenheimer, 1989:186). Women's drug use is implicated as further evidence of the seamless web of patriarchy: 'Through substance use, women temporarily lift the weight of a hostile world which separates them from their *real female selves*' (Ettore, 1992:156; emphasis added). Similarly, other commentators have suggested that some women with drinking problems, rather than being characterized as alcoholics, are more accurately described as exhibiting 'patriarchal defiance syndrome' (Blume, 1990).

Presenting drug use by women as self-medication provides a convenient rubric for a plethora of problems, among them the victimization and abuse of women. Research suggests that as many as 75 per cent of women in treatment for alcohol and other drug problems may have been victims of physical and sexual abuse (e.g. see Miller et al., 1987; Russell et al., 1988; Mondanaro, 1989; Harrison, 1989; Hurley, 1991; Reed, 1991).[8] These rates tend to be considerably lower in community studies comparing abused and non-abused women (Russell et al., 1988). However, not unlike criminological research, drug research which focuses on the relationship between substance use and victimization often fails to acknowledge or 'control for' other variables—such as socio-economic status, family composition, family history of drug use or environmental proximity to drugs—all of which may attenuate or exacerbate the likelihood of drug use. Although there have been few empirically sound studies that address the causal consequences of childhood sexual abuse for women, researchers suggest that, '[i]n all likelihood, a vicious cycle exists in which painful consequences of childhood sexual abuse—such as depression, low self-esteem, conflicted relationships and sexual dysfunction—increase a woman's risk of self-medicative use of alcohol and other drugs' (Russell and Wilsnack, 1991:67).

Clinicians are even less reluctant to attribute causality. For example, Greenleaf quotes cocaine treatment expert Arnold Washton as

---

[8] It is important to note that much of this variation is the product both of different definitions of childhood sexual abuse and differences in methodological approaches, including sensitivity to childhood sexual abuse, sample representativeness, and sample size.

saying that '[b]eing the victim of chemically dependent or sexually abusive parents all but guarantees that a woman will become an addict' (1989:11). Despite the absence of research evidence indicating a direct causal link between childhood sexual abuse and substance use, service providers are often insistent that 'one causes the other' and develop their programs accordingly (Hamilton, 1993:363). Moreover, while the combination of familial drug use and childhood sexual victimization may serve to predispose some women to drug use, current estimates suggest that these variables may over-predict women's illicit drug use. Although there have been no national probability surveys on childhood sexual abuse in the United States, prevalence estimates obtained from surveys of specific communities or geographic regions suggest that between five and 62 per cent of women have been sexually abused as children (Russell, 1986). If current prevalence estimates (using the more conservative definition of sexual abuse) are correct in suggesting that well over one third of women have experienced sexual abuse by the age of 18 (Russell and Wilsnack, 1991:62),[9] the extent of women's drug use and criminality in the United States would appear to have been seriously underestimated.

The identification of predictor variables also tells us little about the process and negotiations involved in becoming and being a drug user or a lawbreaker. Our ignorance in relation to the contents of the 'black box' (Daly, 1992) between women's experiences of victimization and subsequent lawbreaking means that not only is agency discounted, but that there is little room for the role that other kinds of structures and relationships may have in facilitating women's drug use. Within the context of drug research, women's experiences of victimization have largely been examined in relation to treatment and, to a lesser extent, the aetiology of use (e.g. see Hagan, 1988). While the potential connections between victimization and drug-related lawbreaking by women remain largely unexplored, the emerging overlap between female populations studied by criminologists and those studied by drug researchers suggests that studies of women drug users will increasingly both inform, and be informed by, criminological discourse.

[9] Utilizing broader definitions of abuse which included behaviours not involving physical contact, Russell (1983) found that 54 per cent of women in the United States had been sexually abused by the age of 18 and Wyatt (1985) found 62 per cent of women had been similarly abused.

Within criminology, the concept of 'blurred boundaries' between criminalization and victimization in relation to women lawbreakers (e.g. Gilfus, 1992; Maher and Curtis, 1992) represents a potential challenge to the dominant feminist discourse on victimization. Feminist criminological accounts have tended to suggest that victimization is exclusive to women. While girls are clearly more vulnerable to child sexual abuse than boys (Finkelhor and Baron, 1986; Sedlak, 1991a, 1991b) and women more vulnerable than men (Brownmiller, 1975), this focus has resulted in a 'gender-based overlay on victimization and criminalization' whereby only men seem capable of committing crime and only women seem capable of being victimized (Daly, 1992:49). Moreover, the victimization-criminalization thesis raises problems in terms of theorizing women's lawbreaking.

[B]y joining victimization and criminalization, feminist scholars avoid core questions about the conceptual status of 'crime offender' and 'crime victim'. For example, how should feminist scholars represent women who abuse, harm or hurt others? Or women who steal from others? . . . These questions are difficult to contemplate because feminist work in crime and justice has focused almost exclusively on women's legal status and experiences as victims. . . . But where does victimization end and responsibility for acts that harm others begin? How do we characterize women when they do things that are wrong? (Daly, 1992:48).

These boundaries may be blurred for both women and men, but in gender-specific ways. Grounding the theorization of women's lawbreaking solely or even primarily in terms of women's victimization—regardless of whether the victimization at issue is characterized as structural, relational or pharmacological—leaves little room for women's agency. This is particularly apparent in relation to drug research, where the notion of 'crack-pipe-as-pimp' (Ratner, 1993a) exemplifies the denial of agency to women drug users. As an explanation of why women engage in particular behaviours, including lawbreaking and high risk sexual practices, the 'crack-pipe-as-pimp' thesis overdetermines women crack users by positioning them as victims of pharmacology.

The literature in relation to women and crack cocaine is replete with observations that women crack users 'are capable of doing anything for a "blast" of crack' (Anderson, 1990:89). The reference to female sexuality, implicit in such observations, is determined by pharmacology and the 'anything' that these women will reportedly do is inevitably sexualized. Overdetermined by their 'dependence', women crack users who engage in high risk sexual practices are readily positioned as vectors of moral contamination, drug use, and AIDS. For example, in examining sex-for-crack exchanges, Koester and Schwartz have observed that, for the most part, these exchanges are determined by the 'addictive nature of the drug' (1993:192). Although these researchers acknowledge the marginal status of women in the drug economy, their attempt to explain why the women they studied did not seek alternative means of income generation relies heavily on the pharmacological properties of crack.

[Crack's] effects are short-lived, and the desire for more is immediate. Once a user is 'sprung' the compulsion to continue using is overpowering . . . Sex for crack most often occurs while the woman is craving the drug and in a situation where she has little, if any, control (Koester and Schwartz, 1993:194–5).

As victims of crack's pharmacology, these women are incapable of 'taking care of business' or indeed, one suspects, of any intentional activity (see also Allen, 1987).

Pharmacology is also central to several accounts which provide glimpses of women's participation in the drug economy. While Anderson has argued that hapless women crack users are used by drug dealers in order to ensnare 'unsuspecting' or 'weak' men into addiction (1990:89),[10] the notion of the 'drug-dealer-as-pimp' (e.g. see Morningstar and Chitwood, 1987; Goldstein et al., 1992:360) truly denies the agency of women drug users.

[O]n the ghetto street a new pimp emerges. Unlike the traditional pimp, who might wine and dine and 'sweet talk' the girls to get them to 'turn tricks' and at times used physical violence to force them to continue in prostitution, a new style of coercion has developed . . . drugs are more centrally involved in social control. In behaving as a type of pimp, the dealer may get the young woman to try the highly addictive crack, then encourage her to prostitute herself to get more, sending her out on the streets in this manner (Anderson, 1990:88).

The claim that street-level drug dealers deliberately set out to get women 'addicted' in order to guarantee market demand for their product belies the reality that many street-level sellers, particularly those in low-income minority neighbourhoods, are users themselves.

[10] The theme of 'innocent' men being corrupted or enticed into drug use by 'women of the underworld' is hardly new (e.g. see Stanley, 1918, cited in Morgan, 1974:83).

Moreover, as employees—particularly within the context of the vertically organized crack businesses which dominate the market in New York City and many other large urban centres (Johnson et al., 1992)—street-level sellers exercise little autonomy and are rarely involved in profit sharing. For the most part, street-level dealers neither have the need to create additional consumer demand, nor do they perceive their employment in terms of economic rationality or long term planning.

My research finds that while street-level drug dealers participate in the sexual degradation of women, they possess neither the autonomy, power nor inclination to 'entrap' women into drug use or an ongoing market relationship. This is not to deny the existence of a range of situations in which men appear to have gained more direct social control over women involved in the street-level crack scene, including contexts of domestic or intimate relations, sexworker-client transactions, and dealings with male drug users, dealers and 'house men'. However, within this context, although crack has clearly prompted shifts in gender relations, pimps have neither been replaced nor merely reproduced in another form by street-level drug dealers (cf. J. Miller, 1993:24). Indeed, to view shifting gender relations as the simple outcome of a substitution process whereby one oppressor replaces another—either crack the substance or its human agents in the form of drug dealers replacing the pimp—implies a search for a monolithic oppressor.

The 'absence of agency', which Allen (1987) has suggested characterizes the depiction of women's lawbreaking in social enquiry reports and official court documents, is apparent in both popular and academic accounts of women's drug use and related lawbreaking. However, as Allen has noted in relation to social enquiry reports,

it is not simply in relation to *crimes* that there appears a reluctance to describe these subjects as intentional and active: there appears a striking paucity of references to these women doing anything intentional *at all*. . . . There is a conspicuous concern with the women's emotional responses to the material events of their lives, but little expectation that they will normally be the active authors of these events—and every readiness to conclude that they are *not* (1987:90; emphases in original).

That this reluctance is equally apparent on the part of feminist researchers and writers is also clear. Although feminist analyses are more likely to refer to social and economic constraints and the role of childhood victimization and abusive domestic relationships and less likely to resort to explanations involving pharmacology, in the final analysis, most feminist research on substance use is pre-empted by a dual discourse of victimization/dependence. Indeed, the positioning of women as victims constitutes an enduring stumbling block for feminist theory. The dangers of essentialism inherent in the concept of women's victimage and the ensuing silence in relation to their agency and responsibility are 'structural characteristics' of feminist discourse more generally (Allen, 1987).

This well-intentioned perspective inevitably raises ethical dilemmas in relation to women who cannot be made to fit the victim/dependent mould. While women lawbreakers and drug users and the activities in which they are involved often present an unflattering and sometimes distressing picture, the tendency to relocate them within a familiar and sympathetic discourse of victimization may preclude a broader examination of their condition. It may also serve to harm them. This is particularly apparent in relation to sexworkers, where '[t]he social depiction of all prostitutes as victims and sex slaves not only obscures the myriad contexts and experiences of sex work, but more hazardously, exacerbates the dangers of assault . . . portraying all sex workers as victims only encourages attacks on them' (McClintock, 1993:8).

Economic marginalization, coupled with labour market sex segmentation and racial/ethnic discrimination, is conducive to the exploitation and degradation of women in the drug economy. However, in order to understand women's lawbreaking in this context, we need to move beyond mechanistic models of victimization and criminalization and the familiar discourses of external agents controlling women's behaviour.

Readings of Volition

The closer we look at women who are making their way in a man's world, the more they look like men in their profile of physical diseases, their psychological configurations, their criminal deviancies and their addictive patterns (Adler, 1975:132).

An increasing number of commentators, including several highly respected drug researchers, have begun to interpret the presence of women on the streets—in and around drug markets and as drug users—as evidence of increased opportunities for female participation in the drug economy. This thesis appears to have two principal strands. One is the apparently straightforward argument that the presence of women as crack users and drug market participants reflects the emancipation of women in the wider society (Bourgois, 1989, 1995; Bourgois and Dunlap, 1993; C. Taylor, 1993; Wilson, 1993). The second strand argues that the expansion of the drug economy and/or recent shifts in the gender composition of street networks have resulted in a proliferation of opportunities for women in the drug business (Baskin, Sommers and Fagan, 1993; Fagan, 1994, 1995; Mieczkowski, 1994). As Fagan has argued in an important article, 'changes in drugs and drug markets made possible new avenues and contexts for women to participate in drug use and selling' (1994:187).

Both these strands are undergirded by the assumption that male and female patterns of lawbreaking and drug use are converging. This hypothesis is a relatively recent addition to the drug literature,[11] although it is familiar in criminological circles where, known as the 'emancipation' or 'opportunity' thesis (e.g. Adler, 1975; Simon, 1975),[12] it has been largely discredited. As Smart noted in the mid-1970s, the hypothesis of a direct and causal relationship between women's 'emancipation' and female crime represents 'a new phase in the traditional search to locate a monocausal factor to account for female criminality' (1976:75). Despite the fact that attempts to establish causal links between women's 'emancipation' and deviant conduct are notoriously problematic,[13] convergence theorizing appears to be alive and well in the context of drug research. According to Phillipe Bourgois,

[g]reater female involvement in crack reflects in a rather straightforward manner the growing emancipation of women throughout all aspects of inner-city life, culture and economy. Women—especially the emerging generation,

[11] However, it has often been alluded to in some form. For example, Suffet and Brotman note that '[t]o the extent that women gain social equality with men and subscribe to greater personal lifestyle freedom, they may be expected to show a higher rate of illicit drug use' (1976:20).

[12] The argument suggests that increases in female criminality reflect women's increased participation in occupational and social life—in short, their 'emancipated' status. Although Adler's chapter on women and drugs actually says very little about women's drug use, she claims that '[i]t is ironic, although not unexpected, that modern women in assuming the mantle of male power have also become vulnerable to the infirmities of male vice . . . More and more, the temptation is to retreat from the impasse by turning to drugs and other deviant behaviors' (1975:128, 30).

[13] For critiques of this thesis see Smart, 1976, 1979; Crites, 1976; Chapman, 1980; Steffensmeier, 1980, 1983; Box and Hale, 1983; Chesney-Lind and Rodriguez, 1983; Chesney-Lind, 1986; Messerschmidt, 1986; Naffine, 1987.

which is most at risk for crack addiction—are no longer obliged to stay at home and maintain the family as they were a generation ago. They no longer so readily sacrifice public life or forgo independent opportunities to generate personally disposable income. . . . To a certain extent, the emancipation of women has taken place at a faster rate on inner city streets than it has in middle-class suburbs (Bourgois, 1989:643–4).

The crack culture merely provides a 'concrete expression' of 'the growing emancipation of women that is taking place throughout all aspects of American culture' (Bourgois and Dunlap, 1993:122; see also C. Taylor, 1993). Although Bourgois ultimately attenuates his claim that these women are in fact 'emancipated' by acknowledging the role of the crack economy in exacerbating the 'oppression and ideological domination' of women (1989:643),[14] his analysis remains troubling. To the extent that his research attempts to 'do gender', it fails to elaborate the nature of women's participation in the drug economy and the ways in which their gendered status structures this participation. This is presumably information to which, if regarded as worthy of note at all, Bourgois had access. Moreover, the theoretical construct which underpins this work is seriously compromised by the failure to analyze and incorporate gender within the overall framework of 'conjugated oppression' (Bourgois, 1989).[15] In a related effort to explain the gendered forms of violence in the crack economy, Bourgois and Dunlap argue that,

[o]ne way of interpreting the virulence with which many men abuse vulnerable women in the crack scene is as a frustrated attempt by traditional patriarchally oriented men to stave off the challenge to gender roles posed by the growing public presence of addicted women. In short, men on the street are not accepting the new roles that women are attempting to carve out for themselves in the world of substance abuse. Instead males are lashing out at females, and they are desperately striving to reimpose violently the gender order of the previous generation. According to their repressive patriarchal logic, submitting a woman, or even a teenage girl, to violent sex or a gang rape is justifiable since 'she wasn't acting like a lady' (1993:125).

[14] For example, Bourgois notes that '[c]ontradictorily, therefore, the underlying process of emancipation that has enabled women to demand equal participation in street culture and to carve out an expanded niche for themselves in the underground economy has led to a greater depreciation of women as sex objects' (1989:645).

[15] Conjugated oppression is defined as the 'conflation of ethnic discrimination with . . . an economic dynamic of class exploitation to produce an overwhelming experience of oppression which is more than the sum of the parts' (Bourgois, 1989:641).

This account suggests that the 'backlash' against feminism has filtered through to the street-level drug culture where it gains expression in violence against women. Implicit is a desire to comprehend the perceived threat to 'hegemonic masculinity' presented by women crack users. The validity of this argument is ultimately contingent on the degree to which one accepts that women crack users have challenged traditional gender roles and that patriarchal gender relations have been undermined as a result. While Bourgois' (male) informants may perceive this to be the case, accepting such perceptions at face value may misrepresent not only the position of women in the drug economy but the position of women more generally, and that of minority women in particular. A variant of the old 'she asked for it' theme, the notion of a male backlash is neither unique to gender relations in the crack economy, nor does it provide an accurate representation of all such relations.

The second strand of the convergence thesis takes up the slack in Bourgois' original argument. Bourgois and Dunlap effectively retreat from more extreme claims when they argue that, in the final analysis, 'traditional gender relations still largely govern the street's underground economy' (1993:123). This acknowledgement effectively undermines both the perceptions of their informants and the logic of their argument. Their field observations lead Bourgois and Dunlap to admit that selling or dealing opportunities are rarely offered to women and that women are forced to rely on prostitution as an income source (1993:123; see also Bourgois, 1989).

However, others have argued that, in the context of low-income minority communities, traditional gender relations themselves may be criminogenic. Based on an increase in the proportion of female arrests for drug offences from 10.95 per cent in 1980 to 20.34 per cent in 1989 (cf. 21.1 per cent to 32.67 per cent for males over the same period), Wilson suggests that within the 'underclass', 'women have moved readily into drug dealing' (1993:183). In contrast to the other approaches presented here, Wilson argues that it is (minority) women's very domesticity which is criminogenic insofar as it both undergirds their own participation and facilitates that of 'the men of the ghetto': 'the mesh between women's provision of a home base and their lack of mobility and men's lack of a home base but high mobility may be a combination that works well for a sexually integrated drug network' (1993:188). While Wilson acknowledges that women remain excluded from male-dominated networks of 'subcultural theft', she speculates that

[i]t is much easier for drug networks than for theft networks to employ women as well as men, for some aspects of the work lend themselves to the services a woman might provide to the dealing enterprise *just because* she often maintains a stable base in the home, from which, because of child-care responsibilities, she does not range far. Women can provide (a) a place to conduct business, (b) credit (e.g. cash, loans), and (c) communication facilities (a telephone can provide a way to receive and relay messages). . . . What women provide is stability, be they welfare women or other housewives (1993:186–7; emphasis in original).

Wilson insists that 'underclass' women 'can be more easily integrated' into drug distribution networks which follow 'established patterns of normal crime networks, which feature men on the streets in sales and women working, even at drug sales, much closer to home base and in conjunction with the men to whom they are tied' (1993:190). Ironically, it is Wilson's very focus on these women as immersed in traditional gender relations where 'homework is their first priority' (1993:187) which undermines her claim that increased arrests of women for (unspecified) drug offences reflect an 'equal opportunity crime'.

A more convincing thesis has been put forward by other researchers who suggest that the rapid expansion in street-level drug markets prompted by the advent of crack has made it possible for women to make inroads into the drug economy.

While women were consigned secondary, gender-specific roles in these [drug] businesses in the past, the size and seemingly frantic activity of the current drug markets has made possible for women new ways to participate in street networks. Their involvement in drug selling at high income levels defies the gendered norms and roles of the past, where drug dealing was an incidental income source often mediated by domestic partnerships . . . the expansion of drug markets in the cocaine economy has provided new ways for women to escape their limited roles, statuses and incomes in previous eras (Fagan, 1994:210).

Here, the purported elevation of women within the drug economy is attributed to the weakening of male-dominated street networks and market processes (see also Fagan, 1995). This theme can also be seen in the writings of Baskin et al. (1993) who, in asserting a 'new dynamics of crime where gender is a far less salient factor' (1993:417), argue that 'the high incidence of incarceration and homicide among young, inner city' minority males, in the wake of expanded demand for drugs, has provided an opportunity structure for female entry into the informal drug economy' (1993:410–11). A similar logic is reflected in the work of Mieczkowski whose generic focus on entrepreneurial markets as 'highly resistant to control and restriction of entry' (1994:233) leads him to conclude that '[f]emale participation in crack sales represents one aspect of opportunity realization' (1994:233).

Such approaches are united insofar as they all view increased opportunities for women as a corollary of the expansion of this particular (illegal) market despite the many instances where expanded markets (for both legal and illegal commodities) have not been accompanied by the proliferation of opportunities for minority groups and, in particular, for women. The claim that '[t]he decentralization and deregulation of drug selling removed many of the gender barriers to drug selling' (Fagan, 1994:188) belies the existence of highly structured drug markets where male kinship and ethnic ties perform important gate-keeping functions (Waterston, 1993; Maher and Daly, 1996). Claims such as these also rest heavily on the assumption that structural changes have in effect produced changes in the gender composition of street networks. This assumption is informed by an unproblematic acceptance that the demise of men as guardians of social control and as economic role models in the inner city (Anderson, 1990) has been accompanied by a similar erosion of the prestige and authority of female 'old heads'. Indeed, the demise of female 'old heads' is purportedly evident in the emergence of new female role models who, in promoting 'the high life, buying fancy clothes, jewelry, drugs and alcohol' (Fagan, 1994:185), reject the values of hard work and family life subscribed to by previous generations of minority women (see also Lee, 1991).

However, empirical support for the proposed causal linkages between the recent expansion in the drug economy, the weakening of males in street networks, the demise of traditional female role models, the changed status of women, and increased opportunities for female participation in drug distribution and sales is at best weak. As Austin has noted,

[w]ith the ascendancy of crack, the lot of black women who engage in deviant activity has taken a turn for the worse . . . [C]rack usage has driven more black women into lawbreaking, particularly prostitution . . . There has been a decline in the collective and cooperative enterprises associated with networks (which would normally provide women with some protection from violence and exploitation) and a reduction in the remuneration the women receive for their [sexwork] activities (1992:1794).

Ethnographic research suggests that while crack has clearly prompted shifts in the gender regimes which structure social and economic life in and around street-level drug and sex markets, these shifts have not necessarily strengthened the position of women (Maher and Curtis, 1992; J. Miller, 1993; Maher et al., 1996). Where women are represented among populations involved in crack distribution, they tend to be concentrated in secondary roles and/or low-level distribution activities (e.g. Dunlap et al., in press). Indeed, the street-level drug markets studied here provide little in the way of support for either growing female participation or a concurrent breakdown in the hegemonic masculinity of drug markets. Continuity, rather than change, is the story from the streets (Maher and Daly, 1996).

Conclusion

This introductory chapter has sought to problematize the dualism by which women lawbreakers/drug users have been represented as victims (traditional, passive, and dependent) or, alternatively, as volitional (emancipated, rational, and independent). By drawing attention to the ways in which the literature has tended to view women drug users as helpless victims of oppressive substances and/or abusive relations, or as autonomous and volitional maximizers of self-interest, this chapter also raises a number of issues identified as problems of representation in relation to criminalized women. These representational problems, although integral to the production of knowledge in relation to women's lawbreaking and 'deviant' conduct, 'pose knotty, vexing, and contentious questions for feminists' (Daly, 1992:17). As Pat Carlen noted of the 'criminal women' she studied,

[t]he persistence of their nuisances, the violence of their resistances and the audacity of their insouciance before the authorities had gradually marked them, their actions and their files with a criminality that must eventually defy the best jurisprudential attempts to represent them as victims. Nor would they wish to be so represented (1992:12).

While the growing acknowledgement of volition in studies of women's lawbreaking may represent 'a healthy counterbalance to the excessively passive image of women in earlier criminological theories' (Erikson and Watson, 1990:269), patterns of lawbreaking and drug use continue to be sharply differentiated by gender. Moreover, as we have seen, attempts to refute the labelling of women as passive objects by depicting them as active subjects often side-step questions of subordination. As Judith Okely demonstrates in her re-examination of Phyllis Kaberry's pioneering study of Aboriginal women, there is a tendency for analyses of gender relations to conflate 'lack of subservience with absence of subordination' (1996:211). This conflation remains apparent in contemporary studies of gender relations: 'In East Harlem, daughters, sisters, and wives can no longer be beaten submissively and sent upstairs as authoritatively as they were in the past for socializing on the street, or for pursuing careers in the underground economy' (Bourgois, 1995:213). The problem is that activity is confused with equality and presence is read as participation. Again, to quote Bourgois, 'Women on the street, however, are not paralyzed by terror. On the contrary, they are in the midst of carving greater autonomy and rights for themselves' (1995:213).

Part of this problem stems from the fact that such readings are culture-bound: 'The danger is that the Western observer, imbued with an ideology which associates the feminine with passivity, is so astonished at finding individual women elsewhere to be self-possessed that she or he confuses individual agency with Western notions of equality and freedom' (Okely, 1996:211). As this book will demonstrate, the same can be said of the white middle class observer studying domestic cultural formations and, in particular, gender relations in inner-city street cultures. The texts which result are frequently misread as evidence of 'gender complimentarity' implying an equivalence between men and women in terms of power and control (Okely, 1996:230). Rather than providing proof of equality, such readings may serve to submerge, and divert attention away from, issues of structure, power, and domination.

The lawbreaking or income generating activities of women drug users are clearly situated within the context of shifting and, in some instances, severely ruptured social, economic, and cultural relations, processes, and discourses. However, little attention has focused on rendering accessible the discrete and localized contexts through and by which these actions and behaviours are given meaning. Within these contexts, while they may be simultaneously situated both as victims and victimizers,[16] as criminals and criminalized, the women drug

[16] Slightly more than one third (38 per cent) of the women whom I studied grew up in households where they were subjected to physical violence. The sources of this

users in this study defy representation as either passive victims or volitional criminals. As the following chapters seek to illustrate, within the context of the street-level drug and sex markets studied here, women perceive themselves neither as powerless victims nor as emancipated and independent, nor—as their own accounts demonstrate—are they without agency and recourse to innovative forms of resistance.[17] While their narratives contain many of the predictable tropes of poverty, racism, sexism, and violence, these women emerge from their potential victimhood as creative and resilient actors struggling to confront, challenge, and continually re-make the structures which constrain them.

At the same time, their experiences provide a strong counter to the romantic notion of the informal drug economy as the ultimate 'equal opportunity employer' (Bourgois, 1989:630)—as an alternative set of markets free from sexism, racism, and classism. My analysis of the economic lives of women drug users draws attention to the deficits of subcultural theories of crime which posit criminal subcultures as an alternative status hierarchy for the lower class (e.g. Cohen, 1955; Cloward and Ohlin, 1960). It contradicts the conventional wisdom—shaped for the most part by studies of the labour market experiences of minority males in both the formal and informal sectors—that the drug economy functions as a compensatory mechanism. Rather, these women and their lawbreaking activities are situated by social relations and structural processes that permeate both legal and illegal labour markets. The following chapters will attempt to demonstrate how occupational hierarchies within the drug economy serve to reproduce the gender, race, and class relations that structure social relations at a more general level. It is in this sense that the drug economy operates as a site of social and cultural reproduction.

violence were step-fathers, mother's boyfriends and biological parents. Five women (11 per cent) reported having been sexually abused as a child (defined as physical sexual contact); three of these women also came from violent households. In total, 19 women (42 per cent) were victimized by family members while growing up. As adults, 29 women (64 per cent) had been in a physically abusive relationship with a man.

[17] However, as Simone has pointed out in relation to young people of colour, the very existence of the victim label and the resistance it provokes may serve to exacerbate victimage: 'by announcing their intention to victimize . . . [they] attempt to recoup their own status as victims . . . They demand to be viewed as the hunters and "savages" that the general population, preoccupied with crime and safety, is more than willing to see them as' (1989:159–60). Such forms of resistance may ultimately serve to reinscribe behaviour as the cause, rather than a symptom, of marginalization (Austin, 1992:1780).

2

Taking it to the Street

It's magnetic, it seem like once you come here, it's hard to leave. (Princess)

This chapter is about context. It provides an introduction to the neighbourhood, the women who participated in the research, and the complex social relations that constitute street life in the study site. It attempts to give the reader a sense of the settings in which women use drugs, generate income, and seek to avoid the risks of violence and victimization which shape their everyday existence. The first section maps the complex geography of a neighbourhood steeped in the drug culture, and a borderland where the boundaries of legality are continually breached. The second section provides a composite vision of the lives which constitute this work, revealing a group of women whose options have been severely circumscribed, not only by drug use, but by poverty, racism, violence, and enduring marginality. The third section, in describing street life and social networks, touches upon many issues, which, it will be shown, are central to understanding the economic lives of women drug users and to assessing their positioning within the street-level drug economy.

The Neighbourhood

Someone once described Bushwick to me as a neighbourhood past its use-by date—a place where tombstones have been displaced by elaborate brick wall mesas paying homage to the casualties of the drug trade. This is 'The Well'—a squalid stretch of Troutman Street between Knickerbocker and Irving Avenues where drugs rule and just about everyone plays. In a world of relentless poverty and a resounding lack of opportunity, the attractions of the drug economy are apparent. The promise of respite and the potential for remuneration constitute a double-edged holy grail of chemical relief and financial reward. Home to Brooklyn's busiest and 'baddest' drug bazaar and an epicentre of AIDS infection, copping a bag of dope or a vial of crack is as easy as buying a loaf of bread or a carton of milk.

In summer, Bushwick is a pastiche of sensory awareness. When the mercury rises, the neighbourhood is cloaked in the sweet and unmistakable stench of ripe garbage. A steady stream of salsa pulses from the bodegas, ruptured by the occasional burst of rap from a passing car. Drug sellers adorn the stoops and children compete with their customers for space on congested sidewalks. Dealers' lookouts and watchful parents keep an eye on proceedings from wooden frame windows. The banter of childhood is punctuated by dealers calling out brand names that reek of death—*Fatal Attraction*, *Body Bag*, *Homicide*, and *DOA*. Mothers and fathers, aunts and uncles, sisters and brothers pound the sweltering pavements, threading their way through a milieu of drug users, criminals, and assorted street people. Bushwick is a vibrant oxymoron—a neighbourhood where drugs are both a way of life and a way of death.

The curbside distribution and consumption of crack cocaine has been overwhelmingly concentrated in low-income minority neighbourhoods like Bushwick. Despite the media's predilection for attributing a range of social ills to crack, many of these neighbourhoods experienced a massive exodus of human and economic capital over the past two decades. According to Fagan, '[c]rack is both a unique phenomenon and a paradigm for the problems of urban areas. The themes of violence, social trauma and economic marginality are inextricably combined in the processes of crack use and selling' (1989:532). However, just as the effects of economic and social decline vary widely at the neighbourhood level, so too the effects of 'crack' must be carefully differentiated. The manner and extent to which the various 'substrata' of the crack economy are formed and the nature of their involvement in 'criminal or deviant lifestyles' varies widely across regions, between neighbourhoods and 'even between genders', attesting to the 'agency of a plurality of factors' (Hamid, 1991c:833).

By 1988, the phase of curbside distribution and consumption of crack had peaked. With a decline in the overall number of users and the failure of crack to attract new initiates, many previously flourishing drug markets began to contract. In New York City, both market and non-market factors served as catalysts for a city-wide process of shrinkage and consolidation in street-level drug markets (Curtis, 1996). This shrinkage 'led many hard core distributors and users to concentrate themselves in pools which take on the appearance of a vortex: everyone is funnelled into small geographical areas where drug activity is heightened' (Curtis, 1996: 49). Bushwick, the primary study site for this research, is an example of such a vortex.

Described by the *New York Times* as hosting 'the most notorious drug bazaar in Brooklyn and one of the toughest in New York City', Bushwick is an enduring source of arrests, homicides, and HIV infection (*New York Times*, 1 October 1992). Bushwick is no stranger to the drug trade. Ironically, it was once the brewing capital of America and its earliest residents—German immigrants followed later by Jews and Italians—found steady work in the breweries. Between the mid 1880s and the 1920s, Bushwick Avenue boasted elaborate Victorian mansions and the neighbourhood hosted some of the finest churches in the New York area as well as an ornate cinema, the RKO Bushwick. However, the neighbourhood's fortunes changed swiftly with the advent of Prohibition and the Great Depression. By the end of World War II, only seven breweries remained and in 1976 the last two remaining breweries—the Schaeffer Brewing Company and the Rheingold Brewing Company—closed their Brooklyn factories. Bushwick has also generated its fair share of mafia folklore over the years. By the 1970s it had a reputation as a mob neighbourhood under the control of the Bonanno organized crime family. Although New York City's other crime families were reportedly against drug dealing, the Bonannos, under the leadership of Carmine Galante, were involved in organizing a heroin smuggling operation. In 1979, Galante was murdered in a mob-style hit in what was then the 'Joe and Mary' Italian restaurant on Knickerbocker Avenue.[1]

Since the late 1960s, the area has gradually come to be dominated by low income Latino populations, predominantly Puerto Ricans. Dominicans and Colombians, while fewer in number than Puerto Ricans, occupy dominant positions within the local drug markets and command an increasing share of cultural and political resources. Census data reveal that in 1960 the population of Bushwick was 89 per cent white, 6 per cent Black and 5 per cent Hispanic. By 1990 it was 65 per cent Hispanic, 24.9 per cent Black and 5.4 per cent white (Bureau of the Census, 1990). The neighbourhood was the site of massive rioting and looting during the 1977 New York City power

---

[1] Joe and Mary's is now a Chinese takeout.

blackout which resulted in an exodus of merchants and residents, and the demolition of more than a thousand buildings. Bushwick remains the poorest neighbourhood in Brooklyn with a median household income of $16,287—less than half the state-wide median of $32,965. In the poorest sections of Bushwick the median income is as low as $8,662 with the drug market area only slightly higher at $10,859. The majority of Bushwick residents receive public assistance and more than half of all families and two thirds of children live in poverty. Unemployment runs around 21 per cent (twice the city-wide rate), and only 44 per cent of adults in Bushwick report being in the labour force (Bureau of the Census, 1990; New York City Department of Planning, 1993).[2]

The housing stock in the neighbourhood is primarily one and two-family housing, although the drug market area consists of run-down and abandoned apartment buildings set amongst a mix of mostly-defunct light manufacturing and industry, including once-thriving knitting factories.[3] During the 1970s, the decline of Bushwick was accelerated by an arson epidemic prompted by landlords and followed by the demolition of entire blocks of buildings under the federal government's urban renewal plan. While 4,000 new public housing units have been built since the blackout, it has been estimated that almost 10,000 housing units were lost during the 1970s to fire and abandonment. Today, approximately 20 per cent of the landscape or more than 2,000 lots remain vacant. Almost 44,000 people left Bushwick during the 1970s. In 1990 census data estimated the population at 102,572, considerably less than the 137,895 who lived there in 1970.

Residents are confronted by a lack of legitimate opportunities, a dearth of community services, over-pricing of basic goods, rampant slumlordism, an 80 per cent high school drop out rate, endemic violence and one of the busiest and most brazen drug supermarkets in New York City. The density of settlement, due to high levels of overcrowding and doubling up in existing accommodations, means that domestic life in the neighbourhood, especially during the summer months, spills out of the small one and two family houses and

---

[2] These estimates would increase considerably if Bushwick's large population of homeless persons, including itinerant drug users and illegal immigrants, were included.

[3] In 1969, one quarter of all industrial jobs in New York City were located in Brooklyn and more than half the employees in Brooklyn worked in five industries—apparel, food, metal, machinery, and electrical manufacturing (Susser, 1982).

apartments onto the streets. Poverty and unemployment, coupled with a lack of private space and public facilities, have encouraged a vigorous street life and a corresponding diminution of private life. The social organization of daily life in the neighbourhood is dominated by the drug trade and the life chances of users and non-users alike are intricately bound up with the fortunes of the drug economy. Both the drugs themselves and the drug business offer potential relief to those whose lives are severely constrained by poverty and a lack of opportunity. Many residents are caught in a dubious bind.

Preferring the risk of drugs to the pain of withdrawal, many of the Puerto Rican and Dominican residents on the block have clung fiercely to the lucrative trade to help supplement welfare checks or support their own habits. And while many people on the block say they hate the sight of dealers and users on the streets where their children play, many also conceded that these soldiers of the drug trade are less invaders than part of the community's tangled web of blood ties and friendships (*New York Times*, 1 October, 1992).

The active vortex of highly structured drug markets which evolved during the late 1980s underwent considerable changes during the study period. Between 1989 and 1992, drug distribution in Bushwick was characterized by intense competition between drug business owners and constant confrontations over 'turf' as organizations strove to establish hegemony over particular markets. In 1988, 58 homicides were reported in Bushwick. By 1990, this figure had increased to 77 (*New York Newsday*, 21 April 1991).[4] In 1989 a local woman named Maria Hernandez, who had campaigned actively against drug dealers in the neighbourhood, was murdered. One of her killers was a local drug business owner and the other a drug user/employee recruited by the owner to kill Hernandez after she had repeatedly attempted to chase his workers off the block.[5]

---

[4] Much has been made of the crack-violence nexus and the 'fact' that 'crack' has spawned an unprecedented epidemic of violence. However, the absence of an historical perspective in recent accounts of drug-related violence is striking. As Nelli (1976) has pointed out, systemic violence in the context of illegal drug markets has a long history: 'With its numerous gangs and an enormous population providing the richest market for illicit alcohol, New York during the 1920s featured a bewildering maze of shifting rivalries, vendettas, and alliances. More than one thousand gangsters were killed in this urban jungle during the bootleg wars of the 1920's' (1976:172).

[5] In 1991 Harry Santiago, a local drug business owner, and William Figueroa, a convicted drug dealer who worked for Santiago, were convicted of the murder of Maria Hernandez.

Bushwick was also the site of a number of 'stray bullet' shootings during the study period, including the Jefferson-Street death of a 53-year-old woman and the death of a 37-year-old woman on Flushing Avenue.[6] Residents claim that between 1990 and 1992 four members of the community were killed by the police in unwarranted shootings (*New York Times*, 10 May 1992; *New York Times*, 21 May 1992). Between January 1991 and October 1992 there were 23 drug-related homicides within a four block radius of Troutman Street alone (*New York Times*, 1 October 1991). Almost every wall in the drug market area bears a mural to commemorate those involved in the drug trade who have become victims of its violence. Sidewalk 'recordatorios'— temporary shrines at the sites of tragic deaths—are a common feature of the neighbourhood.

During the study period the Narcotics Division within the New York City Police Department recorded 7,323 arrests in Bushwick (Curtis, 1996). In the six-month period between February and August 1992 alone, there were 626 felony drug (sales) arrests, in the 83rd Precinct, 303 misdemeanor drug (possession) arrests, and 7,160 summonses for minor violations aimed at deterring drug traffic in the area. The occupation of the neighbourhood by the Brooklyn North Tactical Narcotics Team during May to August of the same year produced an additional 733 arrests and a three day operation in October resulted in the arrest of a further 150 persons (*New York Times*, 2 October 1992). Despite a sustained policing intervention throughout 1991 and 1992, local residents insisted that the only thing that had changed in Bushwick since the murder of Maria Hernandez was the name of the park which was retitled in her honour. 'Business as usual' continued apace throughout the study period on the block bounded by Troutman and Jefferson Streets and Knickerbocker and Irving Avenues.

The seemingly endless supply of drugs and drug sellers in this section of Bushwick illustrates the failure of traditional law enforcement approaches to curtail street-level drug sales. Neither saturation policing, (street sweeps, road blocks, increased foot patrols) nor specialist operations (including the deployment of a mobile command centre in Maria Hernandez Park, 'Operation Takeback' and a sustained

---

[6] Stray bullet shootings are not unique to the crack trade or the contemporary period. As early as 1931, four children playing in the street in East Harlem were killed by machine gun bullets meant for Dutch Schultz, one of New York's premier 'booze Barons' (Nelli, 1976:150).

intervention by NYPD's elite Tactical Narcotics Team) have affected the availability of drugs in the neighbourhood. This failure has been publicly acknowledged by a former Director of the Mayor's Office of Drug Abuse Policy: 'Troutman and Knickerbocker represents a city, state and national failure to develop a drug strategy that will work in places like Bushwick . . . And our failures are costing us a small fortune in tax dollars and people's lives' (*New York Times*, 2 October 1992). Indeed, there is some evidence to suggest that high levels of policing activity and sustained intervention in the neighbourhood, while they appear to have had little impact on the size and volume of the trade, produced a number of negative consequences.

The police occupation of Bushwick, and in particular, the TNT, alienated many non-drug using residents. Sweeps of the principal drug market locations involved the closure of entire blocks, requiring everyone caught between police barricades to 'kiss the concrete' while waiting to be searched. Such practices incensed many residents (Curtis and Hamid, 1997). Similarly, the impact on the drug market has had unintended consequences, including an increase in the level of drug-related violence (Curtis and Hamid, 1997). The major impact of high volume arrests in the neighbourhood was massive attrition in the ranks of street-level functionaries. The ensuing labour shortage forced drug business owners to replace 'trusted' street-level sellers with 'untrustworthy' drug users: the resultant instability within dealing organizations precipitated violence.

Once newcomers/outsiders entered the vacuum created by TNT, the business of selling drugs was no longer interwoven with social and kinship ties and the potential for violence was greatly increased once these mediating influences could no longer be called upon to settle disputes. In 1992, many shootings and beatings erupted out of soured relationships between managers and sellers (Curtis, 1993:3).

During the study period, drug activity in the vortex was concentrated on Troutman Street and Knickerbocker Avenue, having been displaced from Starr Street and Maria Hernandez Park. Troutman Street, home to the principal heroin market, is a hive of activity 24 hours a day, although during 1991 the police took to closing the street with barricades for part of the day.[7] More than a dozen (Dominican and Puerto Rican) 'owners' control the heroin market

---

[7] The dealers' response to this was simply to walk around the corner to Knickerbocker Avenue where they pretty much conducted 'business as usual'.

with some of the larger organizations employing more than ten street-level operatives. Dealers congregate on virtually every stoop on the block. Supported by 'runners', they hand over $10 glassine bags of heroin to eager customers. In a lucrative market where word of a new or particularly good dope spreads rapidly, labels are important and brand names resonate with popular cultural images: *Jungle Fever, Terminator, Most Wanted, Mambo King, Lamborghini, Double D, Strong Medicine*, and even *TNT*. Traffic moves along the block at a snail's pace. Even the familiar cry of 'bajando' signalling the approach of the police fails to significantly disrupt the trade.[8]

The cocaine hydrochloride (hereafter cocaine HCL)[9] market in the neighbourhood is dominated by Dominican heroin distributors. Powder cocaine, marketed simply by the colour of the bag—mainly *Blue Bag* and *Cherry Coke* during the study period—sells at the far end of Troutman Street and along Irving Avenue for $5 a bag. At the opposite end of Troutman, approximately six principal distribution organizations, also controlled by Dominicans, retail crack at more than twenty sites along Knickerbocker Avenue and Jefferson Street. A number of freelance operators work the edges of this turf controlled by Bushwick's big six. Different brands are identified by the colour of the plastic stopper in the tiny glass vials—*Pink Tops, Blue Tops, White Tops, Brown Tops,* etc. Although crack commonly retailed at $5 a vial during the study period, in 1991 a new business opened on the periphery of the vortex offering two vials for five dollars. Unlike its competitors, this particular brand of crack, which happened to have a red top, was known simply as *Two-for-Five*.

Although Bushwick is an Hispanic neighbourhood, the concentration of street-level drug distribution activity in the area has attracted a large, transient and ethnically heterogeneous drug using population. The influx of drug users from surrounding neighbourhoods produced a noticeable shift in the ethnic composition of the street-level drug using population. Large numbers of African Americans and a discrete minority of European Americans, sizable proportions of which are women, constitute a visible presence in the neighbourhood. In sharp contrast to the small, intimate and tightly knit groups which

---

[8] The proximate translation for this term is 'coming down'.
[9] Cocaine HCL takes the form of a water-soluble white powder which can be administered intra-nasally or intravenously.

generally characterize illicit drug use, the expansion of Bushwick's drug using population has resulted in the proliferation of large over-lapping networks of poly drug users. Although individuals partici-pating in these networks engage in behaviours such as sharing drugs and implements, Bushwick yields little evidence of the dyads or 'rip-ping and running' associations which typified earlier eras of intra-venous drug use (Curtis et al., 1995).

Crack use has clearly had a significant impact on the intravenous drug using community in Bushwick and the behaviours traditionally associated with injecting drug use. This is graphically illustrated in Chapter 6 in relation to sexwork and, more generally, can be seen in terms of shifts in patterns of consumption including the tendency to use multiple substances (heroin, cocaine and crack) and a desire to consume in private. Coupled with recent demographic shifts in the gender and ethnic composition of the drug using population, these factors have given rise to a fluid and constantly changing street scene, compounded instability among drug use networks, and fostered the atomization and isolation of drug users.

These developments have been exacerbated by sustained police intervention in the neighbourhood. The continual police presence and constant arrests have amplified a general air of suspicion and distrust on the part of drug users and increased the probability of users engaging in high risk behaviours, particularly injecting practices, in order to avoid police. As Grund has pointed out, in New York City, 'current drug policies foster less stable settings (abandoned buildings, cars, shooting galleries) where the same injection equipment is used over and over again' (1993:227). The fear of attracting attention clearly militates against regular consumption routines and the forma-tion of stable cohesive user groups. The dwindling number of estab-lished sites for consumption encourages crowding and its concomitant consequences for public health, including the spread of tuberculosis, viral hepatitis, and HIV infection.

The principal site for this study then, was dominated by the pres-ence of several bustling street-level drug markets open for business '24/7' (24 hours a day, 7 days a week). It is within this context, char-acterized by violence, a high incidence of death and disablement, recurrent arrests and a constant stream of HIV infection, that the lives of the women presented below are situated.

The Women

In the course of this research, I observed and recorded details of the lives of more than 200 women drug users in three Brooklyn neighbourhoods (Flatbush, Williamsburg and Bushwick). Unless otherwise stated, the data presented here consist of repeated interviews and multiple field observations with 45 women in Bushwick, the principal study site. All of the women who participated in this study were street-level drug users in one of the poorest neighbourhoods in New York City. The majority used a combination of crack cocaine and heroin on a daily basis. Most were members of racial/ethnic minorities. Nearly all were homeless. Many were mothers and a significant proportion were HIV positive. These women were both the perpetrators and victims of violence and all engaged in law-breaking, principally street-level sexwork, as a means of supporting their drug consumption.

'Representativeness'

I am confident that these 45 women represent the range of ages, life experiences and diversity of drug use histories evident among the full ethnographic sample of 211 women. While I do not want to get into a tortuous discussion of generalizability and have elsewhere justified my decision to present these findings in terms of this smaller group of 45 women (Maher, 1995b), the search for typicality continues to plague both sociologists and criminologists. The positivist nightmare that research participants, individually or collectively, may not be 'representative' or, worse still, that they may be exceptional or idiosyncratic, runs deep. Even anthropologists have been criticized for their failure to justify their choice of subjects in terms of typicality (e.g. Shostak, 1981).[10] The search for representativeness also obscures what the anomalous or the marginal can reveal about the centre and the critical insights atypical voices can yield into power, relations of domination and, perhaps most crucial of all, strategies of resistance (Okely, 1996). A detailed account of the construction of the research project can be found in the Appendix to this volume.

---

[10] Shostak's study of Nisa (1981) has been challenged repeatedly in terms of Nisa's typicality as a !Kung woman.

Demographics and early childhood

The majority of the women who participated in the study were born in the New York area (84 per cent) and more than half (53 per cent) were born in Brooklyn. Four were born in other parts of the United States and three were born in other countries. Most women (64 per cent) were raised in Brooklyn for a substantial portion of their childhood. The mean age was 27.9 years at the time of the first interview and ranged from 19 to 41 years. Less than a quarter (24 per cent) were raised by both birth parents. Approximately one third (31 per cent) of women were raised by their mothers and a further third were raised by female kin. Slightly more than half (53 per cent) grew up in female-headed households. Five women (11 per cent) spent time in institutional foster care during childhood. About a third (31 per cent) came from families where either one or both parents had a history of substance abuse. Ten of these women indicated that at least one parent either was, or had been, a heroin, cocaine or crack user. Almost half the women (49 per cent) indicated that at least one sibling also had a history of substance abuse. One quarter (24 per cent) came from families with a parental record of arrest, conviction, or imprisonment and 40 per cent had a sibling that had been in contact with the criminal justice system.

Victimization and abuse histories

More than one third of women (38 per cent) grew up in an abusive household where they were subjected to physical abuse by family members, including parents, step-fathers, mothers' boyfriends and male kin. Slightly more than one in ten (11 per cent) reported sexual abuse as a child (defined as physical sexual contact). Three of the women who were sexually abused as children also came from physically abusive households. A total of 19 women (42 per cent) were victimized by family members while growing up. As adults, almost two thirds (64 per cent) had at some stage been involved in a physically abusive relationship with a man. Although most women (62 per cent) were not involved in a relationship during the study period, of the 17 women (38 per cent) who were, ten defined their relationships as physically abusive. All of these abusive relationships were with drug using males

Education and formal labour force participation

The overwhelming majority (84 per cent) of women did not complete high school and only one woman in this sample held a college degree. More than half (55 per cent) had never participated in the formal labour force. Four out of five Latinas (80 per cent) and just over half of the African American women (56 per cent) had never held a legitimate job. Most women's labour market experiences were concentrated in the bottom tier of the secondary sector and none held formal sector employment during the study period.

Initiation to heroin and cocaine use

The mean age at first use of heroin or cocaine was 18.9 years with heroin and cocaine HCL initiates (17.5 years) younger than smokeable cocaine initiates (20.2 years). The majority (56 per cent) initiated heroin or cocaine use within the context of a male-female dyad and more than a third (38 per cent) commenced use with either a husband or boyfriend. Between them these women had a mean drug use history of 10.5 years with heroin and cocaine HCL initiates exhibiting a mean of 12.4 years, compared to a mean of 5.6 years for smokeable cocaine initiates. At the time of first interview, all of the women were crack smokers and more than two thirds (69 per cent) also used heroin. Two women subsequently commenced heroin use during the study period. A full account of the women's pathways to drug use can be found in Maher (1995a).

Arrest and conviction histories

Four women (9 per cent) ran away from home as teenagers and 15 women (33 per cent) had been convicted of a criminal offence as a juvenile. About a fifth (20 per cent) had spent some part of their adolescence in a juvenile facility. Almost all women (96 per cent) had been arrested as an adult for offences ranging from shoplifting and prostitution to manslaughter and felony drug sales. Slightly more than one third (36 per cent) had ten or more arrests. A majority (69 per cent) had served a sentence of more than six weeks imprisonment and seven (16 per cent) had done a total of more than five years in prison. Ten women (22 per cent) were on parole or probation and a significant minority (40 per cent) were arrested on charges of drug possession and/or sale during the study period.

Most of these women were sentenced to between one and three years imprisonment.

Homelessness and residential instability

Most of the women (91 per cent) were homeless and alternated between the streets and various short term accommodations including shelters, the apartments of friends and associates, and the homes of elderly males. Only four women maintained a permanent residence (defined as a housing lease in their own or a partner's name) during the study period. By the end of the fieldwork, two of these women had been evicted and another was made homeless as the result of an electrical fire in her apartment.

Reproductive histories

Four out of five women (80 per cent) were mothers. The majority of women (83 per cent) gave birth to their first child during their teenage years. The average age at first birth was 17.6 years with a range between 13 and 32 years. Between them these 36 women had given birth to a total of 96 living children ranging in age from new-borns to 26 years. Some 27 women had given birth to a total of 57 children (59 per cent of all children) while they were active drug users. Thirteen women (29 per cent) were pregnant during the study period. Two women had miscarriages and 11 subsequently delivered during the final trimester of pregnancy. Two of the women who were pregnant managed to stop using drugs and retained custody of their infants. Of the remaining nine infants, six were placed with relatives and three in institutional foster care.

Few (10 per cent) children resided with their mothers. Only four women had custody of their children during the study period. One of these women regained custody of her six children during the study after she stopped using drugs and subsequently gave birth to a seventh child. The three other women each had responsibility for one child during the study period. Of the 86 children who did not live with their mothers, 60 per cent (n = 52) resided with female kin including maternal grandmothers (n = 30), paternal grandmothers (n = 9), sisters (n = 7), sisters-in-law (n = 4) and maternal aunts (n = 2). Seven children resided with ex-husbands or boyfriends and one woman's children were cared for by a female former partner. Four children were independent, four had been adopted and 13 (15 per cent) were currently in institutional foster care.

Health status

By their own accounts, almost half of the women who participated in this study were HIV positive. Fourteen women (31 per cent) indicated that they had tested positive for HIV and a further five believed that they were HIV positive. The remaining 26 reported that they did not know their serostatus. A significant number of the women were infected with viral hepatitis and tuberculosis during the study period. Three women admitted to having attempted suicide in the past and four women had at some stage received psychiatric treatment. To the best of my knowledge, at the end of the study period, two women (4 per cent) had managed to abstain from illicit drug use and seven (16 per cent) were dead. Two of these women died from HIV-related illnesses and five were the victims of homicides.

Street Life

Social and support networks

Social networks provide an important survival mechanism for low-income populations (Young and Willmott, 1957; Valentine, 1978). Specifically, poor women have long turned to other women—kin, neighbours, friends or co-workers—for support and material help. For example, Stack (1974a) documented the 'survival strategies' of urban African American women and the financial and emotional support networks of African women engaged in bootleg beer production have been studied by Nelson (1978). Research on social networks has differentiated between *broad* networks, consisting of a wide range of ties to diverse others which provide a valuable instrumental resource, and *dense* networks which tend to be more closely associated with social support (Campbell et al., 1986; Marsden, 1987; Campbell, 1988). This body of research suggests there are considerable gender differences in social networks; women's networks tend to be dense and kin-based. Compared to men whose networks are more likely to be composed of non-kin and in particular, co-workers, women tend to have fewer ties to non-kin (Fischer and Oliker, 1983; Wellman, 1985; Moore, 1990). Previous research suggests therefore that, compared to men, women are less likely to use personal networks as instrumental resources in terms of employment and career advancement (Fischer and Oliker, 1983).

There is also a growing body of research examining the social networks of drug users (e.g. Hawkins and Fraser, 1985; Kandel and Davies 1991; Krohn and Thornberry, 1991), with particular emphasis on the implications of the drug injectors' networks for understanding and preventing HIV infection (e.g. Klovdahl et al., 1994; Neaigus et al., 1994; Curtis et al., 1995; Friedman, 1995; Needle et al., 1995). However, research to date has failed to pay sufficient or separate attention to the social networks of women drug users. Are they intimate and supportive? Are they relatively stable? Broad or dense? To what extent are they kin-based? Are they primarily same sex networks? Do they function as instrumental resources or survival mechanisms? While my research did not centre on these questions, I was able to learn a good deal about women's networks. My findings bear importantly on the variety and form of income generation, addressed in subsequent chapters (4–7). Thus, I briefly sketch their contours here.

Unlike their male counterparts (who have been portrayed as creating and belonging to complex cultures or subcultures), criminalized or 'deviant' women have rarely been the subject of 'appreciative' studies.[11] Little attention has been paid to the peer group and the influential 'delinquent peers' hypothesis (e.g. Miller, 1958; Cloward and Ohlin, 1960) as it relates to women and girls. It has been assumed that, within mixed sex groups, women and girls will be more influenced by men and boys than by other females. Campbell's (1990) commentary is especially incisive in identifying the two 'interrelated assumptions' in previous research that girls 'do not form strong same-sex friendships, and . . . that it is the influence of male peers which is most powerful in explaining female gang delinquency' (Campbell, 1990:46). The presumed inability to form and sustain same sex friendships is linked to the notion that women and girls are incapable of creating and maintaining cohesive 'deviant' cultures (see also Millman, 1975). However, Campbell's review of the literature finds otherwise: 'girls have equally good (arguably better) peer relations as boys, and their delinquency depends as much on close asso-

---

[11] As Austin has pointed out, the absence of appreciative studies is especially apparent in relation to the Black woman lawbreaker, who, unlike her male counterpart, 'has little or no chance of being considered a rebel against racial, sexual, or class injustice . . . Aggressive and antisocial behavior on the part of black male law-breakers is deemed compatible with mainstream masculine gender roles and is treated like race resistance but the same sort of conduct on the part of black females is scorned as being unfeminine' (1992:1768–9).

ciation with delinquent others as it does for boys' (Campbell, 1990:48).

Although women drug users engaged in frequent and numerous interactions and exchanges with males, their personal networks were dense and women-centred. There are several reasons for this pattern. First, there were few stable female-male intimate relationships: only 17 women (38 per cent) were involved in a relationship with a man, and ten of these women characterized the relationship as physically abusive. Where heterosexual relationships survive the rigours of daily drug consumption by both partners, they tend to be characterized by a reciprocal flow of violence between the street and the 'home' or other makeshift domestic setting. Latisha, a 32-year-old African American woman, described her relationship with her common law husband, Tre, this way.

Last night I went up there, you know, I tricked . . . Took me about an hour and I made money an' I have to tell him how much I made. I made forty-five dollars . . . He call me 'dope fiend' in front of everybody and 'lowlife bitch', 'bitch' suckin' on white face dicks', you know, and this the same money I share with him. I mean after I gave him twenty-five dollars, I took twenty and you know that he smoked it all up, right. I bought me a one-on-one (heroin and cocaine) and a crack, right. I had to give him half of my one-on-one so he wouldn' jump on me an' beat me up—after I gave him twenty-five dollars. Then I had my crack, right an' he want half my crack an' caus I didn't give it to him, he jumped on me an' beat me up and my sweater is all bloodied up from him beatin' on me . . . He knows I got no place to go.

A second reason women's networks were women-centred was that, because street-level sexwork played a significant role in income generating practices, the women spent a great deal of time out of doors 'hanging out' on the stroll with other women (see Chapter 6). Finally, 36 out of 45 women had children. Few of these children lived with their mothers and most either resided with female kin or were cared for by other women. These ties necessitated on-going relationships with the (non-drug using) women that cared for their children.

This section describes the street life and social networks of women drug users. My focus is on women's social relations with others in the drug economy, most of whom are drug users themselves. Curtis and colleagues (1995) have identified a large multi-ethnic 'core' network of street-level drug users in Bushwick who share drugs and injecting equipment on a daily basis. While some of the women in this study were part of this core network, it was dominated by men and, above all, Latinos. Women's social relations are perhaps better characterized in terms of concurrent participation in a number of large, loosely structured and overlapping networks. These networks illustrate the interface between street life and domestic life in the neighbourhood. In addition to gender, participation in these networks is also circumscribed by patterns of drug use, drug use behaviours, economic factors, and race/ethnicity. Women drug users' networks primarily revolved around exchanges designed to promote income generation, drug use, personal safety, shelter, and companionship. These exchanges were usually characterized by the absence of an expectation of immediate repayment and were often embedded in on-going relationships of some form. In many ways they were similar to 'gift' exchanges in relation to the circulation of goods and services among low-income households (Pahl, 1984; Stack, 1974a; Liebow, 1967) and involved a combination of economic motives and social incentives.

Drug users in Bushwick also provided each other with valuable information relating to, for example, the availability and quality of drugs, police activity, consumption sites, and options for shelter. Among the women, the sense of identification as a result of a shared way of life and involvement in illegal activities (particularly among injecting drug users) was strengthened by their awareness of the low regard which the broader community held for women drug users. Institutionalized practices such as drug sharing and needle sharing both forged and galvanized bonds among the women. In a world of extreme impoverishment and deprivation, the sharing of drugs can also be seen as part of a wider pattern of interactions and exchanges involving the transfer of accommodation, clothing, and food, among other things.

Sharing fits the broader context of drug users' lives and finds its function in coping with craving, human contact and needs, and life on the margins of society . . . Both the helping and sharing (as well as the ripping and the violence) characteristic of the subcultures of heavy drug users, are normal behaviors under abnormal or extreme circumstances . . . Without a little help from your friends it is impossible to survive in the tough parallel world of users, dealers and police. In this context, sharing balances the constraints, the ripping and running, the competition, violence and mistrust of daily life . . . drug sharing is an integrating ritual sanctioning a common lifestyle and strengthening mutual ties (Grund, 1993:154).

The ties that facilitated drug sharing varied in strength and content in the study site. Sometimes the motivation for sharing drugs or giving someone a 'taste' was as simple as the desire to help someone who was in a bad way. Such sharing was reinforced by the existence of a normative code among heroin users in relation to helping those who were sick to get 'straight' (i.e. alleviate withdrawal symptoms). For example, Aiesha, a 24-year-old African American woman, described how, on her return to the neighbourhood after a trip to Manhattan to exchange foreign currency (which she had stolen from a date), she encountered a woman who was visibly (dope)sick.

I got me two bags of dope and a bag of coke . . . I went down in the train station. Me and another girl cause the other girl was sick when I got off the train. She was cryin' that she was sick and shit. [Do I know her?] Yeah you probably do know her. She's a white girl and shit, and she said she was so sick and everything. So, I told her come on and shit. We went down in the train station and we got off and shit. Then it wasn't good enough for me cause I had to share with her. So I went and got me some more dope.

Within this context, getting someone else straight can be seen as a way of building up a reserve of 'favours' or 'insurance' which can be called upon when one's resources are low. Sharing drugs then is a survival strategy on the part of street-level drug users. However, within the highly transient drug using community studied here, individuals cannot always count on either the capacity or the willingness of others to do them a favour in return. The latter is particularly true in relation to exchanges with male drug users. While women also got men straight, this was usually done in the context of either a relationship or as a means of negotiating street safety, as is evident in the following quotation where Latisha talks about the sharing practices of one of the European American women.

People out here (are) so streetwise. Everybody's full of shit because once the drugs is gone they're gone. She's turning everybody on so of course they love her. She get anybody high really. She get people high that she knows she won't get nothing back from. Which is kinda dumb—like Panama—you know, they don't have nothing. Panama is very nasty, you aks him (for reciprocity) and he tell you in a minute, he'd say 'So what, you gave me'. I don't know, some people are a glutton for punishment.

As outsiders, European American women were more likely to engage in getting male acquaintances straight and thus frequently ran the risk of 'one-sided exchanges'. However, African American and

Latina women tended to have rather well defined personal networks which determined whom they 'took care of'. This was confirmed on several occasions when African American women used their inter- view payments to 'take care' of their girlfriends. Despite such occur- rences, the absence of friendship was a recurrent theme in women's conversations. Women repeatedly characterized their relationships with other drug users as 'associates' even though, as will be shown, these relations are more complex and perhaps less instrumental than they initially appear. For example, Jo-Beth, a 23-year-old European American told me that she knew,

[a] few women but friendships, no. Some of them say people come before drugs. That's bullshit caus there's a lot of people I really care about—fam- ily and stuff—that I put the drugs before—you tryin to tell me I'm gonna put some street junkie before them?

Working associations between women, and particularly inter-racial associations, were often instrumental and undergirded by the mutual aim of income generation. As Latisha recalled of her working rela- tionship with Verity, a European American woman,

[l]ike me an' Verity did a double date, weekend before las', fifty dollars a piece. [What did that involve?] One guy, we had 'im believe we was gay. I don' mess wi' girls, she don' mess wi' girls, y'know. We jus' wann'ed the money.

Despite claims by other researchers that urban crack users inhabit a 'dog eat dog' world, and even the women's own reluctance to char- acterize their associations in anything more than the most instru- mental terms (e.g. 'there's no friends only associates'), I found that many women did form affective bonds which challenge the image of street-level drug users as cold, callous and self-centred. This was apparent on numerous occasions when women were injured, 'dopesick', or physically ill and other women came to their aid. The following excerpt from my fieldnotes shows that ties between women often arose out of mutual understandings of their shared social position.

Latisha tells me she wants to get a funeral fund together for 'Rosa'. We decide to draw up a list of names and scour the neighbourhood for dona- tions. Latisha describes in great detail how we will use the money to go to the Salvation Army and get her a dress and stockings and a hat and veil (to hide her badly burnt face). Latisha tells me she has already told the police that she owns a plot next to her first husband (who was burnt to death) and wants them to make arrangements for Rosa to have it. She clearly feels there to be a certain symmetry here and tells me that it is up to us to make sure that Rosa isn't 'dumped' in Potters Field. I am not sure where all this is coming from. Latisha was not that close to Rosa and I suspect that what may also be at work is a recognition on Latisha's part that 'it could have been me'. She is, however, genuinely upset and determined to enlist my support to ensure Rosa gets a decent burial. (fieldnotes)

The composition and strength of women's networks are, however, strongly mediated by race/ethnicity (see Chapter 7). I observed this on numerous occasions but it was perhaps most directly evinced when Slim, an African American woman, refused to lend her wig to Candy, a European American woman. At the time Candy was heavily pregnant, looked dreadful and was having difficulty getting dates. Yet when Toni, a newly arrived African American woman appeared on the block later the same afternoon and asked to borrow the wig to wear on the stroll, Slim gave it to her without hesitation. The following extract from my notes shows how these intra-racial bonds affected me in the field.

Walking up the block with Slim who is looking to cop we bump into this tall, rather imposing African American woman. She is selling methadone and asks me if I want some. Slim asks her if she has had the baby yet. The woman pulls up her sleeve to reveal two hospital bracelets and tells us that she had a son on Sunday. Before Slim has a chance to introduce us, word reaches that 'hondo' (the police) is coming up the block. Without warning Slim thrusts her dope cash into my hand and darts off, leaving me standing there with the money and the woman. Rather than draw attention to myself by standing in the middle of the block I decide to head towards the bodega. As I turn to walk away this woman grabs me real hard by the arm with 'Where you going you white bitch?'. I tell her that I am going to the bodega to get a soda—not that it is any of her business. She responds with 'Not with her money you ain't—you wait right here bitch' . . . . (fieldnotes)

This woman was clearly protecting her 'sister's' interests from a (white) outsider. The complexities of women's social networks and their implications for income generation are explored in detail in subsequent chapters. For now, I wish to emphasize that women-centred networks and women's relations with other women were important in facilitating drug consumption (especially getting straight), and in negotiating personal safety and street survival. At the same time, women's relations with men and, in particular, instrumental associations with elderly males, also shaped the composition of their networks. This was vividly illustrated by the various strategies women employed to secure shelter. Once immersed in street life, a constant and recurrent problem faced by women—in addition to the need to generate revenue—was the search for shelter. The nature, form and physical location of accommodations utilized by the women in this sample exhibited wide variation, as did the relationships to which such co-residencies gave rise. Here, social networks were more likely to be male/female as women drug users sought to maximize opportunities for shelter.

The search for shelter

A primary consideration in the search for shelter is personal and material safety. Women frequently spoke about the lack of places to stay where they could feel safe and would not be robbed. This was one of the reasons why the women were reluctant to stay in locations identified as commercial drug consumption sites, most of which were controlled by males (see Chapter 4). As the following accounts indicate, many women recounted being victimized in these locations and all expressed a need to sleep with 'one eye open' in such settings.

Well you know it's so busy over there. And man, I swear to God, I can't hold nothin'. I can't have nothin' there. They took my wick from out my underwear while I was sleepin'. (Sugar)

[You ever stay at Kizzy's place?] No I don't like it there, she robs you when you're there. She robs your stuff while you're there and then say she doesn't know what happened to it. I bought a sweat suit for $75 and when I woke up the top of my sweatsuit was gone. (Rachel)

[Where are you staying now?] The same thing. (Pappy's place) I'm tryin' to find a room. No damn funds. It goes just as fast as I make it. He's a nasty son-of-a-bitch. The older you are on drugs, the more stressful you get. If he don't have a hit every ten minutes, he's throwin' everybody the fuck out of the house with a new crew to come in. He calls the cops on you. I'm tellin' you, he's gettin' bad. He's gettin' super bad. [Are there a lot of people in his place now?] Hell, man, they're sleepin' all over the place. You walk in there you wouldn't be able to find him. It's like an Army base, coming from the field and you sack out one right on top of the other one. There are all bodies all over the floor. You got to step over them and step in between them—all the bodies, I'm tellin' you. (Candy)

Despite the fact that both commercial and non-commercial settings tended to be dominated by drug use, there were significant differences in terms of payment, hospitality, physical accommodations, and personal safety. Women's perceptions of the differences between the two settings made commercial sites a distinctly less attractive accommodation option, as Tameka, a 41-year-old African American woman, indicated.

At Kizzy house, she (another woman) go there. Twenty dollars up front and every time she go in and out she taking Pop or Kizzy a hit or something. And they don't cook no food or nothing. But she went to Dawn house. Dawn cook her a hot meal, she slept comfortable, wasn't worried about nobody running in and out. Over there at least you sleeping comfortable, not looking over your back because, and then she wasn't in a bed, (at Kizzy's house). You all been in the inside so you know how the kitchen is, how they have the crates and that one big chair you can lean your back on. And like you say, one eye closed and one eye open.

Rejecting commercial consumption sites in favour of less commercial settings further restricted women's accommodation options. Many women avoided formal acknowledgement of their homeless status by becoming 'couch people'—alternating between households among extended kin networks or roaming from 'friend' to 'friend' in search of shelter. As evinced in the following quotation from Jonelle, a 32-year-old African American woman, such offers were limited to a shower, brief rest, or perhaps an overnight stay, usually in exchange for drugs.

[So where do you stay mostly now?] Walk the street.[You don't have one particular place where you?] Oh, we got a girlfriend named Jeanette that lives on Jefferson, you know. She let us go up there and wash up or sometimes I might fall asleep up there, but I'm not—I don't consider myself stayin' with her though. [Does she charge you anything to go there?] Not really . . . With her, she's just lookin' to get high. You come with some get high which most likely we'll do, and you turn her on and you know it's cool. [What does she use?] Just crack.

Contingent on the strength and nature of the relationship, women were sometimes able to negotiate longer term arrangements, as did both Sugar and Shorty, Latinas aged 36 and 22 respectively.

I have a room. I was tired of being robbed. [How did you find that place?] Well, I know the girl, Chris. She was from the stroll before. [What, she doesn't work the stroll anymore?] No, she found this white man and, you know, he took care of her. And she's got her own house. [How much do you pay?] Forty dollars a week. (Sugar)

I was living with a friend of mine and her husband, and then this guy came along and started living there too, and they were into getting high and stuff. You know, and I was having a very hard time there, and I didn't have no financial help, as far as my husband working, he wasn't working, I wasn't on welfare or nothing like that. So, finally these guys weren't satisfied with the money we were giving them. They wanted me to support their habit, buy food and pay rent money, you know. [How much were you giving them?] I was giving them $75 a week for both of us, which wasn't bad. I could deal with that, but then they wanted, you know, crack. I had to buy them crack too. (Shorty)

Such arrangements rarely worked out when the household was immersed in drug use. As Shorty's quote suggests, even long-standing relationships between women were rapidly depleted by one or both party's use of drugs. This was clearly the case with the relationship between Dee Dee, a 29-year-old African American woman and her 'homegirl' Rita.

Her name is Rita. She lives in the projects on Marcy. She used to live right around the corner from me. She's one of the first people that we lived with when we came in this neighbourhood. But then they abandoned her building. [Is she somebody that you could stay at her house?] To get in the door it's like you got to have something for them. And I don't really feel like they're such a friend, you know. I told her when I first came there, I said 'Look I got a bag of dope. I'll give you some, all right'. I'm like 'Just give me a wash cloth and a towel. That's all I want to do. I want to take a shower and clean up and then I'll talk to you', you know. So of course I was taking my time. I wanted to relax and really get clean you know. So when I come out it's like a big thing now. It's like 'Well you just walk in my house, and just walk into my shower' and all this, cause all the time I'm in the bathroom she's thinking I'm gettin' high. She think I don't have no more dope. So I played it off like I didn't. I said 'You know what, the bag was so small, I did the whole thing'. And honey she must have caught on fire, right, and when I seen her attitude, and I felt like—and I really had the bag of dope—I just wanted to see how she was gonna act. And she acted just like I thought: 'You ain't got nothin' for me, you're not welcome here'. So when I seen it was like that I said, 'Yeah, well I'll just go, and I won't come again'.

Sometimes women were able to negotiate short term living arrangements with other women drug users fortunate enough to have stable accommodation. As Sugar, a 36-year-old Latina, told me,

I found me a new room. [Yeah, how did that happen?] So you know, uh, Angel, she lives right here on Troutman. She's one of my co-workers. And her old man said, 'Hey let her stay here', you know. And I appreciate that.

[You have to pay them?] She never said nothing like that, but of course I've got to give them something. Yeah, you know. [But I mean they didn't make any kind of formal arrangement?] They just kind of expect you to, when you have, to, you know.

As Sugar's account illustrates, while the need for reciprocity was understood, its terms were often vague, suggesting that conflict would invariably erupt over the precise nature of reciprocal obligations. Such ambiguities precipitated a series of short-lived arrangements and an on-going preoccupation with the need for shelter. The typical pattern then, was of short-lived arrangements. For example, Tameka, a 41-year-old African American woman, lived in a two bedroom apartment on the periphery of the drug market area with her common law husband (a non-drug using Jewish male in his sixties) and her nine year old son. Although her husband did not permit her to rent out rooms, from time to time Tameka allowed both African American and European American women who were part of her personal network to 'stay over'. Below, Tameka explains her reasons for doing this and the limits she sets for herself in relation to houseguests.

[You're kind of unusual in that the girls can come here and rest up?] There's other places, but where there's crowds, in and out constantly, and you have to pay. Whereas, this is my home because I have my kid. It's not a gallery and I don't have a crowd or anything like that . . . only girls. They ask if they could come back and have a shower and sleep. Yeah because I know how it is and I try and stuff to help other people as best I can because I don't know when I might have to go to that person one day, if not for me for my kid or something like that, you know what I'm saying, I don't know . . . but never a crowd because this is my home. I gotta be here after everybody is gone. I could ride the train from pillar to post but my baby, you know what I'm sayin', I can't take him pillar to post and he gotta eat if I don't, he gotta look good if I don't . . . It's bad enough I let the girls come in, even though it be one at a time, but still my neighbours, you know, they see it, my kid, you know, he see it. Some of them he like and then some of them he don't and I don't want somebody here he don't like and have my kid feel uncomfortable, you know I'm saying, in his own house.

For the most part however, women drug users were rarely in a position to extend shelter to each other. For many women this meant that they had to rely on men. Women frequently formed short-lived associations with older males, in which they exchanged drugs, cash or sex (or some combination thereof) for shelter. Although most of these men used alcohol and some also used crack, they were peripheral to Bushwick's street-level drug using networks and were not active participants in street life and street drug use. These men were simply older neighbourhood males who, by virtue of their economic position, were able to offer vulnerable younger women a place of shelter. Women were rarely able to negotiate these relationships on strictly economic terms by paying the men in either cash or crack. Connie, a 24-year-old Latina, maintained that she was able to keep the transaction at a purely financial level.

[Where do you stay now?] At my friend's house on Wycoff. [The friend smokes crack too?] Yes. [You pay him?] Pay him cash, right, in order for me to sleep and take a bath. [He doesn't ask for sex or anything like that?] No, He's an old, old man, no love for me. I tell him I don't like mens. I tell him, and I don't like mens. [You like women?] Exactly. [Well, I don't know. I'm asking. You pay him by the night or by the week?] Oh, I give him ten, fifteen dollars a day.

For Jo-Beth, a 23-year-old European American woman and Candy, a 41-year-old European American woman, both of whom regularly stayed at the apartment of an elderly Latino crack user, crack was the accepted method of payment.

I'm in this old man's house. He's a crack-head. A lot of the girls go there. You give him crack. [Do you find that there's a lot of old guys that smoke?] I don't know. I don't hang out with old guys. I pay my way. (Jo-Beth)

I bought a nickel crack for this old man right here so I can come in here. It cost me a nickel or two to get here. And he's still not happy. If you go out ten times a day, if it be ten times, you got to bring him a bottle (of crack) . . . so I bought him a nickel crack to get in the door and my dime of dope. And this guy done ripped me off of my dime of dope and here I am with his nickel so I can come in this house here, holding on to my dear life because I'm so tired and exhausted. I look a mess. It took me so long to make that damn money and the bastard, me so sick. At least I had that nickel to get in here, you know. (Candy)

More often than not, however, sex was part of the deal. Shorty, a 22-year-old Latina told me about a 'typical' former relationship.

Well, he's the type of guy that used to help all the girls from the Avenue. And they would go up there and take a shower and sleep, you know. He was like very perverted, and to get a place to sleep, you had to do something with him, you know? And, when I was by myself and I was strung out, I could deal with that, you know?

Relationships with older men took different forms. Sometimes these men were dates or former dates who claimed affection for individual women. Tameka met her common law husband as a date in a local bar nine years ago and remained in this union throughout the study period.

He told me, he said 'Look. I'm not worth the fuck, all I want is companionship'. He said 'Look I'll give you $50, you go home with me'. So I said 'Cool, no problem' . . . We never did anything together or anything like that other than lay in the bed and sleep, and that was it, you know. Because I didn't take him for his money and he was used to passing out and they would take his money and leave his door wide open and stuff like that, but I didn't. Because I knew that it was somebody that I wanted to see again who would be there for me. So I knew if I rolled him he wouldn't have wanted me. So I didn't roll him and thank God I didn't, and the man's been there ever since.

For a time during the fieldwork, Peggy, a 34-year-old European American woman, lived with an older Italian man who worked as a numbers runner. Although he did not use drugs, Peggy's boyfriend gave her money to purchase drugs in an effort to keep her off the stroll. The relationship however, was not without its problems.

The man that I live with, I met on the stroll up here. We would see each other once a week, then he would come twice a week, then he would come three times, four times a week, take me to lunch, take me to dinner, take me to the house . . . And then I never moved out. I'm living there eight months already. I mean, he knew what he was getting. But, I cook, I clean the house, I cut his hair. I mean, I wait on him hand and foot. He never was married, so I'm like his baby. You know? So, he treats me like a little girl and he buys me whatever I want. This is going to sound weird to you, I couldn't stay home. I was never home when he got home from work and that's all he asks, that I'm home. He don't care if there's no food, if the house is burning; as long as I'm there when he gets home, that's all he wants. He says, 'I'm going to chain you', and he did one day. I swear to God! He put shackles on my feet. I freaked out.

Even Linda, a 31-year-old European American woman who negotiated a deal with one older man whereby she was given food, shelter, and a few dollars in return for her services as a 'baby sitter' for his elderly invalid mother, found that such arrangements rarely worked to the satisfaction of all concerned.

I've been babysittin' the old lady. I'm still over there but, you know, he's got a lot of problems—he drinks. Yeah, her son. [How much do they pay you for watchin' over her?] You know, whatever. I don't have a set thing, you know. I'm just happy with the roof over my head. [Where do you stay in there?] There's a livin' room and a bedroom like. His mother has the bedroom. And we got the livin' room. But there's two separate beds. [How old is this guy?] Fifty-five. [You don't have to take care of him?] No. [If you know what I mean?] No, only when he gets drunk, real, real drunk. He just wants me to cuddle up next to him. I don't do anything, but I get mad cause he wakes me up. You know, he drinks all night until two, three, four o'clock in the morning, and he has the radio blastin', and then he comes and wakes me up. He goes on and on.

For European American women and Latinas in particular, such arrangements were part of an established trajectory of short-term instrumental associations with older males. As Linda explained, her own recent history (over a two month period during fieldwork) was characterized by four such associations.

Remember I told you I was living on Jefferson. You know that guy died? . . . [Since then where have you been staying?] Well I was staying with this other guy on the Southside, on Bedford, you know. I used to go out with him. You know I give him a blow job to stay there, you know. But then he threw me out 'cause he says, 'I don't want no more injections in the house', you know. He don't get high. He drinks, you know when he got the money. [Since then where have you been staying?] I found this other guy, right. But he got on a program and he was doing good, you know. So then I left there. So now I'm staying with this other guy, this old man, he don't get high or nothing. [How'd you hook up with him?] I used to date him. But now, you know, he just lets me stay up there. He's a little bit off. So I told (him) 'Hey, easy with the sex' (laughing).

Although most women were familiar with the system of short term accommodations developed by the city of New York in response to homelessness, few actually utilized these options. Without exception, the women identified SRO (Single Room Occupancy) or 'welfare hotels' as dangerous, criminogenic, and conducive to drug use. Women preferred to take their chances either on the street or with 'friends' or elderly males rather than in the system. Jenny, a 25-year-old European American woman, began using powder cocaine following the breakdown of a violent and abusive relationship. Evicted from her apartment in Queens because she could no longer afford to pay the rent, Jenny and her two young children were homeless prior to being housed in an SRO hotel in mid-town Manhattan. Her story illustrates the way in which social and economic factors converge with situational factors such as the availability of drugs and the proximity of experienced users/sellers to render homeless women even more vulnerable.

So they got me in the welfare hotel in the Holland on 42nd Street between Eight and Ninth Avenues. And it was like pimps, crack, dope, you know, drug hotel—pimp hotel. And I was, like, I never knew anything about this stuff you know 'cause I came from Queens, in a quiet area . . . He (a crack seller and pimp) conned me into staying with him, and I did you know. I was vulnerable, hungry, you know. I lost my welfare, and they were kicking me out of the hotel; and he had a room in the same hotel which he paid the security guards to have it . . . And I was staying there because I had no other place to stay, and then he turned me out on the streets (into prostitution). I was sniffing dope, coke, and smoking a lot of crack . . . and that's how I became like really hooked because I had a habit and I didn't know.

Jenny's older child was sexually abused in this environment and her youngest was badly burned. Both children were subsequently removed from her care. Boy, a 26-year-old African American woman, was one of the few women who stayed in shelter accommodation from time to time. As she explained, this was not because she found the accommodation attractive but rather because she too had nowhere else to go and refused to sleep on the street. Similar views regarding the shelter system were expressed by the majority of the women, most of whom refused to even contemplate shelter accommodation.

I was scared the firs' time I ever went to a shelter. [When was this?] It was about eighteen months ago. An' I was scared. They took me to a single shelter, I only stayed two days an' I wen' to 116 William Street. Iss called BWS (Brooklyn Women's Shelter), the wors'es shelter ya can ever go to 'cos deres dykes and everythin' there. An' dat taught me a lot. Thassa woman shelter. I wouldn' put ma dog in it. But I havta stay. There's two accommodations dere, dykes and crack. There's nine a y'all inna room. If you look at one person—'You looked at ma woman, I'm gon' kick your ass'. Y'know dykes are the worsest things there ever is. I don' like it, but I havta deal wid it. In nis place you don' get ta lay down. You gotta get up eight a'clock inna morning. An' you don' get ta go back upstairs till, like, six a'clock in afternoon. [What do most of the women do during the day?] I sit ousside. I sit right ousside. But I don' cumulate wid none o' dem nere because once you start ta be frens wid dem, dey're wrapped up in nat system. [So do some women do crack?] Crack it up inside the place, they be crackin' it up ousside the place. Shootin' up. Sellin'. Iss like an animal house.

Previous research suggests that shelter accommodation may be under-utilized by the homeless (Rossi, 1989; Vanderstay, 1992; see also *New York Times*, 7 January 1988). As Rossi suggests, the fact that shelters in Chicago in mid-winter were only 80 per cent full, 'says something about the conditions of our shelters' (1989:199). While the women in this study were critical of the conditions of shelter life, their greatest hostility was directed at those who worked in the system. In particular, women received little comfort or indeed, protection, from the security guards employed to police behaviour and maintain order in the shelter system (see also Rossi, 1989; Waterston, 1993). Guards were widely perceived as being involved in drug use and female guards were frequently cited as being implicated in lesbian relationships with shelter residents. As Boy told me,

[i]ss bad when dere own guards do it. How can da guards protect you when they do the same thing? You got guards dat go tagether. You got guards dat smoke. How can you protect me if you're smokin' an' you a dyke? So you're 'cumulated wid da rest a them. If you have a fight with a dyke, OK, the guard's gonna be onna dyke's side, not your's, so you fucked.

While clearly overshadowed by themes of violence, victimization and drug-related conflict, many of the women reported problems concerning the presence of homosexuality in shelters. As Waterston also noted, 'the language and descriptions residents use in talking about homosexuality reveal a repulsion and disgust corresponding to the larger culture's beliefs about normal/abnormal sexuality' (1993:70). For some women, the shelter system appeared to represent a twisted variant of the popular image of women's prisons as 'full of standover dykes'. The violence and criminality endemic to shelter life also promote the use of instrumental aggression (Campbell, 1993) by women to ward off potential aggressors. As Boy explained in response to a question about how she protected herself,

[o]kay when I went there Tuesday I laid ma law straight, I hadda argument, but dey know me from before, alrigh'. I jus' let you know. OK, iss a certain way you can look at a person, y'know. An' nas wa' I did, y'know. An' by me bein' there before, people know, don' mess wid me, I'm not one a dem suckers. See if you go in nere wimpy, they're gonna kick your ass. But if ya go in nere lay ya law down, an' don' fuck wid no one. Thas all—you don' fuck wid dem, dey won' fuck wid you.

Although women appeared more likely to seek shelter accommodation during their pregnancies, shelters designed to cater for pregnant women were similarly perceived, as the following account, also from Boy, suggests.

Dey placed me inta Saratoga. I don' wanna be dere, y'understan'. I don' like ta be wid a groupa people. Now dey got me inna room, dere's thirteen beds in this room. [Thirteen pregnant women?] Yeah. An' iss like eleven o'clock, I'm ready ta doze off, y'know. Dere playin' cards an' playin' music, an' lights on. Iss like you never can sleep when ya wanna sleep. Ya can't watch TV when ya wanna watch TV. Ya gotta sign fa soap, ya gotta sign fa toilet tissue. Iss jus' like bein' inna detention home. [Do the women fight with each other?] Dey argue like cats 'n' dogs OK. Ya got it inside an' ya got it outside. Right aroun' the corner on the side of the building, is a crack area. Number one crack dealers. [What do they sell?] Crack, dope, heroin, um wass dat stuff, dat orange stuff? [Methadone?] Methadone. Anythin' you want they got, OK? It makes it bad on us. Because at night you hear, 'You took ma money bitch' an' 'Ba, ba, ba'.

These accounts suggest that many of the women perceived the current system of responses to homelessness in a negative light. At best, hotels and shelters fail to provide safe, affordable housing and 'constitute an environment that makes any attempt toward sobriety extremely difficult' (Zimmer and Schretzman, 1991:174). At worst, they provide an environment that serves to amplify drug and alcohol use, foster or cement involvement in illegal activity, and encourage the neglect, and possibly abuse, of children. Viewing both the city shelter and welfare hotel systems as dangerous milieus highly conducive to violence, drug use, and unwanted sexual advances, most women preferred to take their chances elsewhere.

For the majority of women, shelters failed to provide a viable alternative even when the only other option literally meant sleeping on the street (see also Boyle and Anglin, 1993). A small minority favoured the street, not only over the shelter system, but in preference to staying with 'friends' or in the apartments of older males. These were mainly older women who, although they had apartments and/or families, were either unable to or chose not to stay there, as was the case with Princess and Yolanda (below).

[Where did you go when you moved out?] Well I started staying here, there. Mainly I break night a lot so, mainly in the streets. Not that I have to be in the streets. Just that I don' choose to take these drug vices into my family's home. (Princess)

My other daughter lived in my apartment with me, and she had a pair of twins and a new baby girl she had just about three months ago. [What does she say about you using drugs?] She doesn't like it, and sometimes I don't bother to go home at all. I stay in the streets. I don't go home cause I'm disgusted with myself, with my life . . . I say I want help, but every time I go

home I feel this pressure, so I leave because my daughter, she's got this—
well, the baby's father, he's a creep. He steals everything. He's a junkie himself, and she can't see that. (Yolanda)

Sleeping on the street or 'sleeping rough' typically entailed the construction of a makeshift shelter, usually a cardboard shanty or 'lean
to' against a wall or fence. These structures were ironically referred
to as 'condos'. For a time Jefferson Street hosted a row of these
dwellings, some of which, in addition to providing shelter, also
served as consumption sites or 'cardboard galleries' where, for a few
dollars, injecting drug users could 'get off'. Other common locations
for the construction of temporary dwellings were abandoned buildings and vacant lots. The heavy police presence in the neighbourhood
prompted recurrent skirmishes between police officers and drug users
over these makeshift shelters, and the police were constantly demol-
ishing structures and chasing drug users off vacant lots. As soon as a
condo was destroyed, a new fence erected, or a gate put in place,
someone would break the lock or cut through the fence and within
days, sometimes even hours, the condo would be resurrected.

Princess, a 32-year-old African American woman known for her
sharp wit, quick temper, and distinctive dreadlocks, was widely
regarded as the Queen of Crack Row. For a time she even had a
throne—an old battered peacock chair—from which she sold White
Top crack. During the study period Princess expended considerable
energy on constructing makeshift dwellings on Crack Row. Unlike
the usual 'cardboard condo', Princess went to great lengths scouring
the neighbourhood for materials to be used in construction and fur-
nishing. On many occasions these dwellings were quite elaborate, as
the following extract from my fieldnotes suggests.

Today was a sweep day, and as usual, the police were everywhere. They
knocked down all the condos on the lot on Crack Row, including Princess's
which she'd only put up last week. It was made of timber and bits and pieces
of cardboard and inside was an old mattress, a couple of bucket seats out of
an abandoned car, a few milk crates and a large wooden box—in the middle of which she had placed (rather formally), a large ceramic fruit bowl. No
more. As soon as the police moved off the block, Princess started a salvage
operation, dragging the bucket seats, the box and what was left of the
ceramic fruit display out onto the street and setting them up against the brick
wall. (fieldnotes)

Princess rationalized her choice by saying that she preferred to stay
on the street rather than in someone's house because, in her opinion,

either way people were out to rip you off. As she saw it, in some ways sleeping rough may even reduce the risk of victimization insofar as she believed that there was less chance of people thinking that you had anything to steal.

I'll stay here (in the lot), y'know. I paid anywhere I went, but besides gettin' robbed, y'know, 'cos when you stay in somebody's house all they do is rip you off. I've gotten by better in the streets, y'know. That's right. You sleep, fall asleep in the streets, nobody think you got nothin. So they're not gonna search you for anything. You know, you wake up any time you go to somebody's house and you have nothing, not even a wake up (first bag of dope of the day).

For most women however, the high likelihood both of victimization and police harassment meant that condos or other curbside accommodations were not a viable option unless they were in partnership with a male. Following the eviction of Dream from her apartment, three African American couples who had been staying there were forced to relocate to a vacant lot where they established a large communal condo. Dee Dee, a 29-year-old African American woman, described this arrangement.

In the backa da lot, dere a couch back dere. Wen I'm finally pooped, I can' take it no more, I step back dere and fall asleep. An' iss gotta Johnny pump (fire hydrant) das open. [But it's not too good when it rains.] No, but we done made it like a canopy or whatever wid de pallets on each side o' da couch. [How many people are staying over there?] Iss really six of us, but we be in dere at different times. An' if dere's not room for the nex' one we lay a pallet out. We got enough blankets and stuff. We put a blanket on the pallet an' lay out there. [But any one can go in there?] Dey can yeah, there's nothin' stoppin' em, but dey don'. Iss not as popular as dat lot dere. Guess a lot o' people know about it but never think to go in there. Jus' a empty lot, a parkin' lot. An' iss got trees ona sides dat block us out—iss cool for now.

Male drug users who were also part of Bushwick's street networks were neither inclined to nor particularly well placed to provide for women's needs for shelter. Latisha, a 32-year-old African American woman, and her common law husband Tre resided in an abandoned truck for the bulk of the study period. The truck was situated on an empty lot adjoining an industrial estate. Although it was located a thirty minute walk away from the neighbourhood, Latisha and Tre made this journey at least once a day. Overshadowed by a huge warehouse and hidden from the roadside by undergrowth, Latisha and Tre also managed to successfully hide the fact that they lived in this truck from other drug users (and for a time, from me) by claiming that they lived in an apartment in a nearby neighbourhood. Following my first visit to the site, Latisha discussed their accommodation.

It's very hot in the summer. You have to keep the doors open when you're sleepin' and God forbid if you try to put a cover on you, and mosquitoes, my God. [What about rats?] Well, you see the bag hangin' up over the ceiling. Thas where we put the food. If we didn't eat it all we have to hang it up in the ceiling because the rats would smell it and come in. You gotta remember you're on the outside and those are big rats. [What about other people in the neighbourhood?] They know that we're around and we don't bother them or steal or nothing . . . I keep myself pretty much clean, I mean I can't take a bath every day, but we have access to hot water. The guy across the street give us hot water. [So you take a bath over there?] No we fill up buckets, we got a big barrel, you fill the barrel, get in and wash. Outside. Last winter was three feet of snow and I still went outside.

For women such as Latisha who had the 'luxury' of living in an abandoned truck with her physically abusive partner, sleeping rough was rejected as an option because of the undesirable message it sends out and the economic implications of this message. As Latisha explained,

I refuse to just sleep right over here. I don't want people to see me lyin' out here on the sidewalk. Dates come through these areas too and they see a girl laying out here and then they see her back on the street. You know, it's gonna be hard for you, they figure out you ain't shit.

Within the street-level drug economy, homelessness holds highly gendered implications for women's capacity to generate income. Within this context, sexwork, as a primary means of economic sustenance for most women, necessitates a basic level of attention to looks, physical hygiene and, ironically, presentation of moral propriety. For these women, sleeping rough sends out a message that serves to further circumscribe their capacity for income generation and places them at risk both of moral opprobrium and violent victimization.

Conclusion

I've been workin', smokin', that's the whole fuckin' routine, don't you know this. Stay up four or five days smokin', fuckin', jumpin' in and out of cars, smokin' for days 'til you can't take no more of this crash road. The same routine over and over again. You find a place to clean up, you clean up, change your clothes and you're right back out there again. The only thing that changes is the fuckin' weather. (Candy)

I have sketched women's networks, their day to day lives on the street and how these are patterned by gender and race/ethnicity. These networks are more than markers of potential HIV infection. They provide women drug users with opportunities for support, shelter, and sustenance. While drug sharing can be viewed as a defining characteristic of social network composition at the street-level, it is not the only characteristic. The networks of women drug users are undergirded by broader social and structural determinants which influence their positioning in the street-level drug economy. In particular, the existence of dense, women-centred networks in Bushwick can be seen as a response to male domination within the broad 'core' network of drug users described by Curtis and colleagues (1995), and as a marker of the relative status of women within these networks. Women-centred networks serve as a resource for women drug users. While they facilitate income generation and drug consumption (especially 'getting straight'), they are also critical to ensuring personal safety and street survival. And although the considerable evidence of exchange and support patterns among women gives the lie to the stereotype of the predatory thirsty crackhead, care must be taken not to romanticize these networks or their functions. Women-centred networks among street-level drug users must also be seen as adaptive responses to the exigencies of life on the margins. On the street, women drug users are both isolated from conventional sources of social and economic support, and peripheral to the male-dominated core networks of drug using populations.

For drug users in large urban centres and inner city residents, the notion of the 'street' encapsulates a complex of meanings. In the Black vernacular, the street serves as a 'source of practical experience and knowledge necessary for survival' (Folb, 1980:256). Immersion in street life or being 'out there' also includes elements of risk and excitement not always present in everyday life. As Princess noted at the beginning of this chapter, for some women, the street is 'magnetic' and its lure may be every bit as powerful as the lure of the drugs themselves. After two years in jail, 16 months in a residential treatment program, and despite the fact that she no longer used drugs, Rosa often found herself 'back on the block' during her weekend leaves from the program. As she told me during a visit to New York in 1994,

I went around there. Everything is the same. More girls and they look so bad. I feel sorry for them. They are all mess up. But sometime I am scared Lisa, I don' wanna go back out there. I got my life straight up now thanks God but I don't got no job or apartment—the rent is so high you wouldn't believe it . . . Sometime I am so lonely, I am worry for my mental healf. When you out there you ain't got no problem but for to get drugs. Now I got me all, all these problem with my kids, my healf, you know, still in denial with the HIV thing, no job, no money.

For the women in this study, the street is the locus of their daily lives. It is where they interact with others, conduct their business, use drugs, and occasionally, eat and rest. The principal focus of street life in Bushwick is drugs. Drug users are preoccupied with the need to generate income and a large part of street life revolves around income generation and the acquisition and consumption of drugs (see Chapters 4–7). Street life may also afford some women 'opportunities to feel a sense of mastery, independence, individual accomplishment and immediate reward' (Miller, 1986:140). At the same time however, the street provides the premier stage for the harassment and victimization of women drug users. Women drug users were clearly disadvantaged compared to their male counterparts. Men were more able to insulate themselves (for a time at least) from the vagaries of street life. By virtue of their economic position, many elderly males were able to accommodate their own demands for sexual activity and drug use by providing shelter to homeless women drug users. Even homeless men had a relative advantage over women in terms of the risk of victimization and violence at the street-level. Men were less likely to be perceived as the victim-of-choice and more likely both to be able to protect themselves and to engage in the instrumental victimization of others and, in particular, the victimization of women.

Street life both creates and sustains the complex social networks which frame these women's economic lives. The street functions as a distinct cultural and social milieu which evidences 'the same structures of gender relations as the family and the state. It has a division of labour, a structure of power and a structure of cathexis' (Connell, 1987:134). For the women in this study, street life served as the principal locus of social and economic relations. The patterning of these relations is clearly linked to, shaped by, and cannot be separated from, broader cultural understandings of gender, race, and class.

3
Gender, Work, and Informalization

If you a woman, nobody wanna hire you . . . If you a woman and you Black, forget it. Fuck that shit, I'll get mines. (Kizzy)

Previous studies of illicit drug use, distribution, and related activities have been, for the most part, over-determined by the psycho-pharmacological paradigm. The predominance of this paradigm has produced a powerful ideological trope which organizes and diffuses broader cultural anxieties. In attributing the negative effects of drugs to a combination of individual pathology and the pharmacological properties of particular substances, this trope inscribes a particular meaning of drug use. Although, in more recent times, its referents have shifted away from the notion of 'addiction' to embrace a concept of 'dependence', dependency is little more than a euphemism for addiction (Moore, 1992). Both addiction and dependency function as 'keywords' (Williams, 1976) in popular and academic discourse on illicit drugs. Together, they constitute a powerful 'common sense' (Gramsci, 1971) which legitimizes a particular reading of drug use while simultaneously obscuring the possibility of alternative readings.

The depiction of drug users as addicted and dependent has produced a reading organized around notions of passivity, inadequacy, and escapism and has led to the assumption that drug users are, by definition, marginal to economic and occupational life (Cloward and Ohlin, 1960; Chein et al., 1964). Drug users have been portrayed as lazy, amotivational, and parasitic on the formal economy. Bereft of basic normative values, their income generating activities have been characterized as impulsive, random, and pharmacologically-driven. Unable to delay gratification or plan for the future, they contribute little to either production or consumption. Indeed, one could be forgiven for concluding that illicit drug use automatically renders its participants incapable of any meaningful activity.

However, these critical features are not merely evaded. Rather, drug discourse, as presently constituted, is unable to register them. The complex of meaning in and by which Western cultures have historically defined drug use is overdetermined by an extant configuration of pathology and pharmacology which denies and devalues the labour of drug users and restricts their representation as economic agents. The hegemony of the psycho-pharmacological paradigm, reflected in both scientific and popular notions of addiction and dependency, secures the pervasive common sense that drug users are driven by personal and chemical demons alone. Moreover, where women are concerned, the inherent appeal of dependency, secured by reference to psychological discourse which has a long history of feminizing and individualizing dependency, has served to occlude any meaningful consideration of the economic lives of women drug users.

This discourse of dependency clearly undergirds dominant understandings of the 'crack problem'. Since 1985, the media have consistently bombarded the American public with lurid images of crack as a 'demon drug' (Reinarman and Levine, 1989). The form, content, and level of discourse have served to imprint an omnipotent image of crack as a highly potent, 'instantly addictive' drug conducive to systemic violence and 'hypersexual' behaviours. The crack trade has been depicted as immoral, ruthless, and prone to wanton displays of violence. Crack users have been portrayed as unstable, erratic, and willing to 'do anything' for that next hit. Women, in particular, have been vilified as corrupted and polluted by the 'glass dick'. Having abandoned their womanhood with the loss of their 'instinct for parenthood' (*New York Times*, 17 March 1990), women crack users have been held responsible for the creation of a 'bio-underclass' of 'crack babies', said to be lacking the 'central core of what it means to be human' (*New York Times*, 17 September 1989).

Such partial representations have served to distort and obscure critical aspects of drug use behaviour. The inability to 'read' drug use beyond the boundaries of the psycho-pharmacological script belies the variations revealed by ethnographic observations of drug users in their 'natural' settings. Moreover, as Hamid has argued, 'the demonization of human actors proceeds only by removing them from the actual historical, political and economic trajectories in which they are situated. It results from not knowing them personally' (Hamid, forthcoming). While the crack trade is undeniably violent, this is not due to any inherent qualities of the drug or its users but rather to the use of violence as a regulatory mechanism in the illegal marketplace (Goldstein, 1985; Fagan and Chin, 1989). Similarly, violence on the part of crack users is conditioned by factors that extend beyond the psychological and the pharmacological, including the availability of options for income generation at the local level and the politics of gender, race, and class in particular neighbourhoods (Maher and Curtis, 1995).

The discourse of dependency eclipses the role of broader social, cultural, and economic factors. As a small but growing body of research points out, it has also hindered recognition of the relations of interdependence that exist between the formal and informal economies and the 'dependency' that arises out of the vital function of the informal sector in supporting the formal capitalist economy (Perlman, 1976; Waterston, 1993; Bourgois 1995; Hamid, forthcoming). Through the provision of goods and services to those who could not otherwise afford them and in disguising under- and unemployment and stimulating new employment, the informal economy, of which drug users are an integral part, serves to reproduce the relations between labour and capital.

Defining the Informal Economy

The identification of discrete sectors of economic enterprise and modes of transactions which are integral to the formal economy, but are at the same time distinct from it, is not a new development (e.g. Bohannon, 1955; Polanyi, 1957). Low-income urban communities in the United States have a long history of reliance on the informal sector for services such as medical attention, spiritual healing and therapy, beauty and hair care, building, plumbing, painting, and child care (e.g. Liebow, 1967; Stack, 1974a; Valentine, 1978). Within such communities, access is often mediated by social networks and the informal economy represents an adaptation to material scarcity.

In recent years however, a small body of research has identified a global trend towards informalization, exacerbated by economic recession and the transition to post-Fordist regimes of accumulation. Manufacturers in Western Europe and the United States have cut labour costs through de-regulation and other, illegal, methods (Portes and Sassen-Koob, 1987). Trans-national corporations increasingly utilize Third World wage labour to produce their products at subsistence wages while workers in the West have been forced into low paying service jobs and the informal economy. In New York City, informal-sector production traverses a wide range of industrial sectors including apparel, accessories, footwear, toys, sporting goods, furniture, and electronic components (Sassen, 1991:87). In the apparel industry alone, the number of sweatshops in the city rose from less than 200 in the early 1970s to more than 3,000 in the 1980s, employing an estimated 50,000 in-house workers and 10,000 additional home labourers (Sassen, 1991:89). Informal-sector retail activity is experiencing a similar boom, reflected in the growing number of unlicensed sidewalk vendors. More than 10,000 of these informal merchants operate in New York, selling a wide array of goods ranging from faux designer goods to fresh fruit and vegetables (*New York Times*, 9 May 1994).

Two pre-conditions are generally held to be necessary for the creation of informal sector markets. First, the existence of a high demand market for a commodity deemed to be in relatively short supply and, secondly, the existence of state sanctions that manage, regulate, restrict, prohibit or outlaw the commodity in question (Hart, 1987). State sanctions set the terms and conditions of the illegal market: the degree of risk, intensity of competition, the level of corruption of state enforcement agents, and, ultimately, the price of the commodity. Thus the informal sector is in large part created with and by the state.[1] Nowhere is this more apparent than with respect to the market for illicit drugs. As was seen earlier this century in relation to the prohibition of alcohol in the United States, the demand for an illicit substance spawned an outlet for both existing and wanna-be capitalists and created new employment opportunities.

My analysis adopts the broad definition provided by Portes and Sassen-Koob who define the informal sector as 'the sum total of income-earning activities with the exclusion of those that involve

---

[1] For example, Hart has argued that, 'the informal economy is in large part the creature of the state. It does not have any independent existence *sui generis*' (1987:7). However, a one-sided view of regulation as wholly determined by the state denies the role of regulatees and prospective regulatees in shaping the processes by which various forms of regulation are secured (Dixon, 1991; Ayres and Braithwaite, 1992). While not denying the importance of power differentials, in some instances regulation may be better understood as an interactive process, with the content and outcome of specific regulatory strategies seen as the product of complex interactions between the regulator and the regulated.

contractual and legally-regulated employment' (1987:31). This definition entails a recognition that, while many different kinds of activities are conducive to informalization, it is the boundaries of state regulation concerning the processes of income generation, goods production, and service provision that determine informalization rather than the inherent characteristics of particular activities (Sassen, 1991). Some academic literature has tended to attribute informalization in advanced industrialized countries to the existence of immigrant labour forces. Informalization, not unlike Jamaican posses and drug/gun running, is often seen as a 'Third World import'. An alternative view posits informalization as an artifact of underdevelopment or a relic from earlier phases of industrialization. However, both approaches neglect the extent to which the conditions of advanced industrialized economies may actually instigate or promote the process of informalization (Sassen-Koob, 1989; see also Henry, 1982).

The inclusion of what has been called the 'underground' or criminal economy as part of the informal economy is a further point on which many theorists differ. While some insist on a broad definition of informal-sector activity (e.g. Mattera, 1985; Gaughan and Ferman, 1987), others have argued that the proper use of the term describes only 'the unregulated production of otherwise licit goods and services' (Castells and Portes, 1989:15; see also Sassen, 1991:79). For example, many goods and services provided by the informal economic sector are illegally produced and sold but carry only the risk of fines and/or closure, or in the case of illegal street vendors, the likelihood of being continually moved on by the police. In principle, however, the production of clothing in sweatshops, the sale of goods offered by street vendors and the services provided by unlicensed doctors or religious groups that the state does not recognize, could all be undertaken in the formal economy. On the other hand, criminal activities, such as the production and sale of illegal drugs, are excluded from this definition because they cannot legally be undertaken in any economic sector.

From the point of view of understanding social phenomena, in principle it matters little whether the actual goods and services could or could not be provided 'legally'—although the extent and severity of state response/sanction is usually calibrated according to this distinction. Rather, my analysis suggests that, from the perspective of the people involved, the idea that law or legal regulation provides a major demarcation of social life and cultural practice is false, or at best fails to give sufficient weight to 'the power of non-legal social arrangements to "regulate" economic relations in both sectors' (Benton, 1994:236). While illegality remains an important consideration (Castells and Portes, 1989:15), in practice the boundaries between criminal and other forms of unlawful commerce are blurred, and are historically and culturally variable. The institution of a primary division creates, at best, an unnecessary separation and, at worst, a false dichotomy. Moreover, as Benton has noted, the structuralist notion of legal pluralism implicit in much of the literature on the informal sector has left little room for 'a nuanced analysis either of how people perceived what they were doing in relation to the law or of how their "illegalities" may have been shaped by efforts of compliance that were nevertheless left incomplete' (Benton, 1994:227). This leads Benton to conclude that 'it would be sensible simply to abandon the "informal sector" as an a priori construct linked to a separate legal level or sphere' (1994:239).

A further feature which has been used to differentiate formal and informal sector economic activity is the scale of enterprise. While both production and sales concerns within the informal sector tend to be small, modestly capitalized, labour-intensive, and locally based, this is not necessarily the case and the logic of this distinction has not always been apparent (Benton, 1994:226). Another characteristic which has been identified as an 'essential feature of informal production and distribution is that it represents the articulation of market processes with nonmarket features of the social settings where it occurs' (Portes and Borocz, 1988:21). Within the informal sector, some exchanges are secured by barter rather than by cash and recruitment is commonly mediated by kinship and ethnic ties (e.g. Ianni and Ianni, 1972; Block, 1979; Waterston, 1993). Subsistence farming and agricultural petty commodity production in the Third World converts the unpaid or underpaid labour of economically and socially dependent kinspeople and, in particular, that of women, into material value (Portes and Borocz, 1988:22). Research also attests to the importance of informal economic activity in managing the transition from traditional economic societies to modern industrial societies. In Latin America, traditional trading and exchange networks accompanied the migration of persons from rural communities to low-income urban neighbourhoods where they provided the basis of alternative economies and new communities (Perlman, 1976).

The significance of social and kinship networks for informal sector activity has also been recognized in the United States. Studies have documented the role of the informal sector as a crucial adaptive mechanism for migrants (e.g. Dow, 1977) and both literary and ethnographic accounts of life in low-income communities attest to the existence of a strong informal sector in low-income urban communities. These trading and exchange systems, based on social and kin networks, serve to meet the survival needs of the urban poor (e.g. Whyte, 1943; Liebow, 1967; Preble and Casey, 1969; Stack, 1974a; Lowenthal, 1975, 1981; Susser, 1982; Sharff, 1987). The informal economy provides opportunities for income generation and access to goods and services for low income populations that are denied access to formal sector mechanisms because of the inadequate division of labour in advanced industrial economies (Pahl, 1980). In addition to providing an alternative market for jobs, goods, and services, these activities also serve as a kind of 'glue' which gives both 'form and stability to social life' (Ferman, 1985).

In the United States, the informal economy provides at least 12 million people with direct employment (Portes and Sassen-Koob, 1987). Estimates of its dollar value range between $42 and $369 billion per annum (Guttman, 1979; Feige, 1979; Mattera, 1985; McCrohan and Smith, 1986). Estimates of the proportion of the Gross National Product represented by the informal economy also evince considerable variation. Using macroeconomic statistical data, Gutmann (1979) claimed that in 1978 the informal economy represented approximately 10 per cent of the Gross National Product whereas Fiege's (1979) calculations suggest that a figure of 33 per cent may be more accurate. A recent survey of the cash exchange component of the informal economy (which ignored drug distribution and sales and other criminal activities) estimated that the informal economy constitutes at least 11.5 per cent of all domestic transactions (McCrohan and Smith, 1986). These figures are generally regarded as unreliable and the magnitude of activities that escape enumeration, while vast, remains unknown (Portes and Sassen-Koob, 1987).[2]

---

[2] While the crack-propelled expansion of the drug economy undoubtedly contributed to informal-sector growth on both a national and global scale, it is difficult to estimate the proportion of informal economic activity that the drug trade represents. In Bolivia, where it has been estimated that 80 per cent of the entire economy is based on the production and export of cocaine, informal sector transactions have been assessed as equivalent to the balance of trade, rendering the formal economy a 'near fiction' (Jiminez, 1989:139).

While some commentators argue that the growth of informalization in the United States will inevitably be at the expense of the formal economy (Guttman, 1977; Fiege, 1979), others insist that the informal economic sector exists in a symbiotic or mutually-constitutive relationship with the formal sector (Henry, 1988). Similarly, Castells and Portes reject the notion of the informal economy as confined to survival activities on the part of the poor and destitute: '[the] informal economy is not a euphemism for poverty . . . [but rather] a fundamental politico-economic process at the core of many societies' (1989:12–15). Indeed, the 'myth of marginality' serves to obscure the systematic linkages between formal and informal sectors. As Sassen's field research in New York suggests,

the city's larger formal economy creates and/or promotes the informal production of goods and services. It generates demand for specific kinds of products and services . . . the informal sector does not simply result from immigrant survival but is rather integral to the structural transformation of the New York City economy (1991:93).

While 'informal economic processes cut across the whole structure', most of the individuals involved in informal sector activities are poor (Castells and Portes, 1989:12) and many are marked by characteristics—such as immigrant status, race/ethnicity, gender, and age—that render them economically vulnerable. In this sense the informal sector has been seen to perform important disciplinary functions. In providing jobs for those who cannot or choose not to seek them elsewhere, and goods and services for those who cannot afford to pay the 'market' price, the informal economy undermines the power of organized labour, deters low-paid workers from industrial unrest, and serves to reproduce the bottom tier of the labour force (Mingione, 1985). Governments are often complicit with, and at times actively supportive of, informal activities, particularly those not explicitly designated 'criminal'. The existence of squatter settlements in Brazil and the practice of 'doubling' or even 'trebling up' within low-income urban households in the United States, for example, provide governments with cheap, easy 'solutions' to the problems of homelessness and inadequate housing.

A further aspect of mutual interdependence can be gleaned from the way in which the informal economy functions as a source of capital infusion into the formal sector. The flow of informal sector revenues by the relocation of accumulated funds to banks and legitimate investments including real estate, as well as bribes and payoffs to law enforcement and regulatory agencies, is considerable (Block, 1977, 1979; Block and Chambliss, 1981). Benefits may be even more direct: historical analysis reveals that prohibition made a considerable contribution to the formal economy in the United States.[3] During the 1920s, the manufacture of alcohol for industrial purposes increased sixfold, a large proportion of which was diverted to bootleg liquor production (Nelli, 1976:153). However, nowhere is the flow of capital more apparent than with respect to the relationship between the cocaine economy and the banking system. Some banks are 'addicted to drug money'.

Banks, most notably in Florida, have boomed by laundering vast amounts of cash generated through drug prohibition. In Miami so many drug-trade dollars have flowed through the city's branch of the Federal Reserve System that it has not needed to issue new currency for some time and even exports used dollars to other Federal Reserve districts (Woodiwiss, 1988:194; see also Mattera, 1985).

Finally, symbiosis is also reflected in the way that relations between labour and capital in the informal sector mirror those in the formal sector. As some commentators have pointed out, in advanced industrial economies, informalization may represent freedom of choice and a lifestyle alternative for participants. Money is not always the sole or even primary motivation for participation (Ferman and Berndt, 1981). Research strongly suggests that other factors, including autonomy, dignity, and flexible or unstructured working conditions such as the absence of restrictions and regulations—and even sometimes 'fun and excitement' (Henry, 1982)—may be equally important determinants (e.g. see Gaughan and Ferman, 1987;

---

[3] The Canadian liquor industry and the Canadian government were also among the beneficiaries of the 'noble experiment'. In 1929, more than 80 per cent of the production of the Canadian industry found its way onto the American market. While domestic consumption of alcohol halved during the 1920s, liquor revenues to the Canadian government increased by 400 per cent. In the United States, 'respectable' businessmen formed alliances with criminals, facilitating the reverse flow of capital from legitimate concerns to illegal brewing enterprises (Nelli, 1976:151–2; Woodiwiss, 1988:12). A similar history also exists in relation to illegal gambling (Dixon, 1991). During the 1980s, the image of cocaine as a low-risk, high-return venture prompted the investment of legitimate capital, including that of car manufacturer John DeLorean, who was charged with conspiracy to purchase 220 pounds of cocaine, reportedly in an effort to save his floundering car business (Woodiwiss, 1988:204–5).

Bourgois, 1989; 1995).[4] However, not all participants have chosen to enter the informal economy. As Portes and Borocz have noted, '[e]thnicity, race, gender, and age are an additional set of social characteristics which play an important organizing role in the functioning of the informal sector' (1988:21). For some groups, '[t]he existence of socially ascribed negative stereotypes . . . facilitates their willingness to accept unprotected and poorly paid work in general, thus propelling them towards informality' (Portes and Borocz, 1988:22).

Within the informal economy there also exists a distinction which parallels the capital/labour division in the formal economy. Entrepreneurs in the informal economy usually earn more than workers in the formal economy. However, workers in the informal economy earn considerably less than formal economy workers (Portes and Sassen-Koob, 1987). Although in some instances informalization in advanced industrialized economies has produced groups seeking better working conditions, in general, informalization has increased the power of employers at the expense of workers who 'find themselves toiling in conditions reminiscent of the nineteenth century' (Mattera, 1985:38). Informal-sector employers are particularly well placed to circumvent minimum wage and occupational health and safety protections, and research suggests that the relative advantage of informal-sector entrepreneurs is made possible by 'the continuing plight of their own employees' (Portes and Sassen-Koob, 1987:40).

In relation to the drug economy, commentators have been reluctant to make this distinction. The failure to adequately differentiate between drug business 'owners' or entrepreneurs and drug business 'workers' or employees has been exacerbated by the media focus on isolated individual 'success' stories in the 'rags to riches' tradition. Ethnographic research consistently attests to the fact that even at the height of their 'careers', very few crack dealers 'live large'. For the employees of the drug economy—the street-level managers, sellers, runners, lookouts, and touts—the hours are long, the pay is poor, and careers are frequently cut short or interrupted by arrest, imprisonment, or violent death (Bourgois 1989, 1995; Williams, 1989, 1992; Hamid, 1990, forthcoming; Fagan and Chin, 1989). Many street-level

---

[4] Some research suggests that those with jobs in the formal sector may be more likely to secure informal-sector work (e.g. Alden, 1981; Pahl, 1984, 1988). A study of street-level drug dealers in Washington DC also found that approximately two-thirds of those engaged in drug sales also held formal-sector employment (Reuter et al. 1990).

operatives reinvest their earnings directly into the drug economy by way of personal consumption, while for those who are robbed or ripped off, the end of a shift can mean more is owed than earned. For most, the 'crazy money' to be made in the drug economy turns out to be little more than the minimum wage (Bourgois, 1989) and the crack business represents 'a modern, brutalized version of a 19th-century sweatshop' (Kolata, 1989:A1).

The growth of the drug economy, and especially the cocaine economy, must be viewed in a broader context of increasing informalization as a result of widespread economic restructuring, and a concomitant polarization of economic and social life. In New York City, the street-level drug economy may be socially isolated and spatially segregated, but it remains integral to the economic life of the city (see also Sassen, 1991:94).

Women and the Informal Economy

The contraction of the already minimalist welfare state during the Reagan/Bush years made it even more difficult for many people in the United States to satisfy basic needs. These were boom years for the informal economy. Changes in the sectoral composition of regional economies have prompted expansion at both ends of the continuum (both low wage and high income jobs), and the proliferation of small units of production (Sassen-Koob, 1989:61). As the 'primary sector' of good jobs shrinks, the 'secondary sector' of less desirable employment grows (Harrison, 1974). Hourly earnings and skill requirements are dropping while educational achievement and requirements are rising (Braverman, 1974).[5] Like many large urban centres in the United States, New York City, and Brooklyn in particular, has been moving from a unionized manufacturing economy to a more competitive, less unionized post-industrial service

---

[5] A large body of Marxist and neo-Marxist work on dual and segmented labour markets links labour market processes with social stratification (e.g. Dorienger and Piore, 1975; Piore, 1975; Harrison, 1977; Gordon, Edwards and Reich, 1982). This work suggests that the economy is segmented into core and peripheral sectors. The working class is divided between those with secure, unionized, skilled jobs and those with temporary, low-paid, non-unionized, unskilled work. White working-class males tend to have greater access to work in the top tier whereas minorities, women, and immigrants are disproportionately represented in the least-stable, lowest-paying, and lowest-status secondary jobs.

economy.[6] Between 1967 and 1987, more than half a million manu-facturing jobs and over 100,000 jobs in the retail and wholesale sectors were lost in New York City (Kasarda, 1992; see also Drennan, 1991). Since 1965, the number of Fortune 500 industrial firms based in New York has fallen from 128 to 48. Manufacturing employment has decreased dramatically from 865,000 (one quarter of total employment in the region) to 355,000 (less than 10 per cent of the total). New York has shifted from 'a relatively well-off blue-collar city into a more economically divided, multi-racial, white-collar city' (Mollenkopf and Castells, 1991:8).

These changes in regional economies have had a disproportionate impact on minorities (Wilson, 1987). While the annual earnings of young men between the ages of twenty-five and twenty-nine declined by 20 per cent between 1973 and 1986, the decline among African Americans was 28 per cent, and 36 per cent among those without a high school diploma (Sum, Fogg, and Taggart, 1988). The labour force participation of African American males declined substantially from 84 per cent in 1940 to 60 per cent in 1980 (Wilson, 1987:82). Plant closures in cities with large African American populations, such as Detroit and Chicago, have had a devastating effect. During the 1970s, five per cent of African American men and six per cent of African American women lost their jobs as a result of plant closures alone, with African American women taking, on average, twice as long as African American men to find a new job (Amott and Matthaei, 1991:180). Hispanics are also massively over-represented in the declining manufacturing sector (US Department of Labour, 1987) and sectoral decline continues to be an important source of high unemployment among Puerto Ricans (Farley, 1987). The effect of this transformation and, in particular, the shift to a postindustrial service economy has been a changing racial/ethnic division of labour (Bailey and Waldinger, 1991) whereby 'blacks and Latinos have been largely excluded from the most rapidly growing and remunerative occupations in the postindustrial economy' (Mollenkopf and Castells, 1991:8).

[6] This process, often described as the shift to the economic paradigm of post-Fordism, is characterized by a new international division of labour and the globaliz-ation of financial markets. On a local level, the post-Fordist economy is defined by a decline in the manufacturing base and a corresponding decline in the demand for semi- and unskilled workers. Simultaneously however, there has been a marked expansion of the service sector and the proliferation of the new 'information technologies' which have increased the demand for service industry and white-collar workers.

While most studies have focused on the declining fortunes of young men in the labour market, a small body of research suggests that poor minority women may be even more profoundly affected by these changes. While some authors have argued that the relative economic position of women has improved during the last few decades, over-all, women still work in predominantly 'female' occupations and con-tinue to be paid considerably less than men (Acker, 1988).[7] Moreover, for female-headed households and poor minority women the situ-ation is much worse (Goldberg and Kremen, 1987; McLanahan et al., 1989). Recent economic analyses suggest that many minority women continue to experience debilitating economic oppression (e.g. see Malveaux, 1990; Simms and Malveaux, 1989; McLanahan et al., 1989).[8] Historically, African American women have exhibited high labour-force participation rates compared to other groups of women. However, more than three-quarters of African American women's paid jobs have been confined to the secondary labour market and, of these, almost a third consisted of low-paid, low-status jobs at the bot-tom tier of this sector (Amott and Matthaei, 1991:188–190). African American women have been hit hard by sectoral decline and, in par-ticular, the loss of unionized manufacturing jobs. Much formal labour-market research compares African American and other minor-ity women with white women or minority males.[9] However, the

[7] Despite substantial increases in women's participation, female labour-force com-mitment 'is still often less than complete' (Blau and Ferber, 1985:24). Occupational seg-regation remains widespread and continues to be primarily determined by gender (Trieman and Hartmann, 1981; Beller, 1984; Reskin and Hartmann, 1986; Sokoloff, 1992). Women tend to be concentrated in a narrow range of occupations usually encompassing clerical, semi-skilled factory work, and domestic work (Dex, 1987). For every dollar earned by men, women still earn only 64 cents (Hartmann et al., 1985). This situation is exacerbated for minority women who are placed at a double disad-vantage because they tend to work in areas segregated both by sex and race (Corcoran and Parrott, 1992; Sokoloff, 1992).

[8] In a review of Black women's economic fortunes over the last two decades, Corcoran and Parrott (1992) found that while in 1969, Black and white young women worked at roughly equal rates, by 1987 the employment of young white women greatly outstripped that of young Black women. They also found increased differentiation in the labour market behaviour of young Black women over time with employment declining dramatically for high school dropouts and single mothers.

[9] For example, some research suggests that urban African American women may be better placed than their male counterparts in relation to the expanding service sector. In addition to the structural impacts of economic transformation, differential percep-tions of inner city African American men and women by employers—such as the images of threat and fear which attach to Black men but not to Black women—may exacerbate gender bifurcation within the Black community (Kirschenman, 1991).

relatively high incomes of African American women who are full time workers (88 per cent of white women's earnings in 1986) masks other inequalities (Amott and Matthaei, 1991:189). According to Williams (1988), the appropriate comparison group for many minority women may not be white women or minority males but white men, given that minority women, and especially African American women, are more likely to be economic heads of households.

While considerable debate has focused on the economic position of African American women, recent statistics suggest that Latinas, especially Puerto Rican women, comprise an increasing proportion of those women most disadvantaged under the present economic system. Sectoral decline has had a disproportionate impact on '[n]ew immigrant women, speaking Spanish or other languages, [who] are particularly affected by the loss of manufacturing jobs, since white-collar work demands English-language proficiency (Amott and Matthaei, 1991:333). The proportion of female-headed households among Puerto Ricans more than doubled between 1960 and 1980, when almost 35 per cent of all Puerto Rican families were headed by women. By contrast, the percentage of African American female-headed households increased less over the same period; from 21.7 per cent in 1960 to 37.2 per cent in 1980 (Amott and Matthaei, 1991:282, 404). Nationally, almost one-third of all Puerto Rican families receive public assistance, compared to 23.5 per cent of African American families and 5.4 per cent of whites (Amott and Matthaei, 1991:281). In New York City, the highest proportion of female-headed households is found in the Puerto Rican community: 33 per cent versus 30 per cent for African American women and 8 per cent for whites (Rodriguez, 1989:33–34). Puerto Rican female-headed households are also more likely to depend on public assistance and less likely to be in the labour force than either Black or white female-headed households (Rodriguez, 1989:33–34).

In New York City, while the vital function of African American and Afro-Caribbean women as domestic labourers and child carers continues to enable white middle-class women to pursue professional careers (Colen, 1986, 1989), sectoral decline has radically altered the formal labour-force participation of Puerto Rican women. Historically, the cheap, non-unionized, regulation-free sweatshop and piecework labour of Puerto Rican and Dominican women has enabled the garment industry to remain in the city (Sassen-Koob, 1983; Sutton, 1987; Kasinitz, 1992). In recent years, the decline of manufacturing industries, especially the contraction of piecework associated with the garment industry, has exacerbated decreasing rates of formal labour-market participation by Puerto Rican women. In the 1950s, Puerto Rican women in New York had the highest labour-force participation rate of all women. By 1980 their rates were the lowest, despite demographic changes between 1960 and 1970 which would have predicted an increase in their labour-market participation (Rodriguez, 1989:40). Melendez (1987) found that the majority of Puerto Rican women concentrated in manufacturing between 1950 and 1970, did not transfer to the service sector. Nationally, participation rates of Puerto Rican women in the formal economy are 45 per cent compared to 60 per cent for white women and 67 per cent for Black women (Rodriguez, 1989).[10] These women have seldom been participants in the primary sector of stable, unionized jobs, and their position today is even more tenuous.

As the primary sector continues to shrink and men are systematically displaced to the more competitive secondary sector, within some neighbourhoods they are displacing even more marginal labour, such as minorities, women, and undocumented aliens further down the economic job ladder. For many of these women, even secondary sector employment is becoming difficult to locate. The participation of minority women in the informal economy must be understood in the context of these shifts in global and local-level capital. The informal economy, like the formal economy, is stratified, with less-competitive groups such as women and racial/ethnic minorities nearly always bottlenecked at the closed end of the opportunity structure. Within this sector, men often have a wide variety of options for making money while women have traditionally occupied select and/or specialized niches. Agricultural production in the United States, for example, utilizes a mix of labour provided by the homeless, illegal immigrants, drug users, and other economically and socially vulnerable populations. These populations, dominated by minority males, are recruited (typically out of state) to pick tobacco, peaches, and other domestic crops. 'Camp vans' regularly recruit from homeless shelters and bread lines on a 'by the head basis' (Vanderstaay, 1992:32). The lengthy accounts of 'forced labour' provided by Vanderstaay (1992) emphasize the vulnerability of men who are simultaneously poor, homeless, and using drugs.

---

[10] These rates are for women and children aged between 6 and 17 years.

Labour pools provide a further manifestation of the symbiotic relationship between the formal and informal economies in the exploitation of vulnerable male labour. Generally located in minority neighbourhoods in the inner cities, they provide casual day labour for legitimate economic concerns. Companies who contract with the labour pool to purchase the employee's labour are relieved of payroll, taxation, and workers compensation responsibilities, which in principle are assumed by the pool. Much of the work that is performed by day labourers is dangerous work that legal labour cannot be contracted to perform and, for the most part, work that is not covered by existing laws in relation to occupational health and safety. Homeless men, illegal immigrants, and drug users are particularly vulnerable to exploitation by labour pools which recruit from shelters, immigrant communities, and low-income neighbourhoods.[11]

Although such examples clearly speak to the issue of class relations and the nexus between formal economic life on a global level and informal-sector activities at the local level, they tell us little about the role of sex/gender and race/ethnicity in mediating women's opportunities for informal-sector income generation. Although many new immigrants and increased numbers of racial/ethnic minorities found work in the informal sector during the 1970s and 1980s (Waldinger, 1985; Sassen-Koob, 1985; 1986), little is known about the participation of women as agricultural workers or day labourers, or more generally, the impact of sex/gender in structuring participation in informal sector work (Hoyman, 1987). As Sassen-Koob has argued, the greater politicization of women and more traditional minorities with regard to wages and workers' rights may make them more costly and less attractive workers within the informal economy (1983:198). While there exists a literature on the participation of women in what has been called the social or redistributive sub-economy (Stack, 1974a; Susser, 1982), for the most part women are notably absent from studies concerned with participation in the criminal or drug economy.

In order to assess the participation of the Bushwick women in the drug economy, it is first necessary to examine their educational backgrounds, occupational 'choices', and economic opportunities in the formal economy. The following section provides an overview of the formal sector work experiences of the women.

---

[11] During fieldwork for this study, labour pools were regularly observed recruiting day workers for the construction industry in an adjacent neighbourhood.

Women Drug Users' Experiences of Work

Many of the women grew up in impoverished inner-city neighbour-hoods where high-school drop-out rates routinely exceed 50 per cent. Not surprisingly, 38 women (84 per cent) did not graduate from high school. Of the seven women (16 per cent) that did, five were European American and two were African American. One European American woman completed high school but did not have enough credits to graduate and an additional African American woman completed high school while imprisoned during the study period.[12] Four of the seven women had attended college and one had completed a bachelors degree. None of the Latinas completed high school.[13]

Table 1: Reasons For Not Completing High School

Reason*	N
Pregnancy	13
Street Life	6
Ran Away	4
Drugs	4
Fell in Love	3
Boredom	3
Truancy	2
Curriculum	1
Information Missing	2
Total	38

*Women were asked to state the 'main reason' they 'dropped out' of school.

Table 1 indicates that the women gave a variety of reasons for not finishing high school. While it is important to note that pregnancy was not the only reason women gave for not completing high school (only 13 women gave pregnancy as the reason for 'dropping out' of school),[14] of the women who had children, 30, or 83 per cent, first

[12] These women are not included in the seven women who graduated from high school.

[13] With an average of approximately eight years, Puerto Ricans have the lowest levels of schooling of all groups in the United States. The high school graduation rate for Puerto Rican women (52.7 per cent) is significantly lower than that of Black women (74.7 per cent) and white women (87.6 per cent) (Mare and Winship, 1988).

[14] These women represented 28 per cent of the total and 36 per cent of women who were mothers.

gave birth during their teenage years. Early parenthood is widely believed to be a good predictor of future economic instability. Research suggests that 'national data still support the notion that schooling and delayed childbearing are sufficient conditions for most women—black and white—to avoid poverty as adults' (Duncan and Hoffman, 1989:29). However, early childbearing has important functional aspects in the context of low-income minority communities where it is often 'perceived as a viable option that fosters individual growth, family continuity, and cultural survival in an environment where few other avenues for enhancing development are available' (Burton, 1990:5; see also Ladner, 1971; Phoenix, 1988). It is not early childbearing per se which diminishes young minority women's labour-market prospects, but rather, its effects in interrupting or terminating formal education.[15] A study conducted with inner-city single-parent mothers suggests that having a high-school degree is a strong predictor of labour-force participation (Lundgren-Gaveras, 1991). Three of the seven women in the current study who completed high school were mothers. One of these women (an African American) had the first of her two children at age 17, while the other two (one African American and one European American) both gave birth for the first and only time at age 28. All three had at some stage participated in the formal labour force.

Most women had little formal-skills training or employment experience after leaving high school. More than half, or 55 per cent, had never held a 'legitimate' job. Of the 30 women who gave birth during their teens, 64 per cent had no employment experience in the formal sector. Of the nine women in this study who had not given birth to a child, eight had some experience of the formal labour force. A total of 20 women (45 per cent) had some employment experience in the formal economy. Almost all of these women held jobs which fell into the bottom tier of the secondary sector. As summarized in Table 2, collectively these women had experience of 20 different types of legitimate occupations, representing a total of 32 formal labour-force experiences.

---

[15] Other research indicates that early childbearing may have a differential effect on young women based on race/ethnicity with adolescent birth more likely to have a detrimental effect on white than on Black women (Moore and Waite, 1977; Mott and Maxwell, 1981). These studies suggest that white families are more likely to disapprove of early childbearing and Black families are more likely to provide teenage mothers with greater support (see also Ladner, 1971).

Table 2: Formal Sector Work
Experience

Type of Job*	N
Parks and Recreation Attendant	3
Clerical/Office Worker	3
Factory Worker	3
Secretary	3
Cleaner	2
Barmaid	2
Waitress	2
Sales Assistant	2
Dental Assistant	1
Commercial Artist	1
Nursing Aide	1
Receptionist	1
Administrative Aide	1
Token Clerk	1
Telephone Operator	1
Catalogue Model	1
Drug Store Clerk	1
Deli Assistant	1
Cake Decorator	1
Assistant Script Writer	1
Total	32

*Some women had experience of more
than one type of work.

Although none of the women was employed during the study
period, previous research suggests that among populations of heroin
users, Black women may be more likely to be unemployed than white
women (Covington, 1988). Anglin, Hser and McGlothlin (1987)
found that Chicana heroin users in their sample were more likely
than Anglo-American women to be categorized as unskilled and less
likely ever to have participated in the formal labour force. Similarly,
the data presented here strongly suggest that women's experiences of
formal-sector employment are mediated by race/ethnicity. European
Americans, while they comprise only 20 per cent of women in the
sample, accounted for just under half of all women with previous
work experience in the formal economy. And while all the European
American women had some previous formal sector employment
experience, only 44 per cent of African American women and 20 per
cent of Latinas had participated in the formal labour force. Yolanda,
who was 38 years old at the time of her first interview, was one of
the few Latinas with legitimate work experience.

I worked a little in a department store. I worked in a factory, but I never had nothing, you know, important. I'd like to work in an office, something like that, you know, that I can sit there, writing, type or do anything. I should have done something like that but I never had the chance. Cause I feel I'm not stupid, you know. It's just that I never had the chance to do anything and now I'm getting old.

Race and gender are important elements in work stratification and workplace organization: 'For members of both groups (blacks and women), their daily existence as workers is always conditioned by their special status' (Edwards, 1979:197). Boy, aged 26, was one of the African American women with legitimate work experience. Her account is representative of the kind of unskilled employment experienced by minority-group women in this sample.

My first job was a summer job. Cleanin' up da streets for the city [Did you like it?] No. [Why not?] I don' wanna be out dere picking up da trash and shit. And iss hot in da summer. I couldn' take it. [What kind of work did you do next?] Another summer job. I worked in McLaren Pool as a lifeguard. I like-ded that one. [Why?] Cos you get ta see ya friends and ya all can hang out an' y'know, you be gettin' paid. Nobody mess wit you inna job like dat. You be responsible. [After that job did you have any more jobs?] I worked inna pay system, it was like an office place. I worked um, with da folders, y'know puttin' stamps on da folders, straightening out da files. It was alright but you could see dey don' really wan no Black people there. It was only a month or two thing. Dey say they only needed people dere and den—help right now—but you know is caus' you black [What happened after that?] I tried one more job. It was workin' in the factory. An' I couldn' deal with it. I hated it. It was the low pay, four sumpin' an hour but um' it was like puttin' things on shirts and I couldn' deal with it. It was really boring. [What was the best job you ever had?] Workin' in the McLaren Pool. [Why you liked that so much?]. Because I got a certificate ta become a lifeguard. I'm a full term life guard. I got me the papers and all.

Previous research indicates that factors such as flexible or unstructured working conditions, the absence of formal rules, and autonomy and dignity are also important in motivating people to seek work in the informal sector (e.g. Henry, 1982; Bourgois, 1989). The kind of work that Boy enjoyed (pool attendant) and the kind she liked the least (office and factory work) suggest that she would have been a likely candidate for the informal economy even prior to her immersion in drug use.

While most of the 11 minority women with formal sector work

experience felt that their race had influenced their treatment 'on the job' and contributed to their negative work experiences, more than half also drew attention to the ways in which understandings of sex/gender in the workplace were mediated by race. Carol, a 40-year-old African American woman, talked about her short-lived employment as a secretary to a clothing manufacturer in the garment district:

My boss, you know the Jewish guy, after a while he started hittin' on me. Like he got to prove that he some kind of big man, always tellin' me he got cocaine. So he start asking me to stay back to finish this or that and then he ask me if I want a line. I'm like 'Nuh uh, homey don't play that' and he was like 'C'mon, I know *you* girls are really into it'.

The relationship between race/ethnicity and sex/gender in shaping perceptions of legitimate work was also evident among women without formal sector work experience. As Kizzy, a 24-year-old African American woman who had never held a legitimate job told me,

[g]et outta here. If you a woman, nobody wanna hire you. They be like 'Why I train you then you run off an' have a baby'. If you a woman and you Black, forget it. Fuck that shit, I'll get mines.

A similar theme was evident in the account of Rosa, a 29-year-old Latina.

For girls to get a job is hard. For us (Latinas) iss more hard for speaking English. They want to know many thing, you know, ask question: 'Are you on welfare? Where your husband at? How many baby you got? Why you not on welfare?' For me iss too many question because I don't got no (immigration) papers.

In addition to experiences of discrimination and occupational segregation faced by earlier cohorts of minority women, the women in this study were also confronted with a rapidly declining job market. Compared to their parents, these women had restricted employment opportunities and those with the most extensive work experience tended to be older women in their thirties. Many of the parents of the 36 minority women in this sample had been in regular employment and often at least one parent had held a secure job. The women's fathers had been employed in a range of (mostly) secondary sector jobs that included the construction industry, factory work, the merchant navy, and city agencies—most notably the transit authority and the sanitation department. Although few of the women's mothers had completed high school and Latina and European American women were more often described by their daughters as homemakers or welfare recipients, most had at least some formal sector work experience. African American women were especially likely to indicate that their mothers had at some stage worked outside the home. Women's mothers had found employment in a wide range of occupations including security guards, token clerks, factory workers, secretaries, administrative workers in city agencies, domestic and childcare workers, and pieceworkers in the garment industry. Slim, a 29-year-old African American woman, was raised within an extended kin network after her heroin-using father left her mother with four young children to support. Slim's mother worked long hours for many years 'cleanin' white people's houses' before finding a 'steady job' as a hospital cleaner. At the time of the study, she worked as a security guard in a suburban New Jersey shopping mall while raising two of Slim's children.

Not all women provided positive evaluations of their mothers' participation in the paid labour force. Maria was a 19-year-old Latina whose mother had held an administrative position with the Board of Education for many years. During Maria's mid teens, her mother began spending nights away from the home with her boyfriend, leaving Maria to take charge of her younger brother. In fact, Maria attributed her drug use and current lifestyle to a lack of maternal supervision and support.

Like I had to bring him up alone. Like fifteen, sixteen, something like that . . . I gotta make sure his clothes are clean, 'caus my mothers's out fucking with her husband, see my mother two or three days later. Here, she give us twenty, thirty dollars . . . She was working, she wasn't being a mother. She was just like going through the motions. You know if my mother would have been home I wouldn't have been like this today.

Despite Maria's misgivings, it is the steady employment patterns and stable households provided by many of these older minority women that now position them to care for the children of their drug-using offspring. Maria acknowledges that the fact that her mother continues to maintain steady employment places her at a relative advantage in relation to her own daughter, presently being raised by her grandmother. There is little hope that, notwithstanding their drug use, women like Maria and Slim will be in a similar position to care for or support their grandchildren if and when the need should arise.

The combination of regional and global economic shifts and rising expectations of employers with regard to formal education over the last two decades has meant that many of the jobs that had been on offer to women's mothers were simply not available to them.

What is particularly striking about the younger generation of minority women I interviewed is how their educational and formal sector work experiences compare with those of their mothers. While both generations failed to complete high school, more than two-thirds of mothers had formal-sector work experience compared to less than half of their daughters. Their low rates of formal labour force participation, even prior to drug use and criminal convictions, place this group of women at a distinct disadvantage in relation to legitimate employment prospects. By contrast, the European American women in this sample were better educated than their mothers; all had legitimate work experience, and they were the only group to have worked in primary-sector jobs. For these women the shift to participation in the informal economy can best be characterized as a process of 'drift'—with movement between the formal and informal economy precipitated by increasing involvement in drug use and street life. The low rates of labour-force participation of the minority women suggest that their participation in the informal economy was not simply the result of drug use. Most African American women and the great majority of Latinas had few ties to the formal labour market to begin with. For those minority women with formal sector work experience, in addition to the low levels of income, negative perceptions of the world of legitimate work were also conditioned by experiences of racism in the workplace which they felt compromised their dignity and self-respect.

The Informal Economy as a Compensatory Mechanism

[B]lacks and Puerto Ricans, like other ethnics before them, see organized crime as one of the few available routes to success, to financial and thus psychological security (Ianni, 1974:38).

The informal economy has historically served to meet the needs of what have been characterized as marginal groups within the labour force. In the absence of either legitimate opportunities for economic activity or established organizations and turf boundaries, the emergence of crack cocaine presented new opportunities for individuals and entrepreneurs to participate in New York City's informal economy. There is little evidence, however, to indicate that the drug economy has attracted well-educated or skilled participants from the formal economy (Fagan, 1992; Fagan and Chin, 1989, 1991). Participants in the street-level crack economy were drawn from the ranks of the under- and unemployed, those earning low wages, and/or those with long histories of participation in drug use and sales (Fagan, 1992).[16] In distressed inner-city minority neighbourhoods where persistent poverty, structural unemployment, and urban dispossession support a thriving informal sector, the drug economy has become a substitute form of survival. In fact, Williams claims that 'the underground economy, and the drug trade in particular, is possibly the largest single employer of minority youths' (1992:10). For many of these young men, involvement in drug distribution and sales represents a crude adaptation to structural and cultural disinvestment in their futures: a 'rational' choice in the face of poor job prospects and restricted opportunities.

[T]housands of businesses have been spawned as a result of the drug trade . . . These businesses have drawn poor teenagers: the culture of refusal does not just mean that these young people cannot or will not live by conventional rules, but that they refuse to accept *any* subordinate status, convinced that it will allow them to be seen as valueless; they are so determined to escape that humiliation they will not try to advance through the usual channels (Williams, 1992:142; emphasis in original).

Severely restricted access to, and increasing separation from, conventional job networks has meant that for many urban minority males, drug distribution and sales and the oppositional street culture have replaced legitimate work as a primary source of income, respect, and cultural meaning. Crime becomes 'work' and illegal activities a way of 'getting paid' (Sullivan, 1989).

For many young men the drug economy is an employment agency superimposed on the existing gang network. Young men who 'grew up' in the gang, but now are without clear opportunities easily become involved; they fit

---

[16] Some evidence suggests that, among arrestee populations in the United States, women drug users may be more likely to be unemployed than males. A recent analysis of Drug Use Forecasting data indicates that while male arrestees in New York City had the highest rate of unemployment in 20 cities (57 per cent), the rate for female arrestees was even higher, with almost 81 per cent of women arrested in New York City indicating that they were currently unemployed (Drug Use Forecasting, 1990).

themselves into its structure, manning its drug houses and selling drugs on street corners. With the money from these 'jobs', they support themselves and help their families, at times buying fancy items to impress others (Anderson, 1990:244; see also Padilla, 1992).

Similarly, a study of the economics of drug dealing in Washington DC found that drug selling was an 'important career choice and major economic activity' for many poor young Black males (Reuter et al., 1990:xi). In a context where earnings from drug selling considerably surpassed what these young men could expect from legitimate jobs, many poor youths appear to make a 'rational' choice to enter the market (Reuter et al., 1990:85). The most eloquent proponent of the compensatory mechanism claim however, has been Bourgois, whose fieldwork in New York City's Spanish Harlem suggests that the 'underground economy and the culture of terror are experienced as the most realistic routes to upward mobility. Entry-level jobs are not seen by high school dropouts as viable channels to upward mobility' (1989:637–8).

While experience in the informal sector often precedes and replaces conventional work experience for this population, it is important to note that not all roads into the informal economy are economic (e.g. Valentine, 1978:19–20; Bourgois 1989, 1995; Sullivan, 1989). For many racial and ethnic minorities, the prospect of employment in the informal economy is enhanced by experiences or expectations of racial humiliation and harassment in the formal sector: '[b]esides wanting to earn "stupid money", people chose "hoodlum" status in order to assert their dignity by refusing to "sling a mop for the white man" for "chump change" ' (Bourgois, 1989:639). For minority males in particular, in addition to the prospects of independence and upward mobility, employment within the drug economy offers a potential for respect and a sense of dignity not available in the white man's workplace.

They prefer to seek out meaning and upward mobility in a context that does not constantly oblige them to come into contact with people of a different, hostile ethnicity wielding arbitrary power over them. In the underground economy, especially in the world of substance abuse, they never have to experience the silent, subtle humiliations to which the entry-level labor market—or even merely a daily subway ride downtown—invariably subjects them (Bourgois, 1989:642).

To date, little attention has been focused on the role of women in this brave new oppositional world. Given their under-representation

in, and negative experiences of, formal-sector employment, participation in the informal economy would appear to present a similarly
'magical solution' for many low-income minority women. Indeed
Bourgois suggests that 'more women . . . are also resisting exploitation in the entry-level job market and are pursuing careers in the
underground economy and seeking self-definition and meaning
through intensive participation in street culture' (1989:644; see also
Fagan, 1994:186–7). The extent to which this may be the case
remains highly speculative. Little is known about the informal-sector
participation of women in post-industrial capitalist economies or the
impact of sex/gender in structuring the informal workplace. In
Western capitalist economies, where discussion in relation to the participation of women in the informal sector has tended to centre on
the unwaged work of women in the domestic or household economy,
it has been suggested that women are no better off in the informal
economy. In fact Hoyman indicates that, far from providing women
with a 'halcyon experience—an escape from the shackles of the wage
economy', the informal economy 'reinforces the strong division of
roles and the inferior status of women' (Hoyman, 1987:77).

Although women have rarely been either the proprietors or the
beneficiaries of informal-sector activities, this is neither culturally nor
historically invariant. Anthropological research indicates that women
have been successful and independent operators in the sphere of
petty-commodity production. In parts of Southern and Central
Africa, women control the 'shebeens,' or 'yards' where beer is illegally brewed and sold (Bujra, 1975; Nelson, 1978; Malahleha, 1984;
Colson and Scudder, 1988). These shebeens have been the source of
political activism and some women entrepreneurs have managed to
accrue considerable assets and influence as a result. Evidence from
Africa, Latin America, and the Caribbean also suggests that, in some
instances, women market vendors and traders provide a substantial
contribution to family incomes and economic life, and wield considerable power as brokers of credit (Mintz, 1971; Babb, 1984;
MacGaffey, 1987).[17] As Mintz has noted of the Yoruba in Nigeria,
'[p]robably no people on earth has institutionalized women's rights
to engage in trading activity so fully . . . Yoruba women not only

[17] MacGaffey suggests that, in Zaire, the expansion of the informal economy has
weakened mechanisms of male control over women who have utilized opportunities
to become independently wealthy retailers and traders specializing in wax print cloth
and the shipping of fish, beans, and rice (1987:165–83).

have a wholly acknowledged right to trade and to use their capital as they see fit, but they also dominate the internal market system (1971:260).

Similarly, data in relation to women's participation in the 'criminal underworld' in Progressive Era New York suggest that the image of women criminals as 'passive victims of social disequilibrium and the venality and brutality of men' (Block, 1977:5) may be historically inaccurate. An examination of a sample of 311 women drawn from the reports of the Bureau of Social Morals[18] identified 78 female 'entrepreneurs', described as women who 'achieved a management position usually in a vice operation or displayed special business skills such as fencing stolen goods or corrupt bail bonding' (Block, 1977:8). While 22 of these women were known to be married, none actually worked for their partners and only one was reported to be in business with her husband. A total of 18 women were also identified as 'bosses'. In addition to providing goods and services within the informal sector, eight of these women 'entrepreneur-bosses' also made substantial investments in local real estate and legitimate businesses (Block, 1977).[19]

Conclusion

[T]he distributional consequences of the pattern of informal sector work in industrial societies is to reinforce, rather than to reduce or to reflect, contemporary patterns of inequality (Pahl, 1988:249).

While the existence of (sometimes lucrative) employment opportunities in the drug economy for minority males has been well documented (e.g. Mieczkowski, 1986, 1990; Bourgois, 1989, 1995; Sullivan, 1989; Williams, 1989; C. Taylor, 1990), little is known about the extent to which these opportunities are available to, or utilized by, women. Although some research suggests that the rapid expansion in street-level drug markets prompted by the advent of crack

[18] The Bureau of Social Morals was part of a Jewish 'self-defense' organization called the Kehillah, initiated in response to allegations of widespread Jewish criminality during the Progressive Era (1900–1917). The reports from which the data are drawn focused on New York's Lower East Side. For further information, see Block (1977, 1979).

[19] However, Block's conclusion that 'organized crime' was not 'sexually segregated' was not borne out by a subsequent analysis of 263 identified 'drug dealers', drawn from the Bureau's report on Narcotics, of whom only four were women and none of whom worked alone (Block and Chambliss, 1981:48).

cocaine and the erosion of male-dominated street networks have provided new opportunities for women to participate in drug distribution and sales (e.g. Baskin, Sommers and Fagan, 1993; Fagan, 1994, 1995), the nature and extent of this participation remains to be explored. While it may well be the case with respect to minority males that '[t]he underground economy . . . is the ultimate "equal opportunity employer" ' (Bourgois, 1989:630), the introduction of sex/gender as an analytic category produces a different reading of the inter-relations between economic sectors and the distributional consequences of informal sector work. Contrary to the compensatory function which it has been suggested exists in relation to minority males, the drug economy may well have an exacerbatory function for women insofar as it serves to reproduce the gender and racial inequalities which burden poor women, and poor minority women in particular, in the formal economy.

4

A Reserve Army: Women and the Drug Market

My heart pumps no Kool Aid—I don't even drink the shit. (Latisha)

Within the street-level drug economy in Bushwick, options for income generation can be located within three distinct, yet overlapping and inter-dependent spheres: drug-business hustles, non-drug hustles, and sexwork. Drug-business hustles (Johnson et al., 1985) form the 'core' or primary labour market, and non-drug hustles and sexwork constitute a 'periphery' or secondary labour market. Women are virtually absent from the drug business, under-represented in non-drug hustles and grossly over-represented in sexwork. In this chapter I focus on opportunities for income generation arising out of drug-business hustles, while the next two chapters examine non-drug hustles and sexwork.

Drug-business hustles refer to the transfer of goods and/or services directly related to the distribution and consumption of illicit drugs.[1] In Bushwick, drug-business hustles are further distinguished by their location within a structural framework or organization: in theory at least, they offer the prospect of advancement and a potential 'career' path. Non-drug hustles are defined as acts of income generation which, while they may provide revenue for the drug economy, are not directly related to distributing and selling drugs. They include crimes such as robbery, burglary, larceny, and shoplifting, as well as unlawful or quasi-legal activities involving the unregulated production of goods and services (e.g. manual and domestic labour, begging and 'scrapping'). In Bushwick, non-drug hustles did not usually involve structured criminal organizations; most were unplanned, opportunistic,

---

[1] Johnson et al. define drug-business crimes as including drug sales and a variety of associated distribution roles including steering, touting, copping, running, holding, guarding, acting as a lookout, testing, lending or renting works, picking-up, running a shooting gallery and injecting others (1985:61–5).

and committed by individuals or small groups. As such, they are better characterized as secondary-sector activities. The secondary labour-market identified here also consists of street-level sexwork, the primary source of income for women drug users.

Street-level Drug Markets

Crack cocaine has had a profound impact on patterns of income generation among drug users in North America. Research during the late 1980s and early 1990s attests to the salience of crack distribution and sales activity as a source of income generation among drug users in the inner-city (e.g. Bourgois, 1989, 1995; Hamid, 1990, 1991a, 1991b; Mieczkowski, 1990; Johnson et al., 1994). In New York City in the early 1990s, it was estimated that 150,000 people were involved in selling or helping to sell crack cocaine on any given day (Williams, 1992:10). Utilizing a large sample of users of different types of drugs in New York, Johnson et al. (1994) found that crack sales were the most frequent crime and generated the largest cash income. A full third of crack abusers obtained most of their income from crack sales, with one-fifth engaging in four or more crack sales per day. Crack was clearly the most lucrative and frequently sold drug in street-level markets and even drug users active in other forms of law-breaking were unable to generate income from these activities which rivalled that received from crack sales (Johnson et al., 1994).

The advent of crack cocaine has also had a dramatic impact on the distribution and consumption of illicit drugs (Bourgois, 1989, 1995; Hamid, 1990, 1991c, 1991d, 1992a, forthcoming; Johnson et al. 1990, 1991, 1994; Mieczkowski, 1990; Kleiman, 1992; Curtis et al., 1995; Curtis, 1996). During the late 1980s, crack markets in New York City experienced a profound shift in structure. This was characterized by a shift from the old 'dope-den' style of operation known as the 'crack house' to curbside or street-level selling operations. Crack houses had been particularly vulnerable to police raids and it soon became apparent that such operations were not the most efficient way of 'taking care of business' in terms of evading detection and pursuing illegal profits (Johnson et al., 1992). Their successors, street-level crack markets, have been characterized as unregulated markets of freelancers engaged in individual entrepreneurial activity (Reuter et al., 1990; Hunt, 1990) and described as a form of 'capitalism gone mad' (*New York Times*, 12 March 1989).

According to Johnson and his colleagues (1987, 1992), the 'free-lance' model of street-level crack distribution is usually an incipient distribution system within a loosely-organized group of buyers and sellers. Identifying features include voluntary co-operation, flexible agreements between the parties, and the absence of clear employer-employee relationships (Hamid, 1993). Some evidence suggests, how-ever, that once demand has been formally established, competition between retailers may influence the system of distribution and the freelance model may be superseded by a more structured system known as the 'business' model (Johnson et al., 1992). This model, which has come to dominate drug markets in New York City, is char-acterized by pooled interdependence, vertical differentiation, and a formal, multi-tiered system of organization and control with well defined employer-employee relationships (Johnson et al., 1992; see also Mieczkowski, 1990; Curtis and Maher, 1993; Waterston, 1993). Those at the lowest level (generally street-level sales and associated roles) receive minimum compensation with maximum vulnerability (Scharff, 1987). The modus operandi is similar to what Mieczkowski, in the context of heroin distribution, has identified as the 'runner sys-tem'. This system,

is an organized, co-operative strategy . . . designed to market heroin in pub-lic places, most typically at the curbside of public roads or other open locales such as areas in front of shops and stores, playgrounds, parks and school-yards . . . [It] uses individual participants who are organized into a rational division of labor. Interacting cooperatively in accordance with accepted rules, they direct their attention to the successful exchange of heroin for money (Mieczkowski, 1986:648).

In selling crack cocaine, drug business 'owners' usually employ sev-eral 'crew bosses', 'lieutenants' or 'managers' who work in shifts to ensure the efficient organization of street-level distribution. These 'managers' (as they were known in Bushwick) act as conduits between owners and lower-level employees. They are responsible for organizing and delivering supplies and collecting revenues. Managers exercise considerable autonomy in relation to the hiring, firing, and payment of workers and are typically responsible for workplace dis-cipline and the resolution of workplace grievances and disputes. Next down the hierarchy are the street-level sellers who perform retailing tasks involving little discretion. Sellers are usually located in a fixed space or 'spot' and are often assisted by those below them in the hierarchy: lower level operatives acting as 'look-outs', 'steerers', 'touts', 'holders', and 'enforcers'.[2]

Sellers may be assisted in establishing the bona fides of potential customers through a street referral system known as 'steering'. Steerers are usually known users who negotiate an arrangement with the owner or manager, usually in return for a 'PC' or payment in crack. Some sellers attempt to minimize risks by only selling to regular or established customers. In some markets, the volume of new or unknown customers has given rise to an occupational category known as 'zoomers' who sell vials of fake crack: usually soap or peanuts. In neighbourhoods such as Bushwick, which host large drug markets attracting a considerable 'drive-through' trade, it is almost impossible to restrict selling to known customers. Here the function of steerers at the street level is to provide a conduit for the sharing of information. This function assumes particular importance in periods of intensive police intervention.

Prior to the advent of crack cocaine, research on women's participation in the drug economy used one or more of the following to explain women's roles in selling and distributing drugs: (1) intimate relationships with men; (2) restrictions on discretionary time as a result of household and childcare responsibilities; (3) the availability of alternative options for income generation (especially prostitution); and (4) institutionalized sexism in the underworld. Female heroin users were often characterized as needing a man to support their consumption (e.g. Sutter, 1966; Fiddle, 1976; File, 1976; File et al., 1976). They were also described as being 'led' into crime by individual men (Covington, 1985) although this may apply more to white than minority group women (Anglin and Hser, 1987; Pettiway, 1987). The typical pattern was of low-status roles where participation was short-lived, sporadic, and mediated by intimate relationships with men (Rosenbaum, 1981c; Adler, 1985). The availability of alternative sources of income generation for women drug users, such as prostitution and shoplifting, has also been suggested as a factor which may explain their relative under-representation in the drug economy (File, 1976; James, 1976; Rosenbaum, 1981c; Goldstein, 1979; Inciardi and Pottieger, 1986; Hunt, 1990). Some suggest, in addition, that women

---

[2] Runners 'continuously supply the sellers', look-outs 'warn of impending dangers', steerers and touts 'advertise and solicit customers', holders 'handle drugs or money but not both', and enforcers 'maintain order and intervene in case of trouble' (Johnson et al., 1992:61–4).

drug users have less discretionary time than their male counterparts because of household and childcare responsibilities (e.g. Rosenbaum, 1981c; A. Taylor, 1993; Wilson, 1993) which work to preclude full female participation in the drug economy.

Women's peripheral roles in male-dominated drug selling networks (Auld et al., 1986) can also be explained by 'institutionalized sexism in the underworld' (Steffensmeier, 1983; Steffensmeier and Terry, 1986; see also Box, 1983). Steffensmeier (1983:1013–15) argues that male lawbreakers prefer to 'work, associate and do business with other men' (homosocial reproduction); they view women as lacking the physical and mental attributes considered essential to working in an uncertain and violent context (sex-typing and task environment of crime). In the drug economy, in particular, women are thought to be unsuitable for higher-level distribution roles because of an inability to manage male workers with threatened violence (Waterston, 1993:114).

Selling and Distributing Drugs

Since 1989, the displacement of users and sellers from surrounding neighbourhoods has prompted a steady increase in the amount of street-level drug dealing in Bushwick (Curtis and Maher, 1993; Curtis et al., 1995). Although some research suggests that there has been an increase in female participation in drug dealing in recent years (e.g. Baskin, Sommers and Fagan, 1993; Wilson, 1993; C. Taylor, 1993; Fagan, 1994, 1995), the entry of women into this male-dominated field has seldom penetrated up to the managerial level. In three years of ethnographic fieldwork spanning three Brooklyn neighbourhoods, I failed to encounter a single woman who was a business 'owner' and discovered only one woman who worked as a manager. The dearth of women managers suggests that one outcome of more general perceptions of women's unsuitability for drug distribution roles .is the belief that they are unable to effectively manage male workers: '[women's] difficulties in managing male workers may be attributed to the limits of female authority . . . [and control techniques such as] employing the ascribed female attribute of "being nice', as opposed to the more aggressive male technique of threatened violence' (Waterston, 1993:114).

Given the dominance of men at all levels of drug dealing, it has been suggested that, to the extent that women do participate, such participation will be mediated by involvement with husbands and boyfriends. Research conducted in Denver found that only four out of 24 women, interviewed as part of a study of users and street-level dealers, had sold crack. Only two had management roles and all four women had secured their positions through their boyfriends who were crack house managers or distributors. All subsequently lost their jobs when their boyfriends were arrested, the relationship ended, or when they were unable to control their drug use (Koester and Schwartz, 1993:192). For the women in the current study, past experience, rather than present practice, was more likely to conform to this model. For example, Sissy, a 35-year-old African American woman spoke about her short-lived and tangential involvement with the heroin business.

I moved up to Harlem, and um, I hooked up with this guy that was selling heroin. We used to get the quarter bags, and we used to cut it, and the shit used to be good. So I used to tap the bags, the quarter bags . . . I didn't know I had a chippy (mild habit) till like about three years later, when he finally found out that I was messing with it—and all that time he trusted me. And I was handling the money and everything; everything was right there with me. But as soon as he found out that I was messing with it, it was like I was cut off.

Similarly, the experiences of Cindy, a 26-year-old European American woman, in selling powder cocaine, were also mediated by her boyfriend.

He had me workin' with him after a while, you know, to have some extra money for myself. I used to help him sell the coke. I was always with him you know. I would go run upstairs and get the package for him and re-up (replenish the supply).

In the neighbourhoods I studied, the highly-structured nature of the drug markets, coupled with their kin-based organization, militated against personal or intimate sexual relationships between female drug users and higher-level male operatives. To the limited extent that they participated in drug selling, women were overwhelmingly concentrated at the lowest levels of street-level sales. They were almost always used as temporary workers when men were arrested or refused to work or when it was 'hot' because of the police presence.

The most common low-level distribution role for women in this study was as informal or unofficial steerers or touts. This typically involved recommending a particular brand of heroin to newcomers to the neighbourhood in return for 'change', usually a dollar or so. Neighbourhood newcomers were usually white men who may have felt more comfortable about approaching women with requests for such information. Although they only used crack, both Yolanda and Boy engaged in this practice of 'tipping' heroin consumers.

They come up to me. Before they come and buy dope and anything, they ask me what dope is good. I ain't done no dope, but I'm a professional player . . . They would come to me, they would pay me, they would come 'What's good out here?' I would tell them, 'Where's a dollar?', and that's how I use to make my money. Everyday somebody would come, 'Here's a dollar, here's two dollars.' (Yolanda)

[What other kinds of things?] Bummin' up change. [There ain't many people down here with change.] Jus' the white guys. They give you more faster than your own kind. [You go cop for them?] No, jus' change. You tell them was' good on the dope side. Tell them anything. I don' do dope, but I'll tell them anythin': 'Yeah, it's kickin' live man'. They buy it. Boom! I got my dollar, bye. (Boy)

Women's perceptions of 'white boys' allowed them to use this situation to their advantage with some women deliberately seeking out these newcomers in order to 'bum up change' for which they provided little in the way of useful information.

Within the street-level drug economy, the availability of labour is a strong determinant of women's participation in street-level distribution roles. Labour supply fluctuates in accordance with extra-market forces such as product availability, police intervention, and seasonal variations. One consequence of the police activity in Bushwick during the study period was a recurrent, if temporary, shortage of male workers.[3] These 'gaps' in the labour market, produced by attrition as a result of police intervention, promoted instability in the marketplace: the replacement of 'trusted' (i.e. Latino) sellers with 'untrustworthy' drug users (i.e. women and non-Latinos) eroded the social and kinship ties that had previously served to reduce violence in drug-related disputes (Curtis and Sviridoff, 1994; Curtis et al. 1995).[4]

[3] These 'gaps' (which result from short term fluctuations in the labour supply) must be distinguished from what some commentators view as structurally induced 'gaps' of a more permanent nature reportedly utilized by women to gain access to the market (Baskin, Sommers and Fagan, 1993).

[4] A recent study which examined a large core network of injecting drug users in Bushwick (n = 40) found that only 11 people (28 per cent) claimed to have sold drugs and that none of these was a full-time distributor (Curtis et al. 1995).

Early in the fieldwork period, both men and women perceived that more women were being given opportunities to work as street-level sellers than in the past. Such opportunities, as it turned out, were part of a calculated risk-minimization strategy on the part of drug-business owners and managers. As Princess observed, some owners thought that women were less likely to be noticed, searched or arrested by police.

Nine times out of ten when the po-leece roll up it's gonna (be) men. And they're not allowed to search a woman, but they have some that will. But if they don' do it, they'll call for a female officer. By the time she gets there [laughs], if you know how to move around you better get it off you—unless you jus' want to go to jail. [So you think it works out better for the owners to have women working for them?] Yeah, to use women all the time.

As the fieldwork progressed, and the neighbourhood became the site of intensive and sustained policing interventions, this view became less tenable. Latisha, a 32-year-old African American woman, reported that the police became more aggressive in searching women.

[You see some women dealing a little bit you know.] Yeah, but they starting to go. Now these cop around here starting to unzip girls' pants and go in their panties. It was, it's not like it was before. You could stick the drugs in your panties caus' you're a female. Now that's garbage.

Thus, when initially confronted by a shortage of regular male labour and large numbers of women seeking entry-level selling positions, some managers appear to have adopted the opportunistic use of women in order to avoid detection and disruption of their businesses. How frequent this practice was is uncertain; I do know that it was short-lived (see also Curtis and Sviridoff, 1994). While the sustained police presence necessitated shifts in the operations of street-level drug markets in response to specific interventions, most organizations proved highly able to accommodate rapidly changing conditions and to modify their operations accordingly. Indeed, the impact of the sustained police presence in the neighbourhood was arguably felt more strongly by users than distributors (e.g. see Curtis et al., 1995).

While, in the past, most women's experience of the drug business was as the 'girlfriend' of a distributor, this was no longer the case. During the three-year study period, only 12 women (27 per cent) were involved in selling roles. Connie, a 25-year-old Latina, was typical of this small group of women who from time to time managed to secure low-level selling positions. In the following quotation, she describes her unstable position within the organization for which she worked.

I'm currently working for White Top (crack). They have a five bundle limit. It might take me an hour or two to sell that, or sometimes as quick as half an hour. I got to ask if I can work. They say yes or no.

Typically, the managers said 'no' to women's requests to work. Unlike many of the male street-level sellers who worked on a regular basis for this organization and were given 'shifts' (generally lasting eight hours), Connie was forced to work off-hours (during daylight hours) which were often riskier and less financially rewarding. Temporary workers were usually given a 'bundle limit' (one bundle contained 24 vials), which ensured that they worked for shorter periods of time. As Cherrie, a 22-year-old Latina told me,

[t]he las' time I sold it was Blue Tops (crack). That was a week ago. [What they asked you or you asked them to work?] Oh, they ask me, I say 'I want to work'. [How come they asked you?] I don't know. They didn't have nobody to work because it was too hot out there. There was too full of cops.

Similarly, although Princess was well-known to the owners and managers of 'White Top' crack, had worked for them many times in the past year, and had 'proven' herself by having never once 'stepped off' with either drugs or money, she was only given sporadic employment. She reported that,

[s]ometime you can't. Sometime you can (sell for them). That's why it's good to save money also. So when you don't get work. [How come they wouldn't give you work on some days?] Because of some favour that someone might of done or y'know, jus' . . . [It's not like they're trying to punish you?] No, but they will do that y'know. Somebody go and tell them something, 'Oh, this one's doin' this to the bags or this one's doin' this to the bottles'. OK, well they check the bags and they don' see nothin' wrong, but they came to look at it so they're pissed off so they'll take it away from you, y'know.

In addition to their vulnerability to arrest and street robbery, street-level sellers who also use drugs constantly grapple with the urge to consume the product and to abscond with the drugs and/or the money. Retaliation by employers toward users who 'mess up the money' (Johnson et al., 1985:174) was widely perceived as swift and certain. As Rachel, a 35-year-old European American woman told me, '[t]hose Dominicans, if you step off with one piece of it, you're gonna get hurt. They don't play. They are sick people.' In some instances, the prospect of violent retaliation may serve to deter women from selling drugs. As Boy put it,

I don' like dere (the managers') attitude, like if you come up short, dey take it out on you. I . . . don' sell no crack or dope for dese niggers. Because dey is crazy. Say for instance you short ten dollars, niggers come across you wit bats and shit. It's not worth it, you could lose your life. If dey say you are short, you could lose you life. Even if you were not short and dey say you is short, whatever dey say is gonna go, so you are fucked all the way around.

However, considerable uncertainty surrounds the likelihood that physical punishment will be meted out (see also Waterston, 1993:113). This uncertainty can be seen in the following quotation from Princess, who had a long but sporadic history of street-level sales before and after the advent of crack.

It's not worth it. Number one, it's not enough. Come on, run away and then *maybe* then these people want to heavily beat the shit out of you. And then they *may* hit you in the wrong place with the bat and *maybe* kill you.

Such disciplinary practices resemble what has been described elsewhere as the product of a complex interplay between 'patronage' and 'mercy' characterized by relations of dependence (Hay, 1975). Within the drug economy, the unpredictability and uncertainty of punishment may work as a more effective form of control than actual punishment. In Bushwick, the actuality of violent retaliation for sellers who 'messed up' was further mediated by gender and race/ethnicity. In this Latino- and mainly Dominican-controlled market, the common perception was that men, and Black men especially, were more likely than Latino/as to be punished for 'stepping off'. Rachel described what happened after an African American man we both knew had been badly beaten.

[What happened to him? I mean he stepped off with a package, right?] Yeah, but everybody has at one time or another. But it's also because he's a Black and not a Puerto Rican, and he can't, you know, smooze his way back in like, you know, Mildred steps off with every other package, and so does, you know, Yolanda, they all do. But they're Spanish. And they're girls. So, you know, they can smooze their way back in. You know, a guy who's Black and ugly, you know, they don't want to hear about it . . . [B]ecause a girl, if she steps off, they're not gonna kick her ass like they would a guy. And you know, they're very serious about that shit . . .There was about eight of them. They had Joe up against the car. They were beating him up with like a motorcycle chain. I can't imagine the pain he was feeling. They had him pinned up against the car. And they were hitting him across the gut and like in the knees. The screams that were coming . . . They think nothing of really hurting a guy.

Relationships in the drug economy are fuelled by contradictory expectations.[5] On the one hand, attributes such as trust and reliability are frequently espoused as important to drug-selling organizations. To outsiders such as competitor organizations and the police, drug-selling organizations often present as intact social units.[6] For the most part, members are recruited from pre-existing social and kinship networks, which helps to ensure reliability by exploiting obligations that arise out of personal relations (Curtis and Maher, 1993). Ethnic and kinship ties are seen as the best way of ensuring trust among people who cannot rely on the law to protect their rights and obligations (Waterston, 1993). On the other hand, ethnographic informants often refer to the lack of trust and solidarity among organization members. This lack of trust is evident in the constant 'scams' sellers and managers pull on each other and the ever-present threat of violence in owner-manager-seller relations.[7]

The image of crack-using street-networks as a 'cruel world', perpetuated by users and exemplified by the oft-repeated refrain of 'no friends, only associates', is reflected in, and shaped by, the crack marketplace. Characterized as a 'culture of terror', the crack trade is dominated by violent and ruthless individuals with little regard for loyalty or relations of trust (Bourgois, 1989). Such a view contrasts sharply with the relations of trust and reliability that have historically been regarded as essential prerequisites to successful drug distribution by both employers and employees. Among ethnographic informants, the comparison of drug markets pre- and post-crack almost inevitably

[5] Mieczkowski has commented on the similar nature of relationships between members of heroin syndicates in Detroit. Contradictory expectations complicate these relationships. On the one hand, the crew boss expects and demands loyalty and obedience. On the other hand, the nature of the work demands considerable assertiveness and 'street smarts'. Often the very characteristics identified with the latter militate against the presence of the former (1986:658–9).

[6] This view may be something of an urban myth with some evidence to suggest that, especially at higher levels, 'informing or "snitching" has become an integral part of the drug-trafficking and enforcement world, with both small and large operators willing to implicate or testify against rivals or friends in exchange for shorter sentences' (Woodiwiss, 1988:193).

[7] Indeed Bourgois' informants in Spanish Harlem claimed that they did not need to rely on relations based on trust because they were tough enough to command respect and to enforce the contracts they entered into (1989:634).

renders the conditions of labour post-crack as much worse than in the 'good old (heroin) days'. As Ouellet and his colleagues (1993:88) have pointed out in relation to prostitution, a healthy scepticism of any 'rose-colored glasses' rendition of the past is necessary. Almost without exception however, those informants with a history of street drug use pre-crack believed that crack had prompted a shift in employer-employee relations and the responsibilities or obligations that they believed rightfully attached to owner-seller relations. As Candy noted, these days 'when you popped (get arrested), you popped'.

Nowadays, it don't pay to sell drugs caus' they can get busted. The guy ain't going to get you out of jail. He don't care who the hell you are. If you go (to jail), the older times he would work it out. That would be the agreement—that I would work with him if he is goin' to bail my ass out of jail. If I get popped an' get me (dope) sick, come get me. And I'll be illing caus' I got a habit and you better get your ass down here real quick and get me out. The way they workin' nowadays they don't. When you popped, you popped. You on your own.

Violence, or the threat of violence, is endemic to the operation of crack markets by virtue of the nature of the organizations involved and their greater propensity toward its use, both in the pursuit of organizational stability and as a strategic weapon in turf battles (Fagan and Chin, 1989).[8] During the late 1980s and early 1990s, law enforcement strategies altered the equation between drug markets and violence and the 'war on drugs' had profound effects on levels of violence, in low-income minority neighbourhoods (Curtis and Hamid, 1997). In Bushwick, an intensive police presence and large-scale arrests between 1988 and 1992 produced attrition in the ranks of street-level functionaries. The evolution of Bushwick as a drug supermarket was coterminous with the emergence of large corporate-style Dominican-controlled organizations which heightened the traditional rivalry between Dominicans and Puerto Ricans. Puerto Ricans became an increasingly disaffected labour force who strongly resented their Dominican owners. As the gulf between management and labour widened, law enforcement pressures intensified. Mass arrests in the early 1990s depleted the supply of Latinos, prompting further instability in the market and the replacement of Latinos with non-Latinos and heavy drug users.

[8] According to Mieczkowski, '[t]he inability to have normal recourse to third-party resolution may contribute to the tension in such a system and exert a sort of "Hobbesian effect" upon social relationships' (1986:658).

In the drug economy, violence can also be seen as 'a judicious case of public relations, advertising, rapport building, and long-term investment in one's "human capital development"' (Bourgois, 1989:632). In the context of a 'culture of terror' characterized by male-dominated street networks which claim drug distribution and sales as boys' own turf, women who use the streets to sell or buy drugs are subject to constant harassment and are regularly victimized. In response, the women in this study employed several strategies to protect themselves. One of the most important was the adoption of a 'badass' (Katz, 1988), 'crazy' or 'gangsta bitch' stance or attitude, of which having a 'bad mouth' was an integral component. As Latisha was fond of telling me, '[m]y heart pumps no Kool Aid. I don't even drink the shit'. Or, as Boy put it,

[a]c' petite, dey treat you petite. I mean you ac' soft, like when you dress dainty and shit ta come over here an' sit onna fuckin' corner. Onna corner an' smoke an you dressed to da teeth, you know, you soft. Right then and there you the center of the crowd, y'know what I'm sayin'? Now put a dainty one and put me, she looks soft. Dey look at me like 'Don't fuck wid dat bitch, she looks hard'. Don' mess wid me caus I look hard y'know . . . Dey don't fuck wid me out here. Dey think I'm crazy.

'Acting bad' and 'being bad' are not the same. Although many of the women presented themselves as 'bad' or 'crazy', this projection was a street persona and a necessary survival strategy.[9] Their instrumental rhetoric stands in sharp contrast to the middle-class feminine concept of expressive aggression. Their use of protective strategies, expressed in the cultivation of a 'self-protective reputation for craziness' (Campbell, 1992:13), resembles that of their male counterparts: 'to survive, force must be met with more than unspoken anger or frustrated tears . . . the best line of defence is not attack, but the threat of attack (Campbell, 1993:133).[10] But, unlike their male

[9] A study of street vending in Washington, DC by Spalter-Roth found that women street vendors adopt a number of strategies to protect themselves from harassment from male customers, vendors, and police. As one informant reported: 'You learn very fast to be as quick and as vulgar as they are, because if you do the standard female thing of being coy and shy and try to back off gently, they take it as encouragement and it gets worse' (1988:174). To outsiders, the distinction between offensive and defensive aggression in such situations is not always apparent.

[10] Campbell's research suggests that, among young female gang members, the containment of anger in the face of victimization results in a shift of allegiance from an expressive to an instrumental representation of aggression: 'Aggression in their lives is a means of survival . . . the indisputable law on the street is fight or get beaten. The reasoning that leads women to this instrumental use of aggression is *not confined to*

counterparts, for women, reputation was about 'preventing victim-ization' (Campbell, 1993:140). Despite the external manifestation of aggression and toughness in terms of posture and rhetoric, and the pre-emptive use of aggression, women were widely perceived (by men and women alike) as less likely to possess the attributes associated with successful managers and street-level sellers. These included the prerequisite 'street cred' and a 'rep' for having 'heart' or 'juice': in general, masculine qualities associated with toughness and the capac-ity for violence (Waterston, 1993). As Bourgois has pointed out, '[r]egular displays of violence are necessary for success in the under-ground economy—especially the street-level drug-dealing world . . . [which] requires a systematic and effective use of violence' (1989:631–2).

The desirability of these characteristics appears to work against the employment of women in street-level drug distribution insofar as they are perceived as deficient in them.[11] While on face value, many women appear to manifest these traits, the reality remains that men and women are 'far from equal in their power to make their own rep-resentations stick' (Campbell, 1993:143). Women's abilities to 'talk tough' and 'act bad' were apparently not enough to inspire employer confidence. Prospective drug business employers may need to feel that someone is capable of actually 'being bad': '[e]mployers . . . are look-ing for people who can *demonstrate* their capacity for effective viol-ence and terror' (Bourgois, 1989:632; emphasis added). Perceptions of women drug users as unreliable, untrustworthy, and unable to effec-tively deploy violence and terror are integral components of the sex/gender regime within the street-level drug economy which place would-be female sellers at a distinct disadvantage.

Sale and Hire of Drug Paraphernalia

Although both crack stems/pipes and injecting equipment or 'works' were illegal commodities in Bushwick, the sale of crack paraphernalia was controlled by the bodegas, or corner stores, whereas needles and syringes were the province of the street. Men dominated both markets

the gang. Wherever women face lives of brutal exploitation that destroys their faith in the value of trust and intimacy, they will be driven to it (1993:140; emphasis added).

[11] According to Miller, 'the ability to maipulate [sic] people or "con" people into giving you their money *without resorting to violence*' (1986:164; emphasis added) is an essential prerequisite of a 'successful' street woman.

although women were sometimes employed as part-time works sellers. Men who regularly sold 'sealed' (i.e. new) works generally had established suppliers (typically men who worked in local hospitals) from whom they purchased units called 'ten packs' (ten syringes). The wholesale rate for ten packs varied. Sometimes it was as low as two or three dollars but more often it was $5 per pack, or a unit cost of 50 cents each. Retail prices for works also varied, with sealed works generally selling for $2 each, although sometimes they fetched as much as $3 depending on general availability and the need of individual consumers. As a male informant told me,

[f]ive dollars a pack bring you twenty. You giving five dollars a pack and you got fifteen dollars more (profit), you know. Sometime you got more 'caus you got people that come down there, 'two-for-five' you know, buy two sets for five dollars, you understand what I'm sayin?'.

The benefits of selling needles and syringes were twofold: the penalties were less severe than those for selling drugs and the rate of return was higher compared to the street-level sale of either heroin or crack. Street-level drug sellers typically received a ten per cent cut on each unit of drugs sold. Drug sellers made $1 on each $10 bag of heroin they sold and 50 cents on a $5 vial of crack, compared to works sellers who usually made at least $1.50 per unit, depending on the purchase and sale prices.

Women who sold works were less likely than their male counterparts to have procured them 'commercially'. More often they 'happened across' a supply of works through a family member or social contact who was diabetic. Women were also more likely to sell works for others or to sell 'used works'. Rosa, a 31-year-old Latina, described in detail the dangerous practice of collecting used works strewn around the neighbourhood. While she often stored them and later exchanged them for new works from the volunteer needle exchange (which was illegal at the time), Rosa would sometimes select the works she deemed in good condition, 'clean' them with bleach and water, and re-sell them. Injecting equipment, including cookers and cottons, as well as needles and syringes, could also be hired from local 'shooting galleries'. Prices varied according to the establishment but typically ranged between $1 and $3 or a 'taste' of the drug to be injected. Given the scarcity of female gallery owners, women had few opportunities to generate income through the hire of injecting equipment (see the next section).

Although crack stems and pipes, in addition to the ubiquitous Bic lighters, were available from neighbourhood bodegas at minimal cost, many smokers chose not to carry stems on their person. These users, almost exclusively men, were from outside the neighbourhood. Their reluctance to carry drug paraphernalia provided the women with an additional source of income in the form of a 'hit' in exchange for the use of their stem. Sometimes these men were 'dates' but more often they were 'men on a mission' in the neighbourhood or 'working men' who came to the area on Friday and Saturday nights with the express purpose of getting high. As Boy told me,

I be there on the block an' I got my stem and my lighter. I see them cop and I be aksin' 'Yo, you need a stem, you need a light?' People say 'Yeah man', so they give me a piece.

Initially, it struck me as strange that these men did not purchase their own stems given their low unit cost of a dollar or two, even if they discarded them immediately after use. However, the demand for stem rental was seen to increase over the study period as the police presence in the neighbourhood intensified. An additional benefit for those women who rented their stems was the build up of crack residues in the stems. Many users savoured this resin, which they allowed to accumulate before periodically digging it out with 'scrapers' fashioned from the metal ribs of discarded umbrellas. Stem renters, then, not only benefited directly in terms of a 'hit' and/or a dollar or two, but accrued additional indirect benefits in the form of accumulated crack residues in their stems.

Some women also sold condoms, an ancillary form of drug-related paraphernalia in Bushwick. Although condoms were sold at local bodegas, usually for $1 each, many of the women obtained free condoms from health outreach workers. Sometimes they sold them at a reduced price (usually 25 cents) to other sexworkers, 'white boys' and young men from the neighbourhood. Ironically, these same women would then have to pay the considerable mark-up charged by the bodegas when they had 'smoked up' all their condoms.

Operating 'Shooting Galleries'

A wide range of physical locations were used for the purposes of drug consumption in Bushwick. Although these sites were referred to generically as 'galleries' by drug users and others in the neighbourhood, they differed from the traditional heroin 'shooting gallery' in several respects.[12] Bushwick's 'galleries' were dominated by men because they had the economic resources or physical prowess to establish and maintain control. Control was often achieved by exploiting women drug users with housing leases. Such women were particularly vulnerable, as the following quotation from Carol, a 41-year-old African American woman, illustrates.

I had my own apartment, myself and my daughter. I started selling crack. From my house. [For who?] Some Jamaican. [Yeah, how did you get hooked up with that?] Through my boyfriend. They wanted to sell from my apartment. They were supposed to pay me something like $150 a week rent, and then something off the profits. They used to, you know, fuck up the money, like not give me the money. Eventually I went through a whole lot of different dealers. Eventually I stopped payin' my rent because I wanted to get a transfer out of there to get away from everything cause soon as one group of crack dealers would get out, another group would come along. [So how long did that go on for?] About four years. Then I lost my apartment, and I sat out in the street.

The few women who appeared to maintain 'successful' galleries operated with, or under the control of, a man or group of men. Cherrie's short-lived attempt to set up a gallery in an abandoned, burnt-out building on Crack Row is illustrative. Within two weeks of establishing the gallery (the principal patrons of which were other women), Cherrie was forced out of business by the police. The two weeks were marked by constant harassment, confiscation of drugs and property, damage to an already fragile physical plant, physical assaults, and the repeated forced dispersal of gallery occupants. Within a month, two men had established a new gallery on the same site which, more than a year later, was thriving.

This particular instance of differential policing is explicable in terms of a set of practices that have their roots not only in 'individual' police discretion, but in light of the larger picture of policing low-income urban communities.[13] Here the primary function of

[12] While consumption settings in Bushwick more closely resembled heroin shooting galleries (see, e.g. Des Jarlais et al., 1986; Murphy and Waldorf, 1991) than crack houses (see, e.g. Williams, 1992; Inciardi et al., 1993), many sites combined elements of both and most provided for polydrug (heroin and crack) consumption (see also Geter, 1994). For further details see Maher (1995b).

[13] Historical research indicates that the policing strategy adopted in relation to working class gambling in the inter-war period in Britain was 'one of differentiated rather than universal enforcement. The place and time of the behaviour, and the age,

policing is not so much to enforce the law but, rather, to regulate illegal activities (Whyte, 1943:138). As such the beat police officer must, to some degree at least, 'conform to the social organization within which he [sic] is in direct contact' (1943:138). Within the highly gendered context of the street-level drug economy, police officers exercise considerable discretion in deciding which activities to ignore, which to police, and to what extent. Field observations suggest that the reason the police did not interfere as much in relation to galleries controlled by men was that they assumed that men were better able than women to 'control' galleries and thus minimize problems of violence and disorder. An alternative view would suggest that in this instance, as in many others, police harass women drug users simply because they can.

Other factors contributed to women's disadvantage in operating galleries, crack houses, and other consumption sites. Male drug users were generally better placed economically than the women in this sample, most of whom were homeless and without a means of legitimate economic support. When women did have an apartment or physical site, rather than open up opportunities for their entrepreneurial activities, this made them a vulnerable target either for exploitation by male users or dealers (as in Carol's account) or to harassment by the police (as in Cherrie's). Even where women claimed to be in control of particular locations, field observations confirmed they were not. One woman, Kizzy, continued to maintain that she was the 'boss' of the gallery which operated from her apartment, even as she complained to me about yet another unwelcome house guest imposed on her by her (male) cousin.

She's stayin' ere 'cos a ma cousin. Cos she, she sucks his thing—he demands ma money from them . . . [How come you let her stay?] I changed my mind. You know why, caus' I told the bitch, and then she gonna go ask my cousin. Who the fuck is he, this is *my crib*. She want to be a stinky little dumb bitch, and gonna try to get permission from them too. I'm the boss.

In this situation, the attribution of ownership and control were confounded by the conflicting accounts that emerged in relation to economic transactions, rule setting, and rule enforcement in Kizzy's apartment. However, according to most of those who were familiar with the establishment, Kizzy's cousin Pops had the upper hand.

sex, status, and class of the actors determined in practice what was, and what was not, permissible . . . What was treated as deviant in practice did not match the formal definitions of illegality' (Dixon, 1991:267).

[Let me just ask you, in your opinion who runs Kizzy's place, her cousin Pops or Kizzy?] You said it, the first one. You don't go in there honey because you think you're getting a break, shit. Not there. Pops doesn't give breaks. (Tameka)

Thus in Bushwick the presence of a man was a prerequisite to the successful operation of drug consumption sites. The only real choice for those women in a position to operate galleries or crack houses was between the 'devils they knew' and those they did not.

Copping Drugs

Many women supplemented their incomes by 'copping' or purchasing drugs for others. These others were usually white and almost always men. At times they were dates, but often they were users who feared being caught and were prepared to pay for someone else to take that risk. As Rachel explained,

I charge them just what they want to buy they have to pay me. If they want twenty dollars they have to give me twenty dollars worth on the top, because I'm risking my free time. I could get busted copping. They have to pay me the same way, if not, they can go cop. Most of them can't because they don't know the people.

Those who cop drugs for others perform an important service which is integral to the functioning of the drug market. As Biernacki suggests in relation to heroin, 'they help to minimize the possibility of infiltration by undercover agents and decrease the chance of a dealer's arrest' (1979:539). In Bushwick, the copping role attracted few men and was generally regarded by both men and women as a low-status, peripheral hustle: those who copped drugs for others were looked down on and 'viewed as failures, as persons who are not competent enough to manage their addiction or who do so with little style and no character' (1979:539).[14] Nonetheless it was difficult to ascertain whether the low status ascribed 'copping agents' was a product of the feminization of this particular hustle or whether, following Biernacki, the fact that it yielded low returns for high risks and was universally regarded as low status, meant that it was 'left to the girls'.

[14] Biernacki was concerned with the attribution of social status among heroin addicts based on the hustles they employed. He found that heroin addicts who participated in dangerous hustles with low rewards had low self-esteem: '[those] who, for example provide street services for other users—appear to be attributed one of the lowliest statuses in the heroin world and correspondingly most often think of themselves in similar deprecating terms' (1979:540).

Most women viewed the female-dominated nature of the job as a product of their differential positioning in the marketplace in relation to contact with outsiders. Within the context of a parallel sex market, outsiders could readily approach women to buy drugs under the guise of buying sex and thereby minimize the risk of dealing with undercover police. As Rosa recounted,

[y]ou would (be) surprise. They'd be ahm, be people very important, white people like lawyer, doctors that comes and get off, you'd be surprised. Iss like I got two lawyer, they come saying, you know they give me money to go, to go and cop. And they stay down over there parking . . . [How do you meet them?] Well down the stroll one time they stop and say you know, 'You look like a nice girl though, you know, you wanna make some money fast?' I say, 'How?' So they say, you know, 'Look out for me.' First time they give me like you know, twenty dollars. They see I came back, next time they give me thirty. Like that, you know. I have been copping for them like over six month already.

Sometimes this function was performed in conjunction with sexwork, as Latisha's account demonstrates.

He's a cop. He's takin' a chance. He is petrified. Will not get out his car . . . But he never gets less than nine bags (of powder cocaine). [And he sends you to get it?] And he wants a blow job, right, OK. You know what he's givin' you, a half a bag of blue (blue bag cocaine). That's for you goin' to cop, an' for the blow job. That's two dollars fifty (worth). I can go to jail (for him) caus' I'm a piece of shit.

Women also felt that given the reputation of the neighbourhood as very 'thirsty' (i.e. as having a thirst or craving for crack), male outsiders were more likely to trust women, especially white women, to purchase drugs on their behalf. Often this trust was misplaced. The combination of naive, inexperienced 'white boys' and experienced, 'street smart' women produced opportunities for additional income by, for example, absconding with the 'cop money'. This was a calculated risk and sometimes things went wrong. When they did, women sometimes received severe beatings from the angry 'client'. More often it meant 'laying low' for a few hours while the angry client drove around the neighbourhood in search of the woman and his cash and, usually, a more trustworthy woman to fulfil the original mission. A safer practice was to inflate the actual purchase price of the drugs and pocket the difference. Rosa explained this particular scam.

He think is a ten dollar bag, but issa five dollar. But at least I don't be rip-pin' him off there completely. [But you're taking the risk for him.] Exactly. Sometime he give me a hunert (hundred) dollars, so I making fifty, right? But sometime he don't get paid, he got no second money, eh. I cop then when I come back the car, he say, 'Dear, I cannot give you nothin' today,' you know. But I still like I say, I gettin' someting from him, because he think is a ten dollar bag.

Similar scams involved the woman returning to the client with nei-ther drugs nor money, and claiming that she had been 'ripped off' or, less often, short-changing the client by tapping the vials (removing some crack) or adulterating the heroin or powder cocaine (cutting it with other substances). These scams attest to the diversity of women's experiences as copping agents and indicate that, while marginalized with respect to most drug-business hustles, many women were astute in making the most of the limited opportunities that came their way.

Street Docs

The practice of injecting those who are unable or unwilling to inject themselves, either because they are inexperienced or have deep or col-lapsed veins, has been documented by others (e.g. Johnson et al., 1985; Murphy and Waldorf, 1991). Those performing this role are referred to as street 'docs' (Murphy and Waldorf, 1991:16–17). In Bushwick, men typically specialized in the provision of this service which was often extended as part of an established shooting gallery or consumption site. For example, Sam, a Latino injector in his late thirties, lived in one of the makeshift condos located adjacent to the principal heroin copping area. Those who were in a hurry to con-sume or who had nowhere else to go would use Sam's place to 'get off'. In addition to a supply of works (both used and unused, the lat-ter obtained from the underground needle exchange), Sam provided water and a range of 'cookers' and 'cottons'. Sam had a reputation as a good 'hitter' and injected several of the women in the sample on a regular basis. He provided this service in exchange for a few dol-lars or, more often, a 'taste' of the substance to be injected.

Only one woman in the sample, Latisha, capitalized on her repu-tation as a good 'hitter' by playing the street-doc role. At one stage, Latisha had a regular arrangement with a young street thug named Crime, who had only recently commenced intravenous heroin use and was unable to 'hit' himself. While experienced women injectors were as likely to have the requisite level of skill, they were less likely than men to be able to capitalize on it because they did not control established consumption settings.

Conclusion

Cat got busted. Yeah, the other night. And she was set up. She was in the train (station) and we were all smoking. And Crime and these other people were selling (on the corner). She finished smoking everything. She had no money left. She walked around the corner to speak to them. Like six cops rolled at once. The kid threw the package on the floor. It ended up in front of Cat. I don't know where the money ended up. They took Cat. It was no product on anybody, but they (the police) put it on her.

Cat was convicted and subsequently imprisoned. She was not the only woman in this study arrested for selling drugs who happened merely to be in the wrong place at the wrong time. Some women, like Jenny, were arrested as a result of their cohabitation with male sellers. Jenny was arrested when her pimp/boyfriend's hotel room was raided by the police and a large quantity of crack was found. Although the case against her was 'constructive' possession with intent to sell, Jenny pleaded guilty, was subsequently convicted, and served one-and-a-half years in prison.

The findings presented here serve both to challenge and to contextualize the conditions of female participation in the drug business. They stand in sharp contrast both to analyses of official data, and to studies which highlight increased female participation in the drug economy. For example, in a study of women crack users in Miami, Inciardi and his colleagues found that drug-business offences (mainly street-level sales) represented a much greater proportion of crimes committed by women (94 per cent) than that found among two earlier cohorts of female heroin users (28 and 34 per cent respectively). The women in this sample were also significantly less likely to engage in prostitution (Inciardi et al., 1993).[15] However, such accounts provide little insight into the positioning of women in street-level drug markets.[16]

[15] Seventy-six per cent of this Miami-based sample of 197 women crack users (a combination treatment/street sample) reported drug business crimes in the 90 days prior to interview (Inciardi et al., 1993:120–2).

[16] Inciardi et al. (1993) claim that while the women in their research reportedly preferred drug sales to prostitution, drug shortages, rather than a segmented labour market, were what served to prevent them from exercising their employment preferences (see also Inciardi and Pottieger, 1986).

While disparate images of women's participation in drug distribution and sales may be the product of differences in study samples (including racial-ethnic variation in drug market organization, neighbourhood-level variation, variation in the kinds of drugs sold, and when the study was conducted), they also reflect differences in the methodological approaches utilized by researchers. Virtually all North American studies of women drug users have employed one-time interviews. The ethnographic approach used in this study reveals that in the absence of a temporal frame and observational data, interviews may provide an incomplete and inaccurate picture. The one-time interview also misses the changing and fluid nature of relations in the informal economy. For example, for a short period there was a perception in Bushwick that 'new opportunities' existed for women to sell crack. That perception faded as it became clear that owners and managers were 'using' women to evade the constraints imposed on them by law enforcement and police search practices. Ethnographic approaches, then, can offer a more dynamic and contextualized picture of women's lawbreaking. While such approaches are relatively numerous in the study of adolescent and adult men in the United States (e.g. Sullivan, 1989; Anderson, 1990; Padilla, 1992; Bourgois, 1995), they have rarely been utilized in the study of women and girls.

This chapter suggests not only that considerations of the status and positioning of women in the drug economy need to differentiate between the respective market sectors in which men and women typically generate illegal income, but also that generalizations about the nature and extent of women's participation in drug distribution typically fail to distinguish between the different types of 'models' which characterize drug-distribution networks and the particular organizational forms they take at the neighbourhood level. Indeed, the fact that the women in this study were markedly under-represented in street-level sales positions reflects a number of features identified here, including fluctuations in the availability of labour in accordance with extra-market forces and the 'business' model which characterized drug distribution in Bushwick. While, in theory, the built-in supervision and task differentiation of the business model should have provided opportunities for both men and women (Johnson et al., 1992), my findings suggest that sellers were overwhelmingly men whose involvement was further mediated by ethnic/kinship ties.

The theoretical tools used by researchers to examine women's participation in the drug economy have also been inadequate. Women drug users have rarely been studied as members of social networks or as participants in collective or group-based activity. Nor have they been viewed as economic actors in illegal markets governed by organizational constraints, occupational norms, and workplace cultures. Those making a general claim about 'women's emancipation' in the drug economy ignore the obdurateness of a gender-stratified labour market and the beliefs and practices that maintain it. Those making the more restricted claim that male-dominated street networks and market processes have weakened, thus allowing entry points for women, need to offer proof for that claim. Assertions of women's changing and improved position in the drug economy have not been well proved. Nor are they grounded in theories of how work, including illegal work, is conditioned by relations of gender, race/ethnicity and sexuality (e.g. Kanter, 1977; Game and Pringle, 1984; Messerschmidt, 1993).

Of the four elements that have been used to explain women's restricted involvement in drug economies of the past, I found evidence of change in two: a diminishing of women's access to drug selling roles via boyfriends and husbands, especially where drug markets are highly structured and kin-based; and decreased economic returns for street-level sexwork. Because few of the women had stable households or cared for children, I cannot comment on changes (if any) in discretionary time. Institutionalized sexism in the underworld was the most powerful element shaping women's experiences in the drug economy: it inhibited their access to drug-business work roles and effectively foreclosed their participation as higher-level distributors. All the elements of underworld sexism identified by Steffensmeier (1983)—homosocial reproduction, sex-typing, and the qualities required in a violent task environment—featured prominently in Bushwick's street-level drug economy.

The 'new opportunities' said to have emerged with the crack-propelled expansion of drug markets from the mid-1980s onwards were not 'empty slots' waiting to be filled by those with the requisite skill. Rather, they were slots requiring certain masculine qualities and capacities. These qualities, while presented as 'human' are both gendered and raced. Their significance and the symbolism used to convey them was evident in the women's use of instrumental aggression. While fluctuations in the availability of labour appear to produce temporary ruptures or gaps which precipitate sporadic and short-lived opportunities for female participation in low-level distribution roles, highly gendered understandings continue to be reflected in, and shaped by, perceptions of women as unreliable, untrustworthy and incapable of demonstrating an effective capacity for violence. Ultimately these perceptions serve to reinforce the marginal status of women as a reserve army of labour within the drug business.

The formal organizational characteristics of highly-structured drug markets, the distribution networks which sustain them, and the cultural practices and beliefs of the social actors who inhabit them, work together to foster both sex/gender and race/ethnic segmentation in the (illegal) workplace. It not only remains the case that, as Klein and Kress observed almost twenty years ago, '[w]omen are no more big-time drug dealers than they are finance capitalists' (1976:4), but moreover, that this division of labour appears to permeate the street-level distribution hierarchy. With few exceptions, opportunities for income generation within this hierarchy—ranging from higher-level managerial and distribution roles to minimum-wage positions as street-level operatives—continue to be monopolized by males.

5

Jobs for the Boys:
Street Hustles

[What do you mean two different systems?] Wake up and smell the coffee baby. Men got their thing, we got ours. (Candy)

This chapter focuses on women's involvement in a range of income-generating activities which, while clearly drug-related, are not confined to the drug economy or its participants. These non-drug hustles fall into two categories: 'criminal' hustles and 'unlawful' hustles. 'Criminal hustles', such as street crime, are those activities which are prohibited by criminal law per se and cannot legally be undertaken in any other economic sector. In distinguishing unlawful hustles from criminal hustles, this chapter relies on the conventional definition of 'informal sector' activity as that which is marked by the absence of state regulation (Castells and Portes, 1989; Sassen, 1991). Unlawful hustles are those acts of income generation which could theoretically be undertaken in the formal economy if appropriate regulatory conditions (e.g. paying taxes, obtaining licences, registering businesses, having premises and work conditions subject to state oversight) were met. They constitute the 'unregulated production of otherwise licit goods and services' (Castells and Portes, 1989:15) and are unlawful, not per se, but because regulatory conditions are not met. Their unlawfulness stems not from the activity itself but from the failure to observe the stipulated regulations (Williams, 1967).

Such a distinction may, however, invoke an artificial separation. As Benton has noted, a priori categorizations of economic activities as inhabiting distinct spheres of illegality 'make an awkward scaffold for observed behavior' (1994:224). In practice, unlawful hustles are interstitial activities, located in the interstices between legal and illegal economic conduct. As such, their legal status is often ambiguous. In Bushwick, both criminal and unlawful hustles were identified by drug users as 'street hustles'. They were part of a domain of

income generation intimately connected with street life in the neighbourhood, and, while not directly related to the distribution and sale
of illicit drugs, they provided a vital influx of revenue into the drug
economy. Criminal and unlawful hustles were not mutually exclusive; in theory at least, an individual was not confined to either category. Those fortunate enough to be able to identify and act upon
opportunities to generate income from unlawful hustles also participated in criminal hustles—sometimes switching between the two categories several times over the course of a day. While some unlawful
hustles evinced a degree of organization and planning, most street
hustles (both criminal and unlawful) were unplanned and opportunistic, and were usually undertaken by individuals acting alone or
in concert with one or two others.

'Unlawful' Hustles

Drug-using male members of the underclass have a greater variety of possible economic strategies than women. Potentially violent criminal activity and
all but the lowest levels of drug dealing are dominated by men. Men, even
those with limited educational skills, can more readily find jobs as manual
laborers through temporary labor pools (Koester and Schwartz, 1993:192).

Male drug users in Bushwick generated income from a range of
sources including unlawful activities such as begging or panhandling,
recycling aluminium cans, washing car windscreens and odd jobs.[1]
One notorious slumlord retained a permanent crew of male drug
users for odd jobs, building maintenance, and caretaking roles. In
addition to providing a cheap supply of labour, these men served as
a source of 'cut-rate' (i.e. stolen) supplies, including power tools and
building materials. Male drug users were more likely than women to
have the kinds of previous experience, knowledge, and skills—
whether gained formally or informally—which were in demand in the
local-level informal economy. As one man told me, '[w]ell, you know
I do a lotta things. Like I do electricity or electrician work. I do
plumbing, I do mason, you know, like carpentry, you know.' Men
were also more likely to have the contacts necessary for the deployment of these skills. As the same informant noted, '[p]eople know me

[1] I conducted a small number of interviews with male informants who were partners of women in the study sample about their relationships. In addition to extensive
participant observation of gender relations between these couples, I also spoke to the
men about their income-generating activities.

and like some people refer me (to) other people's places, places that people own their own business, you know, and they know that I am capable, what I am capable of doing. So if they need me, and say they get a spot open for a couple of days, you know, they give me a shot.' Of course the opportunities for male drug users to participate in unlawful hustles is also related to the fact that their services come very cheaply.

While, with few exceptions, women rarely held regular—or even irregular—jobs in the informal sector, several men managed to obtain informal-sector work on a regular basis. For example, Latisha's partner Tre retained a stable position assisting on a milk delivery truck every morning from 7.30 am to 10.30 a.m. As he described it, 'I make like, I only work three hours a day so I get like thirty dollars a day so that's like ten dollars an hour. It's off the books . . . I'll never give up the milk truck thing because it's constant and I can rely on it.' However, it was not merely manual work but, rather, a particular and gendered form of labour that Tre was paid for. As he elaborated,

See basically it's like this, you know, we're helpers but we're not really. They consider us watchers. We're supposed to be there on the truck to watch the truck. That means, in other words, when he (driver) pull up to the stop, we're supposed to get out the truck and keep walking around the truck until he finish the work and get ready to go again. So we're supposed to be watchers.

Although Tre claimed that he did in fact help out with the delivery work, the 'strong-arm' or minder role was his 'official' occupational function from his employer's point of view insofar as it was necessary to protect both the merchandise and the (formal sector) employee from potential predators. This could also be seen in the case of Charlie Thomas, the neighbourhood slumlord referred to above. While Charlie clearly derived considerable economic benefit from his crew of male drug users, they also provided him with a degree of informal protection as he moved around the neighbourhood. The employment of women was not perceived to have these additional benefits.

Scrapping, a practice which involves the retrieval of 'scrap' metal from abandoned buildings, rubbish-dumping sites, factories and sometimes telegraph poles, was a common and exclusively male means of generating income in the study site. Indeed, the only flourishing formal-sector activity in the study site was the scrap-metal business.

Although it is hard work, scrapping nevertheless brings in a regular daily income. Scrappers are routinely seen around the neighborhood pushing shopping carts filled with odd pieces of metal. They are good at spotting the valuable types (copper and aluminum for example) and can wring profit out of sites (abandoned buildings or heaps of garbage) that appear valueless (Hamid, 1992b:232).

Although 'the scrap' in question is often legally-abandoned material, some of the scrapping that took place in the study site could be classed as theft and, in some instances, burglary. In Bushwick 'scrappers' operated according to an arrangement whereby each worked a fairly well-defined area or territory. They tended to be cautious about revealing their sources and most were careful not to divulge precise locations. Once retrieved, scrap was redeemed for cash at one of several local scrap-metal yards. A male informant explained.

I go out scrappin'. Well, the best place I would go is down by the railroad tracks or the side street by the factories caus' people dump garbage there. [Where do you sell it?] Oh there's several places you sell it. The best is Dependable Scrap Metal. Caus' he pays higher prices. Copper over there is eighty cents a pound. Brass is fifty and aluminum is forty cents. Stainless steel is twenty cents.

This particular informant chose to haul his 'scrap' a considerable distance to a nearby neighbourhood, claiming that prices in Bushwick were too low because of the number of men who engaged in scrapping. Prices for scrap also varied according to whether metals are stripped (i.e. taken out of their receptors). The removal of valuable scrap such as copper wiring from pipes was a physically demanding and labour-intensive task.

For the most part, women did not participate in these forms of unlawful informal sector work nor did they appear to enjoy 'comparable' gender equivalents—for example baby-sitting or domestic work. 'Gendered' work such as baby-sitting is usually home-based and those who would willingly employ drug-using labour outside the home may be reluctant to welcome drug users into domestic settings. Women's lack of opportunities were also structured by a double standard whereby, although male drug users were perceived as an erratic and unreliable source of labour (Faupel, 1991), popular images of women drug users may render them even more so. The three 'exceptions' to this pattern of exclusion from unlawful hustles all involved highly gendered forms of domestic labour. Esmeralda, a 28-year-old Latina, managed to obtain an apartment in one of the buildings owned by Charlie Thomas. Charlie gave Esmeralda sporadic payments (a few dollars here and there) in return for her attempts to clean and maintain the lobby and the stairwell. This was no easy task considering the traffic in and out of the building occasioned by the crack dealers who frequented the stoop and the heroin dealing operation located on the third floor. Linda, a European American woman, received 'free' accommodation in return for 'baby-sitting' an elderly woman, and Carol, an African American woman, had a regular arrangement with an elderly and visually impaired Italian man in a nearby neighbourhood whom she took grocery shopping.

In relation to unlawful hustles then, women drug users are disadvantaged relative to their male counterparts. To the extent that women drug users are represented within this sector, they appear to be confined to a traditional 'pink collar' ghetto of domestic labour whose workforce extends beyond women drug users.

'Criminal' Hustles

Some of the men enjoyed the action. This was their chance to be on top, them in control and society on the cement, telling people to give it up, give it up, their fingers on people's shelves, in their pockets, against their bodies (Bearak, 1992:A18).

Drug using males in Bushwick generated the bulk of their revenue from criminal activities such as theft, burglary, stripping motor vehicles and street crimes such as robbery. This is illustrated in the following quotation from Cookie, a 25-year-old Latina.

They're like cavemen. If they could eat each other, they would. Very *thirsty* out here—I mean, hardly any white boyz comin' down here no more. They grab the white boys, every single white boy that come, they scalp him. They let him cop, before he gets to Putnam or when he gets to Flushing, that's it—he's gone. They take all his shit and plus they beat him up. Pretty soon we ain't gonna have no walkin' dates. They go on the Avenue and under all the lots that we take the dates—the tracks—they go back there and they wait for them.

While the victimization of 'white boyz' by male drug users held obvious benefits for those women who acted as 'copping agents', it also meant less business for sexworkers in terms of a dwindling pool of car-less or 'walking dates'. During the study period, there was a shift in 'victims of choice' from 'outsiders' (both 'white boys' who came to cop drugs and 'walking dates') to victims within the drug-using community. Victims were increasingly women drug users. As Peggy, a 34-year-old European American woman put it, '[i]t's more rugged turf, because you have a lot of vultures that walk around. You know, the guys that wait on the girls to come out of the cars to rob them. Girls are always gettin' beat up.' However, it was not only money that male drug users were after but also drugs, something that was regarded by the women as particularly callous. Women were frequently robbed and beaten for their drugs. As Latisha noted of Crime, a notorious neighbourhood male who specialized in victimizing women drug users,

[h]e made a girl hit (inject) him. After he took her drugs. He made her sit there and hit him. [That's cold.] You know it. [But he doesn't have any other way of getting stuff, right?] No. Gotta do what he doing. The only thing he knows is that knife in his boot, right?

On the street, the tenuous relations between genders were under-girded by the threat and reality of male violence. These relations were reinforced by an apparent lack of collective solidarity between the women (but see Chapter 7). As Boy saw it,

[d]e guys, dey stress the females. De guys out here kick the girls' ass. Thas where the girls got to watch OK? You got the girls competitioning each other, and you got the guys victimizing them, see? Thas the line out here. [How come the girls don't get together and kick the boy's ass?] Because they're having their little rival, you know, all the girls are rivals. They're tryin' to out-beat each other.

In particular, women were conscious of the multitude of ways in which male users 'disrespected' them. Again Boy noted,

(men are) bitches . . . because since they got on crack I learned dey ain't no self respect for nobody. Dey treat you like shit. Straight up, like shit. Disrespect—dey lose all respect. Treatin' em like a dog—word!

Participation in non-drug hustles, like drug-business hustles, is highly regulated. Men and women concentrate their efforts in particular areas and divisions of labour are primarily structured by sex/gender. In the following sections, I examine women's participation in a range of non-drug business crimes: shoplifting, robbery and theft, conning and gaming, burglary, and violent assault.

Shoplifting

Shoplifting or 'boosting' has historically provided an important source of revenue in low-income inner city neighbourhoods. However, in Bushwick the decline of formal sector economic activity meant that this old gendered standby was no longer a viable option for women drug users. Most of the women with histories of heroin use prior to initiation to crack reported having engaged in shoplifting or 'boosting' as a means of supporting their habit. In contrast, crack cocaine initiates in this sample were unfamiliar with shoplifting in the context of drug-related income generation.[2] Women with histories of shoplifting as an income generating strategy reported that they were often accompanied or assisted by males. This was because the men possessed contacts for off-loading or 'fencing' the proceeds. This type of shoplifting—as the account of Rosa, a 31-year-old Latina, attests—was not done in a random or indiscriminate way. Rosa's 'boosting' (done in conjunction with male heroin users who 'taught her everything') was firmly embedded in a local context in which shoplifting was both possible and 'tolerated' because of the function it performed in redistributing scarce resources.

[What kinds of things would you steal?] Les see, the coat—you know the feather one? [The down?] Yeah, is easy to sell. Les see, some people buy, you know, they would go to the store to buy a coat, right, so we would say, you know, we could get it for you, you know, get it for you—give us less money. [Which people?]. No no no, regular people that, they was lookin' in the store to buy so we would say you know, 'We could get that for you, just wait ousside and you pay us less money . . . What do you want? We can get it for you' . . . They be waiting . . . [This was before the electronic tags came? Did that change it?] Oh yeah, 'for they put that thing it's difficult to steal you know. [So back then you would steal stuff from the store—what other things, anything else? What about like robberies, robbing stores and robbing people?] No, only stealin', I'm not gon' hurt nobody.

As Preble and Casey (1969) have noted, heroin users in low-income communities typically receive local support for their income generating activities in exchange for providing a supply of cheap goods. Rosa's account illustrates how the nature and strength of both the formal and informal economies within given neighbourhoods struc-

---

[2] Some of these women did, however, report engaging in shoplifting as teenagers in order to obtain consumer goods for personal consumption.

ture opportunities for income generation. The fact that Rosa and her male cohorts knew who to approach shows how 'crime'—as a form of redistribution—produces 'complex chains of interaction resulting in local tolerance and shelter . . . for illegal activities' (Sullivan, 1986:386).

However, things have changed since the research of the 1960s. Lorraine, a 25-year-old Latina, also had a male 'ripping and running' partner in the early stages of her drug use career. Together they would go boosting, 'doing the malls'—Kings Plaza, Coney Island—all over. 'I would steal it, he would sell it. We'd split the money evenly and get high together'. Lorraine and her partner have long since separated. In addition to maintaining a heavy heroin and cocaine habit, Lorraine also used crack. She supported her consumption by working the stroll, and as she put it, '[o]nce you're here, it's a rut, I don't think you can get out'. Similarly, Jo-Beth, a 23-year-old European American woman from Long Island, reported that after she lost her office job she began to finance her heroin use by 'boosting' with a girlfriend out in the malls on Long Island. As her use of heroin increased, Jo-Beth began hanging out on the Southside. When her car broke down, she decided her shoplifting days were over and moved in with one of the local Latino dealers.

The rich detailed histories of shoplifting provided by many women also illustrate the ways in which opportunities which result from the overlap between legal and illegal work are structured by sex/gender. In her early days of heroin use, when she only had a 'chippy', Latisha utilized her casual employment in a department store to steal managers' name tags which she and her male partner subsequently used as a cover for their shoplifting activities. As she told me,

I used to work at Smith's (a large department store) before they closed. I used to take name tags. I used to take the manager's name tags. We used to go there, me and my old man.

It seems an ironic twist that the managers at this particular store were all males. According to Latisha, it was not only the name on the badge but cultural expectations in relation to the gender of the wearer that confined their use to her male partner. While the name itself may have gone unnoticed had Latisha worn one of these badges, the fact that a woman was wearing a manager's badge would have served to draw attention. Just as their legitimate use was restricted to men so too was their illegitimate use.

The apparent lack of participation by women crack users in shoplifting has not gone unnoticed by other researchers. Unfortunately, some have attempted to attribute the failure of women crack users to follow what has been seen as a traditional female career trajectory to the pharmacological properties of crack. For example, Koester and Schwartz have argued that crack users are incapable of displaying the degree of planning and skill necessary to generate income from shoplifting. Moreover, their inability to delay gratification means the 'time lag' between stealing and selling the merchandise is 'incompatible with the pharmacological properties of crack' (1993:94). While consistent with the characterization of women crack users as passive victims of crack's pharmacology, this argument precludes consideration of the role of social and economic factors in structuring women's economic decision-making. Implicit in accounts which invoke the discourse of pharmacology is an absence of agency. The crack-crazed woman is rendered incapable of making rational or sensible decisions about income generation.

Accepting the accounts provided by the women in this study necessitates an understanding of the degree to which their economic fortunes are tied to the fate of the local economy. Within this context, women drug users display considerable ingenuity in interpreting and defining the opportunities available to them. I spoke at great length with the women about boosting and why they no longer engaged in it. Their accounts were consistent and characteristically simple, the most common response being 'Whatcha gonna steal down here?'. Looking around Bushwick—where the bodegas are at least three to a block—it is obvious that fast food, condoms and Bic lighters are the only legal commodities that do a roaring trade. There is nothing to boost and no stores to boost from in this neighbourhood.

Robbery and Theft

The lack of participation by women in street robberies could also be partly attributed to an absence of viable targets in the neighbourhood. Latisha recalled how 'once-upon-a-time' she and another girl had a 'regular thing' stealing gold chains from people as they came out of a now defunct grocery store on a busy avenue. Her account illustrates how the nature of the formal economy influences the opportunities for income generation that are available in the informal economy.

There's a girl, now she's in jail, name Raka. We used to do things like that over here . . . [How is it that you and she got together?] She was robbin' this guy with this other girl and the girl ran and she couldn' see nobody and I was just standin' there watching them and she goes 'Yo, Latisha' and she was surprised that I responded, you know, and I blocked the guy and threw a bottle at him and hit him in the head and he ran and then, after that, like a couple of days, like everytime seem like we always be (dope) sick together. Somebody rich come out and she say, 'I'm gonna push you into this guy, push you into him and snatch his chain, we'll run and I'll pass it'. After like five or six times we started hangin' out together. [Who you did this to?] These were people maybe comin' out the grocery store, in front of Putnam. When that store opened a lot of people used to stop there and we used to wait for them to come out.

Latisha and Raka used to take the stolen chains to a local jeweller who fenced them in exchange for cash. Ironically this service no longer exists: the jeweller was murdered during a robbery on his store in 1991.

Most women engaged in various forms of theft in order to support their drug consumption during the study period. The most common form of theft resulted when women reneged on their undertakings to cop drugs for others. As noted in Chapter 4, women frequently reported that they would either abscond with the money or return only to pretend that they had been robbed or 'ripped off' or else they would pretend that the drugs had cost more than the market price. The second most common form of theft among the women was stealing from their families. As Boy told me,

I used ta steal you know. [Yeah, like boosting from the stores?] No, only from my family. I never stole from nobody else . . . I have been down to where you steal from your mother, my sister, I have even got down to stealing my fuckin' baby's milk a while back.

Boy recounted this particular incident at great length—detailing how she stole the coupons for her baby's formula from her mother's house and cashed them in at a local bodega for well under the market value. Such incidents reveal the gendered forms lawbreaking takes. Stealing from one's family—and in particular the acute sense of awareness that this involved 'taking the food out of the mouths of babes'— certainly had a higher emotional price for many women than participation in generic street robberies. This is evident in the following quote from Boy.

After you do it and you smoke it, it hurts, thas when the fuckin' stress comes, that depression stage. But can you change it? Can you come back home? Hey Boy, you did this for a fuckin' cap, a three minute high, and it's gone. What da fuck you gonna do now? You can't go home, so I'm gonna stay out here onna street.

Within the heroin-using subculture, drug users are believed to employ what Faupel (1991) has described as 'the principle of social distance' in order to define appropriate victims for hustling behaviour. Many of the women told me that they had stolen from their families and friends, which would be regarded as a severe violation of this principle. Yet their accounts also suggest that their lack of participation in street crimes such as robbery can also be attributed to a propensity to minimize the social distance between themselves and potential victims. As Candy noted,

[i]f I'm sick, I'm gon do anything to get my money, I don't care. (But) I don't think I could bop a little ol' lady walking down the block, could be my moms.

Women picked victims they knew more often than men. The tendency to minimize the social distance between themselves and their victims meant that women were less likely to victimize strangers. As Latisha put it,

[Do you think that it's harder for a guy to make money out here than a girl?] No, caus if they so bad, they go and stick somebody up. [What a woman couldn't do that?] I wouldn't. I may go in somebody pocket you know but I wouldn't, not just cold blooded stick somebody up. [What other kinds of opportunities do women have to make money besides work on the stroll?] I don't know. The Avenue (stroll) is the only opportunity that comes to my mind.

According to Messerschmidt (1993), crime is a resource for 'doing gender' or, more precisely, for 'doing masculinity'. Street robbery provides a particularly vivid example of this phenomenon whereby males 'show and affirm' their masculinity (1993:84). In low-income minority neighbourhoods, where young men are routinely deprived of other resources to accomplish masculinity, robbery provides a resource for constructing a specific type of public masculinity—the 'hardman': by 'making a fool of his victim', the stick-up artist constructs *an angle of moral superiority* over the intended victim' (Katz, 1988: 174, 169, emphasis in original). Street robbery is portrayed as 'a rational practice for "doing gender" and for getting money' (Messerschmidt, 1993:107). However, Messer-schmidt has very little to say about how women 'do gender' in such settings: 'Within the social setting of the street group, robbery is an acceptable practice for accomplishing gender' (1993:108). While street robbery and other forms of crime may be a source of status, reputation and respect for males—a way of proving that the perpetrator is 'a man among men' (1993:110)—the experiences of the women in this study suggest that crime does not function as a resource for 'doing femininity' in the same way. The theoretical categories advanced by Messerschmidt for 'doing gender' cannot simply be inverted in order to understand the relationship between 'doing crime' and 'doing femininity'. Indeed there were no instances in this study where crime by women could be interpreted as a way of separating from all that is masculine.

Regardless of how others saw them, when it came down to it, women simply did not see themselves as 'bad' enough to do the kinds of things that men did. Doing stick-ups meant *being bad* as opposed to merely *acting bad* (see Chapter 4). In the street-level drug economy 'badness' is synonymous with maleness. While some women were able to 'fake' it, to the experienced observer—whether potential street predator or prospective drug business employer—badness was indelibly associated with masculine capacities for violence and terror. As Candy put it, Bushwick was not 'Hollywood' and she was neither Thelma nor Louise.

[Could girls get a hold of like guns and go in and rob stores or people—do they do that?] They could do it but it's not done, right? It's not Hollywood. This is the real deal out here . . . See what I'm sayin'? So they (girls) work their con—they go for their own kind of bullshit.

The sexual division of labour in the drug economy was not some-thing to be messed with. As Boy saw it, men had strong vested inter-ests in maintaining sex segmentation in the informal economy. Treading on their turf—in this instance robbery—would almost cer-tainly invoke violent retaliation.

[Why do you think women stick to, like turning tricks when they could do like rob people and shit, do all the things that men do?] Dat ain't their style, is not their style. The guys would get pissed and the guys would start rob-bin' the girls. Dey take it now, rob da girls, you know it, dey take the shit, like the money dey make from trickin' and stuff, guys rip 'em off, dey be *bad* out here.

Although none of the women reported having engaged in either armed robberies or muggings during the study period, many of them were involved in a form of theft specific to sexwork which they termed 'viccing'(see Chapter 6).

Conning and gaming

'Cons' are a specific type of larceny which involve the manipulation of trust. Biernacki's study of heroin users suggests that forgery and confidence games are dominated by whites and women, a feature he attributes to a greater capacity by these groups to establish credibility and trust (1979:543–4). For the women in this sample, although cons or 'gaming people' were almost always undertaken in concert with males, they were typically seen as 'female things' and women exercised considerable control both in the execution of the offence and the distribution of the proceeds. Although only a small minority of women participated in this type of activity, they had all at some stage been arrested for it and done felony jail time. An interesting example is Latisha's 'meat game', described below.

It was a scam. I would always have a male partner. I used to get all this meat (from the supermarket), about $200 or $300 worth, you know like the best fillet mignon. You steal, but you don't steal. You don't put it on your person and you don't put it in a bag. You let them bag it up. Meanwhile they think you are goin' to pay for it because who in the hell would think that you are not goin' to buy it. You put all that stuff in the shopping basket and I don't even have coffee at home half the time. [So how do you get out of the store with it?] In most neighbourhoods, no offence, but they trust white people so much, if you're white you're right. I would see these white couples going on, 'Hey honey put these in the car' and the lady would still be on the line. This is what I would do. I would go into the store and I would say 'Honey, put this in the car' and I would give him a fake set of keys and he would go and leave me on the line. I would go and talk to the girl and while I am talkin' I would break a bag of sugar or flour and that would be my out to get off the line and go put that sugar or flour back. I would say 'I am not goin' to pay for this. I have spent like $400 here'. I would say it with an attitude that would like scare her, make her nervous. Then I would go 'No offence to you sweetheart, but could you continue to ring this while I go and change the sugar or flour'. In the meantime, I would always wear a scarf or hat, I would take it off, go around the other aisle come out and that's it. My partner had gone through the checkout.

Despite the fact that she always had a male partner, the 'meat game' was clearly Latisha's con. Although technically Latisha could be viewed as merely carrying out the 'decoy' or 'sexual media' role (Steffensmeier, 1983) while her partner escaped with the goods, the con itself is much more complicated and extends beyond simple theft. Understanding this particular con necessitates a contextual reading in which gender and race are central. Latisha's 'meat game' successfully exploits dominant cultural understandings of race and gender. Latisha is Black, as is her accomplice. They dress up and go to a middle class neighbourhood. She calls him 'honey'. Latisha plays the fact that, as a Black woman, she is already under suspicion. She calls the racist bluff. As a Black woman, ostensibly about to spend a considerable sum of money, Latisha manipulates both gender stereotypes and white racism to her advantage. The con then, is concerned with more than the instrumental value of the theft. It is about 'getting over' in which Latisha plays a central role. 'Getting over' in the meat game involves a subtle and subversive invocation of gender and race. Without the 'getting over', there would be no con. Removed from its context and reinscribed within the narrow confines of criminological discourse as theft or larceny, the con is mis-interpreted: Latisha becomes the 'decoy' and her agency is denied.

Burglary

Quantitative research suggests that burglary is the most sex segregated of all index crimes with the exception of rape (Shover, 1991). My research confirms this pattern. Many of the men in the neighbourhood were involved in factory burglaries which they referred to as 'geesing' or going on a 'geese'.[3] Latisha was the only woman in this study who regularly participated in burglaries. Although she maintained that her role was secondary or that of an accomplice, Latisha strongly resisted any implication of passivity. As is evident in the later half of the following quotation, she was anxious to demonstrate her agency and her value as an active participant.

Well, I plan on goin' onna geese—meaning to burglarize a factory. It's gonna be open. [What do you mean it's gonna be open?] Yeah, they're gonna be working there. And stuff is stacked in the yard, OK, and the person that I'm goin' with—it's really their geese, and, you know, they need me as a decoy, you know. They prefer me they say because they know that I'm a good

---

[3] A broader definition of a geese includes a range of 'riots' or 'gigs' involving theft which are designed to generate income (e.g. see Sharff, 1987:36). In this context however, the use of 'geese' appeared to be reserved for burglaries.

lookout. And plus I work, you know, I like to carry stuff too, you know; and, uh, I don' wanna get busted, so I ain't gonna take no chances on lettin' them get busted. In other words, I be fully awake, you know, and aware.

Despite her strong sense of worth as an active participant, Latisha's male partner frequently ripped her off on the proceeds, as she told me of another 'geese'.

We went to this factory on a burglary together. [What kind of factory was it?] Soda. We made like $110. [What did you take?] Bout seven cases of soda and ten cases of beer. [So you both did it together?] Well, OK, he go in the trailer to make a case, right, caus so many cases are not together no more, so he had to make a case. He make the case, I take it across—it's a track, but a long track—I take it across the track and stash it in the bushes. And I just take one case, one case, I keep goin' back and forth, stack 'em the bushes. Then, when he comes out after the last case, we leave 'em in the bushes. We go find somethin' to put 'em on, like, one a those thing, like a dolley. We go find one of them, then I climb over the fence, then he passes 'em over to me. After we got out the factory he started actin' real nasty like. Caus he was over, he didn't need me no more, so he was like 'Look, put the cases like this, put the cases like that.' I put them one way, and he say, 'I didn't tell you put like that, put it the other way'. Just being an asshole caus he thought I would be aggravated and I'd say, never min', fuck you, and leave. An' I hung in there, an' hung in there. He couldn't get rid of me . . . He tryin' to chase me away. So, he had like forty five dollar on him, right, so he goes, 'Here take this twenny dollar an' get lost'. So I said, 'No, cause I entitled to half this, I went in there and if we woulda got busted I was goin' to jail too and I got a warrant.' An' he said, 'I don' give a fuck, take this twenny dollar or I beat you up.' So I took the twenny.

Tre, Latisha's common law husband, saw things somewhat differently. As he explained,

If I take the female with me, I can get four, five case (of soda). Say I wanna get ten, I hand her out these cases, now she don't carry them, it too heavy. Now I got to climb out their trailer, sit them on the floor, walk them out the back, you know what I'm sayin'. Stash them and come back and then get the rest of the stuff and you know, but she want half the money, you know. You know like, come on, give me a break.

Even though he is emaciated and clearly not in the best of physical health, Tre clearly views Latisha as a member of the 'weaker' sex with a limited physical capacity. This view of women, in terms of biological or physiological (as well as emotional) attributes is not uncommon in the drug economy and is used to undermine women's participation as social and economic actors. It is also used, as in this instance, as a justification for exploiting women's labour power. By downplaying the (physical) role of women in the actual offence, men also reinforce their own sense of self-importance and accomplishment. Thus not only do they get to keep the lion's share of the proceeds, but they also get to feel good about it.

Women have few opportunities to participate in activities such as the 'geese'. Both Latisha's and Tre's accounts illustrate the inequities that structure male-female co-offending relations. As Tre suggests, women continue to be confined in rhetoric, if not always in practice, to a secondary role. Moreover, women's vulnerability to physical abuse and victimization renders them unable or unwilling to enforce compliance when men renege on deals or attempt to rip them off.

Violent Assault

While not an income-generating activity, violent assault is included here because most non-domestic assaults in the study site related to robberies or economic conflicts over drugs or money. Assaults typically took place in the context of street robberies, disputes over drugs, and conflicts in relation to money. Women were rarely the perpetrators of robberies, although they were frequently the victims and were often assaulted in the process. I also witnessed several altercations over drugs in which women were involved: none of these disputes involved weapons. The most common form of female violence, however, was when women used violence against others in order to fend off threats to their economic wellbeing.

While women were clearly conscious of the need to avoid victimization by being seen as having 'heart' or 'juice' (see Chapter 4), more often this was framed in the negative—in terms of not being seen as a 'pussy' or a pushover. As Candy told me,

[w]hat else is there to do out here besides uh, you know, to make money? You can't get a legit job [What about ripping another girl off or . . . ?] Well, they do that too. Some girls. I don't. They'll bull you and take your money. If you're a pussy, you're a pussy. You ain't going to give it up, you got to fight. You going to fight me to get my money. You got to kill me first. [Well, when you say fight, you mean fist-fight or . . .] Right, that's right. Go to blows. [And you'll fight them?] You understand what I'm saying? If they take it once, they going to take it all the time. Nine outta ten times, they're all mouth. They're all bark and no bite. You know, just try to talk big and action but it comes down to being nothing.

Candy's comment that most women were 'all bark and no bite' is interesting in light of the relatively few incidents, either directly witnessed or recounted to me, involving violence between women. Such violence, when it occurred, almost always took the form of 'stand-up' fights. Despite the availability of firearms and the violence endemic to drug markets, few women carried weapons. The following excerpt from my fieldnotes indicates that even where such incidents could be classified as 'systemic violence', occupational disputes among women were settled without resort to weaponry.

I bought Lucy a pear juice and we were chilling out when a blue van pulled up driven by a Spanish guy with a white girl in back. The girl got out and started shouting at Princess calling her a bitch and a ho. Both girls took their jackets off and Princess kicked off the red boots she was wearing. They started laying into one another right there on the block. As the fight erupted everyone started crowding around to watch. A couple of the black guys on the block came over initially to try and help Princess, but the guy in the van said 'Let them fight fair'. So everyone backed off and let them go at it. Even a police car from the 83rd Precinct stopped to watch but didn't interfere. The fight lasted a couple of minutes. Finally the owner of White Tops came over and separated them. The white girl got back in the van and they sped off. I think Princess got the worst of it. She was complaining bitterly that her opponent had 'fought dirty' by pulling her dreads. Her face had been smashed into the door of the van and she had a big lump on the side of her head with a cut in the middle of it. Blood was streaming down the side of her face.

Princess later explained to me that the white girl had accused her of selling dummies (vials of fake crack). What is interesting is that this dispute was settled in the 'old fashioned way'. Despite the drug trade's reputation for elevating certain forms of weaponry to the status of cultural icons (including the much-esteemed 9mm pistol and the ubiquitous baseball bat), here was an old-fashioned fist-fight being used to settle a drug-business dispute. The experience of the other women confirms that, where they were involved in violent encounters, women typically 'took care of business' without resorting to weaponry.[4] Occasionally, a woman might carry a folding knife or box cutter, but these were infrequently used.

[4] This finding is supported by a report on self-identified inmate substance-abusers by the New York State Department of Correctional Services which indicates that of 2,546 female substance-abusers, only one per cent or 19 women were committed to prison for weapons charges (Department of Correctional Services, 1990b). Similarly, national surveys of inmates in state correctional facilities indicate that less than one

Even though women were more often the victims of violent crime (including assault, robbery, rape, and homicide), there were occasions when some of them did get violent with others. Princess was one of the few women in this study whose rap sheet identified her as a 'violent offender'. Although she had served twelve months in prison for assault, the story behind this particular incident suggests that she may have been just as much the 'victim' as the 'aggressor'.

I got arrested for assault—I did twelve months. [Tell us the story behind that?] Well, I was back on Delancey Street. There was this club over there, called the CBGB's. And you know the skinheads, these guys? Well I woun' up cuttin' one of them up because they had surrounded me and they pissed on me—and for no reason. [What do you mean they surrounded you and pissed on you?]. Y'know I was sittin' in a parking lot and I was smoking (crack). It was a Sunday so it's not open—the booth, y'know. So these guys they came into the parking lot, I guess to take a leak, I don' know what they went back there to do. So as they were coming out I say, 'What are you sayin?' They thought I was a homo or a faggot or something, I don' know. They say, 'You're not a woman, you're a fuckin' faggot'. I said, 'What are you talkin' about?'. So they jus' took this shit out and jus' pissed on me. And I got up to walk away and he shoved me back down and I jus' . . . I had the razor in my hand, and I jus'. . . Well, the state picked it up because he was a ex-correction officer. So I got indicted, and then I wound up gettin' a year flat for it.

Violence by women was overwhelmingly retaliatory in nature with most instances involving a threat to personal security or economic well-being. The story related below by Lady B., about how she cut a date's face with a broken bottle, was typical of the kind of violence engaged in by women. Lady B. is a 32-year-old Jewish woman from Mill Basin (Brooklyn). She had worked the stroll in Bushwick for about two years before this incident occurred. Lady B. is about 5'1" and weighs about 80 pounds. On this particular occasion, she picked up a date who promised to give her twenty dollars, in return for which she agreed to purchase crack for him and accompany him to a nearby motel.

per cent of women are imprisoned for weapons offences (Bureau of Justice Statistics, 1991). However, a study based on an imprisoned sample of females involved in robbery and assault found that 70 per cent of robberies and 78 per cent of assaults involved some kind of weapon—usually guns and knives—with most (66 per cent) women reporting that they routinely carried weapons for self protection. This, the authors interpreted, was an indication of their 'readiness to use violence' (Sommers and Baskin, 1991:9).

Like yesterday, I had a pretty bad experience with a guy. He took up most of my night . . . You know I tell them 'Whatever you want to do, lay the cards out on the table. Either I'll say yes, or I'll say no' . . . Later on, everything he wanted was different. He was talking about fucking me in the ass, and this and that. In the beginning I took care of him like he wanted. But all this time is going by and he is not giving me money. Anyway, he had me copping for him, and after the third time I said, 'You know, you said you would take care of me.' He said that he had to go over to his house to get more money. At this point, all he had in his mind was gaming me . . . In the middle of the highway he wanted to throw me out. I didn't know where the hell I was, how to get back, plus I didn't have any money at this point, and he is being a real scum-bag. Obviously everything he said was lies. He wasted a whole night of mine. I could have been making money. I could have been doing anything . . . So the bottle of soda that I had, I broke it and I cut him with it. I didn't stab him with it, I cut him with it. But, I don't get mad easy. For me to get mad it really takes a lot. This guy really hurt me . . . You know, it was fucked up with him. I don't go around cutting people. That was fucked up.

Lady B.'s account reveals several key themes. First, like Princess's account, it suggests that incidents where women appear to be the initiators of violence[5] are often the culmination of a string of events to which women respond with the use of violence. Second, it challenges the tripartite model of drug-related violence proposed by Goldstein (1985). While Lady B.'s story is clearly related to drugs and income generation, her use of the broken bottle to cut her 'date's' face does not 'fit' any of the three types of violence outlined by Goldstein. More generally, incidents like this defy simple categorization. They are not explicable with reference to a single variable or readily categorized as a distinct 'type' of violence. Without knowing the recent history of the stroll in this neighbourhood and without appreciating the background of this particular incident, categorizing it as a particular type of violence—on the part of either party—is, at best, misleading.

Conclusion

Similar to the way that certain societal conditions and attitudes that are prevalent in the general society restrict the life chances of many of its members, these same conditions are also operative in the heroin world and func-

---

[5] My research suggests that the police are called in many such incidents.

tion to restrict participation in certain hustles to particular kinds of addicts (Biernacki, 1979:540).

Constructions of work in the street-level drug economy are both raced and gendered: 'particular kinds of addicts' participate in particular kinds of hustles. The distributional consequences of these gendered and raced patterns of work tend to reflect broader social and economic inequalities. In particular, cultural beliefs about gender take the form of oppositions between male and female and between the practices, appearances, obligations and rights that are distributed according to sex. Perceptions of both men and women drug users in relation to 'getting paid' are linked to, and informed by, these broader cultural understandings. Gender is a central organizing principle in the distribution of opportunities for income generation at the street level, illustrated in the following quotation from Lady B.

[Why don't girls strip cars, scrap metal—you think the guys would get upset if you started doing that?] Yeah, they would probably try and get over if I came along. But it's too heavy and I don't have the tools . . . Some girls can do that but with a guy. The one girl I know who strips cars by herself is a dyke—she's a Mack truck mechanic. Most of these girls don't know nuttin' about cars.

Cherrie, a 21-year-old Latina, was one of the few women who did know something about cars. Prior to her initiation to crack use, Cherrie was taught a set of 'masculine' crime skills by her brother. As her account indicates, Cherrie prided herself on having the requisite knowledge and skill to steal cars. Her account is also evocative of the hedonism and excitement sometimes involved in car theft—features typically confined to accounts which emphasize the role of motor vehicle theft in affirming masculinity (e.g. White, 1990).

I wanna talk about the cars I told you about. My brother teach me how to steal cars when I was what, 14. We used to go to Coney Island every Winter. We used to break all the game, into all those stores, all those new stores on Coney Island, we used to break them up. Candy stores from Coney Island, the rides, the smoke stores for Coney Island, and any other stores for Coney Island. The rides, the go-carts, we used to steal them. We steal a lotta shit from there and then we start stealin ah Buicks—real cars. Used to take the hangers and pull em through the window and open doors. We used to take the screwdriver and pop the lock, and take out the wires and attach them together and used to brrrm brrrm, turn on the car, and we used to take off with the cars.

Although she clearly retained these skills, Cherrie supported her crack use during the study period through a combination of sexwork, hustling from her nearby extended family, and sporadic bursts of street-level drug sales. Both Cherrie's acquisition of these skills and the fact that she no longer used them in the context of her street life and crack use indicate that women's options in the street-level drug economy are structured by gendered constructions of social meaning and appropriate behaviours. This was borne out as I spent day after day in the field watching and recording struggles by individual women to generate income. My fieldnotes reveal a typical day's hustling for Boy as including: intermittent hits of crack in exchange for the rental of her stem; panhandling a total of 70 cents; purchasing a stolen bedspread from a 'stressing' male crack user for one dollar and after a long hustle, finally re-selling it for two dollars; obtaining free condoms from health workers and selling them to other women on the stroll for a quarter each; and finally, trying for over an hour, without success, to pick up a date.

One may ask why, if things are so bad, do women not go elsewhere? Reminiscent of images of 'battered women' who seem unable to leave their batterers, the women in this study rarely left the neighbourhood in order to pursue income-generating activities. Like 'battered women', however, the Bushwick women did not stay because they 'liked it' or because of the crack-based equivalent of 'learned helplessness'. Rather, they stayed because they saw themselves as having nowhere else to go, or nowhere that provided a realistic alternative. The sight of emaciated and often dishevelled women with pock-marked skin, abscesses, open wounds and, at times, bruised faces and battered bodies, was familiar and drew little attention in the neighbourhood. And while their physical condition was not regarded as unusual in this context, it would arguably have drawn attention to them in mid-town department stores or suburban shopping malls.

Similarly, although most of the women were aware that, for the price of a subway token, the going rates for street-level sexwork in Manhattan provided opportunities to increase their earnings,[6] only one woman ventured into Manhattan on a semi-regular basis. The first tier strolls in Manhattan demanded a standard of physical attractiveness, grooming, and well-being that many women could no longer

[6] This was the particularly the case below 14th Street in Manhattan where women were able to work without a pimp and to keep the money they earned.

accommodate and thus, in reality there were few opportunities for upward mobility. For these women, leaving the local stroll in search of greener pastures risked not only finding themselves unable to compete in the broader marketplace, and the resultant injury to severely depleted supplies of self-esteem, but it also meant potentially losing their 'steadies' or regular clientele. As Candy put it, '[b]etter to stay here where you know you're gonna get someone to go out for ten dollars than to go in there (Manhattan) and get passed up by some guy who pays twenty'. At least they knew the turf in Bushwick and could usually hustle up a few dollars. If not, there were always their 'associates'—perhaps someone owed them a 'favour' and would be willing to 'take care' of them. Crime-as-work rarely strays far from home. Most types of income-generating crime are highly localized, intra-class, and intra-racial in nature. The Bushwick women's 'choices' are not dissimilar to those of others and are 'irrational', in the sense of spurning greater rewards elsewhere, only from an external point of view. Subjectively, the 'rational' choice for women like Candy was to work locally, not to go to Manhattan or anywhere else.

Women's lawbreaking, like men's, takes gendered and raced forms although it is men's lawbreaking, especially street robberies and stick-ups committed by minority group men, that continues to dominate legal and cultural constructions of drug-related crime. Gender differences in patterns of street hustles reflect the articulation of broad cultural beliefs with local expressions and conditions. Like drug-business hustles, non-drug hustles in Bushwick were, for the most part, dominated by men. The exceptions were shoplifting (which was no longer a viable option) and various forms of larceny or cons. Most women drug users in Bushwick did not perpetrate street robberies, steal cars, commit burglaries, or engage in scrapping or other forms of unlawful informal sector work. Their participation as economic actors was restricted. They showed no signs of being 'career criminals' nor were they part of any street crime 'underworld' (cf. Inciardi et al., 1993).[7] Finally, while women rarely benefited from criminal non-drug hustles, they were not excluded from participation. For the most part, the participation of women drug users in predatory street crime was confined to the role of victim.

[7] Inciardi et al. have suggested that 'street addicts and "career criminals" are increasingly the same people, and that the heroin/cocaine addict's world and the street crime underworld have essentially converged into one . . . serious drug involvement by female criminals is more extensive now than even in the very recent past' (1993:113).

6

A Hard Road to Ho: Sexwork

[Were there any other ways you could make money?] Only whoring, I had to walk. I slipped out of reality. I had a hard stroll. (Dream)

Sexwork was the only income-generating activity consistently available to women drug users in Bushwick. Despite the recent influx of women into the drug economy, their participation as producers largely revolves around sexwork, and their presence has been most strongly felt as consumers. This has prompted major changes in the operating contexts of street-level sex markets. In New York City, the advent of crack cocaine and the concomitant flood of sexwork initiates lowered the going rates for sexual transactions, encouraged 'deviant' sexual expectations on the part of dates, engendered relations of competition and hostility, and promoted the atomization and social isolation of women drug users. These factors have rendered street-level sexwork less lucrative, more demanding, and increasingly violent (Maher and Curtis, 1992). However, women have not been passive recipients of these changes. Cumulative market processes and shifting social relations have created a pool of increasingly economically marginalized women for whom 'viccing' has emerged as a form of resistance. Ironically, it is this very resistance which serves to (re)produce them as 'criminal' women. In this chapter, I describe these changes and their impact on the positioning of women in the street-level drug economy.

Crack-induced Participation in Street-level Sex Markets

Street-level prostitution in New York City has traditionally been stratified. The most lucrative prostitution strolls are located in Manhattan and a hierarchy of second-tier street-level sex markets are dispersed throughout the city. In Brooklyn, prior to the crack era, prostitution strolls were spread over a wide geographical area and there was a clear hierarchy among them. The preferred strolls, where working conditions were better and income potential was higher, were located near major transportation arteries, such as Williamsburg's Southside. The worse strolls were located in isolated, interior neighbourhoods, such as Bedford-Stuyvesant and Bushwick.

The evolution of street-level prostitution markets in these neighbourhoods has been directly tied to the fate of local drug markets, to which they function as an adjunct. Recent changes in the structure, functioning, and locales of drug markets can be seen as constitutive of changes in street-level sex markets. The city-wide 'drying up' and consolidation of drug markets into 'drug vortices' has been mirrored by parallel shifts in sex markets. The hierarchy of sex markets within this second tier has broken down in tandem with the breakdown of street-level drug markets in many neighbourhoods. Some of the second tier sex markets have dried up, while others have been forced to absorb displaced women, resulting in an increasingly heterogeneous population of sexworkers (e.g. in terms of race/ethnicity, age, drug use, and sexwork experience). This process has arguably widened the gulf between the two tiers.

For example, the 'drying up' of drug markets on Williamsburg's Southside had a debilitating impact on the once busy sex trade and many of the women who worked the stroll on the Southside followed the drugs down to Bushwick. When drug trafficking became concentrated in Bushwick, the local stroll began to draw women from surrounding strolls (some better, some worse) which were becoming less viable as money-making locations. Most of the women in this study felt that the conditions of work and wages in Bushwick were a real step down for them, while a few indicated that it was about the same or slightly better than where they had come from. As Jonelle, a 32-year-old African American woman put it,

[d]e difference between here and M'hattan is da guys are so cheap over here. All dese bitches around here is crack heads so every trick you get now wanna give *crackfare*. [They don't wanna give you cash?] No, I'm sayin' crackfare because dey know what these bitches be doin'. Every bitch over here is a crack head, so dey just wanna give you that amount ($5).

Many of the women had worked other strolls in Brooklyn and some had experience in other parts of New York. Lorraine, a 25-year-old

Latina, was one of the women who followed the drugs from Williamsburg's Southside down to Bushwick.

[Is it harder down here than it was up on the Southside?] There's no money out here. I haven't even got a date. Imagine. You know I would over there. Down here, I been out for like two hours. There's fuckin' customers, but I don't know what they're looking for. They got a lot of girls over here.

Candy is a 41-year-old European American woman who has been a sexworker, or as she put it, a 'ho', for about seventeen years. She is well placed to describe recent changes in street-level sexwork in the neighbourhood. As she told me,

[m]any moons ago I started off down by the Star Diner. There was three girls—Jo, Ellen and myself. OK. By the train station, there was three of us out there. That was about fifteen years ago when it was real discrete. We had to do all the talkin', you know . . . 'it'll cost you a few dollars, you can give us a present if you want, you know, you can give us money for a meal', you know. It was so much different and more fun back then too. [Did you have friends among the other girls then?] Those were friends. Now, these girls out here are just for the drug and theirself—no friendship, everyone's out to cut everyone's throat. [Back then were you all using drugs?] Of course, that's mainly what the whole deals about—drug using, you know what I'm sayin? You not out there caus you need love, you can get that any damn where, you know what I'm sayin' . . . We were friends and we'd help one another out whether we were right or wrong . . . We'd stick together, it's like I said, do a favour, call somebody up, go get a bag of dope . . . These people don't know how to be hos.

Candy's comments suggest that crack use changed relationships among the women; they became more competitive, cut-throat even. All the women agreed that 'crack' had increased the number of women 'on the street' and had had a significant impact on the kind of work they did, the remuneration they received, and the interactions that occurred in and around street level drug and sex markets. As Boy told me,

[c]rack progressed more women out on the street. You see things you ain't never seen before; girls changin' clothes on the street, shit dat females would never do, dey do now, you know, dat you would never see before—in dis day and time you see now . . . You have got to look in back of you all while you walk out here. Because dey'll rob from their mama. Dey don't care if you're pregnant. Dey don't care. Once dey want dat hit, they'll fuckin' kill you.

The inter-relation between crack use and income-generating strategies has also influenced patterns of consumption, with many intravenous heroin and cocaine users commencing chronic crack use in the context of street-level sexwork. 'Crack' created a vicious circle, producing a rapidly deteriorating work environment which entrenched its use as an integral feature of street prostitution. Sexworkers who were intravenous drug users readily incorporated crack into their consumption repertoires. As Keisha put it, '[d]ey wan' a pebble, a rock, sumpin' ta get dem high enough where dey can get de nerve up ta do this'. Many women perceived the effects of crack as conducive to getting on with the business of street-level sexwork. As Verity explained,

[Is crack the main drug you use while you're working?] [y]eah, because I can't go out sober on a date, because I don't like what I do and I do it for my (dope) habit. So I gotta be high on somethin' before I get into that next car.

This was confirmed by Keisha who suggests that, given the deteriorating and dangerous conditions of street-level sexwork in Bushwick, crack may be perceived as better suited to such conditions than heroin: '[i]f I can stay level on crack, das better dan doin' dope where you goin' sit outside an' nod out in da middle o' da street an' don' remember whatcha' doin' an goin' asleep.'

Rosa was a 31-year-old Dominican woman who came to Bushwick in 1988. Although she had been using heroin and speedballs (cocaine and heroin mixed together) intravenously for fifteen years, she was not a crack user. Rosa walked onto a stroll dominated by crack smokers.

It was problem because you know, they want get a hit and you wanna get a dope you know . . . They ones that crackhead, they even go for fi' dollar, three dollar. Yeah, we charge fifteen caus we need it. Like now I always try to get twenny-five because like, I remember the crack, the coke, the dope and I try to get more. But the one only smokin' crack they don' care to go for fi' dollar, because right there they got a bottle . . . [Do the dates all wanna go with them caus they're cheap? And so what did you girls do about this?] Yeah, we fight or watch them go out and when they come back rip 'em off. Two of you together and we say, 'I share with you whatever she got'.

Like Candy's account, Rosa's suggests that relations among women sexworkers are certainly 'not what they used to be'. Interactions between the women were increasingly characterized by competition and mutual hostility. Where they were not victimized first by dates or male users, some women victimized other women for increasingly hard-to-get cash and drugs. In a period in which 'poly-drug use' has become a fashionable catch-all however, Rosa's distinction between crack smokers and poly-drug users suggests that the social and economic relations which characterize multiple substance use differ from those attributed to more exclusive forms of drug use. These distinctions may yield important insights into the relationship between crack use and high-risk sexual practices.

Previous research has posited a market correspondence between the minimum price for sexual exchanges and the retail unit price of drugs (Goldstein et al., 1992; Hoigard and Finstad, 1992). The low unit price of crack in Bushwick (typically $5) corresponded to what was generally regarded as the minimum rate for oral sex. The correspondence between these commodities was made explicit by widespread references to $5 blow jobs as *crackfares*. Many women who held out for $10 as their lowest price for a blow job were heroin users, with $10 corresponding to the market price for a bag of heroin. Some research also suggests that the relative brevity of the crack high may be an important factor in structuring the frequency with which women both generate and spend income derived from sexwork (Goldstein et al., 1992; see also Koester and Schwartz, 1993). As Jonelle noted in relation to crack users, 'when dey want another crack, dey go back'. The high frequency of sexual transactions may underpin the correlation between crack use and high-risk sexual behaviour, accounting for the stronger association some researchers have observed between high-risk behaviours and crack use, than injecting drug use (e.g. Edlin et al., 1992).

Most women, however, were poly-drug users. More than two-thirds used heroin as well as crack. During the study period, two women who were crack smokers at the time of the first interview began using heroin. Many women believed strongly in the power of heroin as a remedial medicine and, in particular, as a potent antidote to the effects of crack. As Latisha explained: 'The crack gets so speedy and somebody tells you, I know how you can stop, you know, that speedy feeling—get a bag of dope'.

Changes in the Price, Structure and Nature of Sexwork

How can you compete against all these bitches who's givin' it away? (Latisha)

While the price of sexual services provided by street-level sexworkers varies over time, at any given time there are generally agreed-upon minimum prices (Hoigard and Finstad, 1992). Although all the women smoked crack, they universally identified it as a culprit in limiting their ability to make money.[1] As Latisha noted, women who sold themselves for less than the 'going rate' made it difficult for everyone.

We got a girl we call 'Two Dollar Mindy' . . . Mindy will stay with a date forty-five minutes an' come back an' she wanna get down on (share) a crack. . . . Two Dollar Mindy don't care about nobody, nuttin'—long as she got two dollars. I've never seen a girl stay that long in a car an' come back an' she wants to get down. On a good date, she got four—she come back an' she need a dollar. [What do you girls think about her doing that?] Oh they be talk, that's why they call her Two Dollar Mindy. Why would you pick up a girl for ten when you can get one for two?

'Crack' was repeatedly identified as having lowered the minimum prices for sexwork by flooding the market with novice sexworkers and increasing the potential for violence, both from 'asshole dates' and male crack users. This is reflected in the following quotation from Boy.

Oh man, dey be go so low as a cap ($5 vial of crack)—dependin' on how bad the person is stressin'. Dey lose all the respect of yourselves—just totally bizarre if you ask me . . . The dates are rougher and nastier too. You're always gonna run into an asshole out there but there's more assholes now. With the girls, it's let's see who can beat each other, the majority of women try to challenge each other. It's pathetic . . . it's just fucked up, dey just want that hit so bad—they're not pathetic, they're sick.

In the early stages of fieldwork, I could not be sure who these 'others' were that engaged in price-cutting. As a novice ethnographer, I embarked on a mission of my own to locate the 'other' or, as Keisha described her, the 'real crackhead'.

---

[1] In comparison to figures cited in previous research, current rates for sexwork appear to be extremely low. For example, Courtwright et al. (1989) suggest that the minimum rate for sex in New York City during the early 1940s was $10. Research in Harlem in the late 1970s and early 1980s indicates that the market rate then was $20 (Johnson et al., 1985).

Dey (dates) want fi' dollar ($5) blow jobs, fi' dollar this. I told this guy, I said 'Baby I lay down on a bed and fuck for fifty dollar and better'. He said, 'Huh', I said 'For dat fi' dollar bullshit you had better go and see those other girls'. I turned him down. He thought I was one of the *real crackheads*. Dey expect you to do a blow job for fi' dollar or dey expect you to fuck somebody for fi' dollar.

As fieldwork progressed and my relations with individual women strengthened over time, it became clear that the 'other' was often the self, as indicated in the following quotation from Rosa.

[And if like guys ask you for five, you would go?] Well, believe or not meantime I'll be doing it because I'll be desperate or if you sick for five dollar, need another five, four dollar for the day. So it's like, you know. Not every time though but you know, I have done it. Everybody have done it, believe me. [Well it's hard for me, because some girls say 'No, I never do that, she do it'. It's always everyone else who does it.] They lie, because everybody have done it, believe you me.

As Peggy, a 34-year-old European American women, explained, in practice, everyone had their 'bottom price'.

I don't go out for less than twenty-five—over here, anywhere. I'll let twenty cars pass me, they can go. I don't know them. They don't know me, they can go. Two dollars. They go out for two dollars. I mean if I was sick—don't get me wrong—if I was dopesick and I needed a bag of dope, I'd go for ten dollars. I'm so sure I would. I'm sure any junkie would.

While the drop in price was prompted by a drop in standards on the part of these others/selves, this change was also accompanied by inflated expectations on the part of dates, which many women viewed as insulting and disrespectful. From the dates' perspective, this meant paying less and getting more. As dates' expectations increased and prices decreased, women's assessments of the value of their labour shifted accordingly. As Candy summarized,

[What has changed most about your work out here?] I'd be gettin' more then than I'm gettin' now, caus of this crack shit or they wanted to get laid more than they do now caus of this AIDS thing OK . . . Now they don't want to pay no more than ten dollars and you don't want no more.

Such expectations on the part of dates are not unrealistic, given that anyone who read the newspapers in the New York area could hardly have avoided repeated reports that, in some neighbourhoods, blowjobs could be had for as little as 50 cents. Elevated expectations on the part of dates also increased the likelihood of violence. Because they saw them as 'crackheads', men felt that they could do 'anything' to women who used crack. As Boy put it,

I don't care how good ya look, you can have diamonds on, everything, rubies. Dat does not matter because ta dem you're pronounced a *crackhead*. 'I can do anything I want ta this bitch if I want ta'.

Women who smoke crack are widely believed to be prepared to 'do anything for a hit' (Anderson, 1990; Inciardi et al., 1993). The reference to female sexuality is implicit and the 'anything' that these women will reportedly do is inevitably sexualized. Increased expectations on the part of dates—fuelled by sensationalist media reports—also included a significant proportion of requests for kinky or 'freaky' sex.[2] Most women agreed that, with the widespread availability of crack, the numbers of such dates had increased. A small minority of women participated in sexual acts beyond what they regarded as 'normal' in order to procure money or drugs. However, contrary to the findings of other research (e.g. Inciardi et al., 1993; Ouellet et al., 1993), most women strongly resisted such transactions.[3] Requests for 'non-normative' sex predated the widespread availability of crack and were entertained by women who had developed particular skills. Masochists were not uncommon among dates and one woman specialized in S&M services. Sometimes women who were unfamiliar and 'untrained' in relation to sado-masochistic sex were prepared to engage in what they saw as merely 'kinky' sex. Dream, a 39-year-old African American woman, just happened to be picked up by a masochist one night and to her surprise found that, in addition to the 'easy money', she enjoyed 'beating his ass'. As she recalled,

[w]e went to a hotel. [How much did you get behind that?] Forty-five. [Wow! What, he wanted special considerations or something?] He was—he's what

[2] Definitions and meanings attached to 'freaking' vary geographically. As Inciardi et al. have noted, while in Miami it was originally confined to women crack users who engaged in oral sex with other women, the term freak refers to 'anyone who trades any type of sex for crack' (1993:59). According to Koester and Schwartz, from the perspective of the woman, freaking is defined as non-normative sexual acts: '[p]erforming sexual acts that they do not perceive as normal or something they would willingly do is called "freaking" ' (1993:196). For most of the women in my study, 'freaking' included lesbian sex, group sex, bestiality and sexual acts involving urine and faeces.

[3] This may be partially due to the over-representation of intravenous heroin and cocaine users with a history of street-level sexwork prior to the advent of crack in this study.

you call, uh, sadist. He wanted his ass whipped. [What's he, uh, white or Puerto Rican, or what?] White. [And you did it good I hope?] (Laughing) I enjoyed it. I enjoyed it. I really did. [Did he enjoy it?] Yes, he did. He came all over hisself.

However, some dates tried to take advantage of what they believed were desperate women, or women who would 'do anything', in order to indulge their sexual fantasies, as the following example from Peggy, a 34-year-old European American woman, illustrates.

There was this one guy in a Mercedes, a stretch Mercedes, a limo and he used to come by and he just wanted the girls to smell his sneakers and shit on his face. He'd give them a $100. They didn't give a fuck (sic). They been out for six or seven days. They haven't showered or anything, so he had a good old time. Yeah, but you know, it's weird, but it's the truth . . . the more money people have, the more odder they get in bed. It's the truth, it is.

Rarer reports involved instances of women engaging in acts involving what was regarded as gross sexual degradation, as is evident from Keisha's account.

I was down south and dere ya have what dey call base house. I went dere one time with my fren (male) and I never seen nuttin' like it. Check it out, dere was this one bitch an' dis guy makin' her eat doggy doo—for a hit. [No, get out of here!] Word. I was buggin'. I mean dese girls will do anything. Dey ain't got no respec'.

The relative rarity of such accounts among the women in this sample may speak to the purported differences between street-level sexworkers and women who work the 'crack' and 'freak' houses described in other research (e.g. Inciardi et al., 1993). However, some of the accounts presented to researchers (including some of those presented here[4]) bear the hallmarks of 'urban legends' or myths (Brunvand, 1983).[5] Although, as Koester and Schwartz have argued, these stories 'are significant as indicators of the level to which this humiliation might be taken' (1993:197), it would be unfortunate if extreme cases of 'hyper-degradation' were necessary in order to counter the 'hypersexuality' hypothesis. The terms of sexual encoun-

[4] In some instances such stories may be a function of the research enquiry—i.e. if you enquire about bizarre acts, you will find them—or merely part of subcultural urban folklore. Either way, research which fails to actually observe such incidents leaves us with few clues as to their veracity, frequency, and meaning.

[5] As Brunvand notes, '[l]egends can survive in our culture as living narrative folklore if they contain three essential elements: a strong basic story-appeal, a foundation in actual belief, and a meaningful message or "moral" ' (1983:21).

ters for the women in my study were negotiated up front and typically involved the payment of cash (as opposed to the promise of drugs). Most transactions took place either in the date's car or on the street. I found little evidence that women were so desperate that they were willing to do 'anything' for the 'glass dick'. Almost all women took exception and offence—despite the greater amount of money involved—to 'non-normative' sexual transactions. This can be seen in Boy's outraged response to such a request.

I had man stop in a car, 'If you let me piss in your face?' I said 'What!' I said 'Get the fuck away from me'. I said 'I'll make a deal with you. Go home to your wife, piss in her face and you can save a lot of fuckin' money'. He said 'I don't have a wife' an' I said 'That's why, what wife would stay with you. And at night you get in the car and you want to piss in my goddamn face'. I wouldn' even say shit like that to no fucking body. Thas how dey are, y'know, de way dey treat da girls, y'know, an' what the girls havta go through ta get the money—it ain' worth shit. One guy stopped a car las' night an' tol' ma girlfren'—'You shit? Do you shit?' In other words he wanna her to shit in his face. Y'know shit (sic) like that, I jus' cannot relate to. [How much did he want to pay her for something like that?] Fifty, summin' like that. He could pay me two hundred. A person could righ' now pay me two hundred dollars, I'd say 'Hell, no'.

Within the confines of the operating conditions of street-level sexwork however, some women are able to manipulate opportunities to their advantage. The ways in which these women 'resist' the oppressive conditions of their working existence both refutes the hypersexuality hypothesis and denies a simple reading of them as victims of pharmacology. Both women's perceptions of, and responses to, requests for 'non-normative' sexual activity indicate that they are not in fact prepared to do 'anything'. Most women maintained fairly clearly defined limits in relation to sexual conduct, reinforced by the occupational norms of street-level sexwork, which they felt were important to maintaining a sense of dignity and self-respect.

Increased Competition and Hostility between Sexworkers

We were standing like three or four girls on a corner. And if a car stopped, it was like, 'He stopped for me, he stopped for me', you know. [Did you all fight over the dates?] Well, uh, it depends on who was there. Some of us are more dignified, you know. We'll just walk a little bit faster than the other one. Linda had tried to cut my throat, and I said, 'He stopped for me'. And she said 'What for bitch?'—she's like she didn't hear me. And when she got there and he said, 'No, I want the girl behind you', I was like 'Na, na, na'. (Rachel)

Women were identified as belonging to one of two categories of sexworker: those with experience of street-level sexwork prior to initiating crack use ('the professionals') and those who began sexwork subsequent to using crack ('the new girls on the block'). All but one of the European American women had participated in sexwork prior to commencing crack use, as had nine of the African American women and 13 of the Latinas. These women were less likely to engage in sex-for-crack transactions with only 22 per cent reporting sex-for-crack exchanges, compared to 50 per cent of the second group. Many of the women in the earlier cohort viewed the more recent initiates with contempt and often went to considerable lengths to distinguish themselves from these 'new girls on the block'. The earlier statement by Candy that 'these people don't know how to be hos' was representative of the strong views held by many of the women in the pre-crack cohort. As she elaborated,

[y]ou don't have to be beautiful, can be the ugliest bitch on the street. Bitch on the corner look like a Bowery bum and he'll pick her up and you're standin' there. They call themselves men and some of the girls out there really look like shit. I'm no raving beauty but there's a way to do everything—take care . . . I'm out there most of the time and here comes a girl looking dynamite, really stecked out, she can't pick up a date for jackshit and here comes this stank bitch lookin' terrible and dirty and she'll pick up a date faster than I will . . . I be there for hours and don't make a dime and here's this filthy bitch making money left and right.

While all the women agreed that street-level sexwork had come to be more competitive, the earlier cohort sought to draw attention to the ways in which crack and individual crack users were responsible for this change. According to Candy,

[t]he girls be runnin' after the cars now callin' them down and girls would *never* do that. [You think there's more girls out here now?] Hell yeah. New ones. Young ones, and they love the young ones. What can I tell you? They don't want nothin' old like me. The old guys, they feel old, so they want the younger ones. I had a guy ask me for a twelve year-old. He offer me $100 for a twelve-year-old girl. I'm gonna get Lisa, you know, I'm gonna get her. Without makeup and shit, she looks like a young girl—a kid. She's a kid anyway, so without makeup. She get in the car for five bucks for that crack. Crack is worse than dope.

In particular, many of the 'professionals' expressed the view that the 'new girls' were the *real crackheads*: i.e. the women who were willing to 'do anything' at any price. As Jo-Beth, a 23-year-old European American women, explained,

Normally you try to ask for fifteen for a blow job. These girls do it for five— less. That's, that's, you know, that's self-degradation. You can't even blame the men because of course if you can get a blow job for five instead of ten or fifteen, you're going to take it. It's like someone selling me a bag of dope for five dollars; of course I'm going to buy your dope instead of the dope for ten, you know.

While some women emphasized the pharmacology of crack and the pathologies of the 'real crack head', others were philosophical and interpreted these changes as a function of a simple market equation whereby 'more drugs equals more girls equals fewer dates'. Latisha first came to Bushwick in 1988. Prior to this she had worked a 'Black stroll' in nearby Bedford Stuyvesant, where the dates were predominantly African American and most of the girls had pimps.

[Do you think girls on the stroll over here compete more or less here than they did over there?] More, caus there's more drugs around so you need more money. There's more girls and less dates.

Within any given sex market, some women always earn more than others. Earning capacity is structured not only by the location, level, nature, and form of particular markets but also by patterns of drug consumption and attributes such as race/ ethnicity, physical looks/attractiveness, street smarts, and the willingness and ability to provide special services. Considerable evidence suggests that, even prior to the advent of crack, sexworkers engaged in price cutting and sex-for-drug trades (e.g. Goldstein, 1979; cf. Hoigard and Finstad, 1992:41–2). Among the many legacies attributed to crack cocaine, however, has been the institutionalization of rate cutting and sex-for-drugs transactions as defining features of street-level sexwork (Goldstein et al., 1992; Ouellet et al., 1993; Ratner 1993b).

Sex-for-Crack Exchanges

Although the exchange of sex for drugs is not a new phenomenon (Goldstein, 1979), several recent ethnographic accounts have highlighted its significance and frequency in inner city drug use settings

(Bourgois and Dunlap, 1993; Feldman et al., 1993; Inciardi et al., 1993; Ouellet et al., 1993; Ratner, 1993b). Within this context, women crack users have been sharply differentiated from earlier cohorts of women drug users who exchanged sex for drugs.

[N]either the 'strawberries', 'skeezers,' 'head hunters,' and 'toss-ups' (the crack 'house' girls who provide oral sex for just a few cents worth of drugs), nor the crack-house 'freaks' (the 'house girls' who have public sex with other women for similarly small amounts of drugs), have any parallel in either the heroin subculture or that of the old-style brothels (Inciardi et al., 1993:96).

My findings do not support these claims. Almost half the women in this study reported having bartered sex for drugs (usually heroin) on at least one occasion during their drug use careers. Sometimes this was in the context of a relationship but more often these women described themselves in terms of the 'bag brides' identified by Goldstein (1979), who found that slightly more than one third of the 33 female heroin users in his study had engaged in sex-for-drugs transactions.[6] Thirteen women or 29 per cent reported engaging in at least one straight sex-for-drugs exchange involving no cash transaction during the study period. These women were both more likely to be crack initiates (50 per cent) and more likely to be Latinas (75 per cent). Indeed the experiences of Latinas suggest that, as crack initiates, many may not have had opportunities to learn other hustling skills. This relative lack of opportunity, combined with a unique drug-sex career trajectory, may render Latinas more likely to engage in sex-for-crack exchanges (Maher, 1996). Yet most research to date has failed to explicate the relative proportions of crack-induced initiates to sexwork or to distinguish between women with histories of street-level sexwork pre- and post-crack. Even a recent study which suggests significant differences between 'street prostitutes' and 'crack house whores' fails to relate these differences to either drug use history or sexwork careers. The authors suggest instead that variable sex work practices can be attributed to the different physical spaces in which sex takes place (Inciardi et al., 1993:67–8), a claim I shall challenge below.

While sex-for-crack exchanges may be the norm in the 'crack house' scenes described by some research (e.g. Inciardi et al, 1993;

[6] A study of 170 pre-crack cocaine users in Miami between 1979 and 1981 also found that 47 per cent of women had exchanged sex for cocaine (Morningstar and Chitwood, 1987).

Koester and Schwartz, 1993), such exchanges were not routine in the street-level scenes on which this research focused. With the exception of car dates and the less-frequent motel dates, the women in my study spent most of their day on the street. There were no 'crack houses' in Bushwick where women could enjoy an unlimited supply of well-stocked willing traders in exchange for sex. When sex-for-crack transactions occurred, they took place in the same physical sites as sex-for-cash transactions—i.e. in dates' cars or vacant lots. Sex-for-crack transactions typically yielded lower dollar returns for the amount of time spent than sex-for-cash transactions. With the exception of the handful of steadies some of the women had, most transactions, whether sex-for-cash or sex-for-crack, involved strangers. Thus it is highly unlikely that, in the context of the present study, sex-for-crack transactions worked to alleviate the climatic and physical discomforts of street-level sexwork, minimize the risk of arrest, or reduce the potential for client violence (Ouellet et al., 1993). Indeed, as suggested below, sex-for-crack transactions may actually increase the potential for violence against women.

While all women resisted sex-for-crack transactions in principle and more than two-thirds did so in practice, it was difficult to solicit information from those women who did engage in sex-for-crack exchanges. Initially, most women were extremely reticent about admitting to sex-for-crack transactions. This particular cultural silence was hardly surprising given the prominent and pejorative spectacle of the debased 'crack ho' in popular culture. However, when observations and interviews began to suggest that this phenomenon was more frequent than originally suggested, women were concerned to make the point that it was not so much that such transactions were refused outright but rather, like the five dollar blowjob, they took place under particular conditions and always involved a compromise of principle. In their conversations with me, women saw a strong need, and often went to considerable lengths, to emphasize the conditions under which such compromises were seen as necessary. As Candy's account suggests, sometimes some women do exchange sex for crack, but neither frequently, readily, nor easily.

OK. If I was stressin' real bad and a guy tell me he's got two or three caps I might do it. I'm sorry, I'm no better than anyone else. Shit, I don't put myself on a pedestal, if I was stressin' bad enough I'd do it. But then after I do it—I think—you muthafucka, man you give me two bottles and I gotta suck your dick . . . I get so mad at myself sometimes.

Goldstein et al. have suggested that some women crack users delib-erately 'get over' by encouraging men to smoke so much crack that they are incapable of performing the sexual act, which places women in a position of relative power whereby they get to use the drug with-out providing sexual services (1992:358–9). However, the experiences of the women in this study strongly suggest that withholding sex until men have smoked too much is not an effective strategy and may increase the risk of violence. Rachel, a 35-year-old European American woman, described this risky practice in the following terms.

You just don't know. Sometimes they will smoke and smoke and you know they can't do shit. But then they still want you to suck and suck and suck. He's like spent all this money and so he thinks he's gotta prove himself or something you know. I mean OK, so you gave me a few caps, doesn't mean I'm going to suck your dick all night. Things can get nasty then.

As Inciardi et al. (1993) have suggested, the fact that cocaine appar-ently interferes with men's sexual potency and their ability to 'come' often prolongs sexual activity. This makes the women's lot more difficult, increases the potential for violence, and may exacerbate the risk of HIV infection (Inciardi et al., 1993:99). When a date is expe-riencing difficulties associated with ejaculation, women may find themselves the victims of male sexual frustration. As Rachel explained, the regular 'everyday' risks of street-level sexwork were compounded by the debilitating effects of crack use on male sexual performance and the consequences of frustration.

I don't like to take drugs on dates because it takes much longer and when they do cocaine they cannot come and it takes much longer and some of them get crazy and when they can't come they want to blame you for it. It just makes everything real risky. [How long does it take to do a blow when a guy's been smoking crack?] About 15, 20 minutes. Without, about four min-utes.

It is not surprising then that most women resisted sex-for-crack transactions on grounds of principle and pragmatism. In a deflated sex market, women were keenly aware that it was both time con-suming and dangerous to support consumption through sex-for-crack transactions. As Jonelle, who had worked as a 'professional' prosti-tute in Chicago told me, *smoking dates* or sex-for-crack exchanges, were dangerous and 'unprofessional'.

They fail to realize that crack affect everyone different—you know what I'm sayin'. Whereas I might take a hit and sit here an' be cool, another person might take a hit and get to trippin', ya know what I'm sayin', they might think anything—flip out.

Part of their resistance was also couched in the inevitability of street-level gender relations whereby men constantly 'got over' on women and ended up getting both 'the head and the drugs'. As Candy explained, women have even less control in the context of sex-for-crack transactions.

He smokin' so lovely everytime he tell you 'OK, you can take a pull', you take a pull an' he wants you on the dick right away. 'Let me enjoy the fuckin hit if you want me to smoke wit you'. You take a hit and you're down there and ain't even let the shit out your mouth yet. You know what I'm sayin'. He fuckin' smokin lovely while you're just suckin' rubber lovely.

My research attests to the existence of—if not total adherence to—a strong set of normative codes and values in relation to street-level sexwork. This can be seen both in the women's insistence not just on 'cash' but on 'cash up front', and the demarcation of certain body parts and activities (e.g. kissing on the mouth or breasts) as off limits. However, as usual, the existence of norms does not mean that people are successful in adhering to them (e.g. see Faupel, 1991).[7] Moreover, subscription to these norms hardly places women in a position to enforce compliance. What did emerge was that women strongly felt that 'successful' sexwork involved the ability to discriminate among clients and between sex acts, and to negotiate the price and the duration of the transaction. While adherence to such norms by both parties provides women with some degree of protection from exploitation, it does not protect them from being raped, ripped off or robbed by dates.

To the degree that they could be effectively mobilized, occupational norms in relation to street-level sexwork placed these women in a better position than women who have been described as consistently or exclusively trading sex-for-crack (e.g. Koester and Schwartz, 1993:193). Compared to the various 'crack house' scenes (e.g. Inciardi et al., 1993), the occupational norms of street-level sexwork appear

---

[7] For example, Faupel has argued in relation to heroin addicts that 'criminal addicts are guided by a rather well developed normative system. The existence of such norms does not mean that addicts are always successful in adhering to them. Like other people, addicts occasionally violate norms' (1991:59).

to afford these women some element of control. By contrast, the norms of the crack house effectively render women completely powerless insofar as these transactions appear to be characterized by an absence of negotiation: 'women in crack houses resign all control of their bodies and their sexual self-determination to the crack house owner and customer' (Inciardi et al., 1993:76). As documented by Inciardi and his colleagues, in the crack house the rule is whatever the male wants, however he wants it, for whatever he is prepared to pay, and for as long as he deems necessary. In my study, sex-for-crack transactions were characterized by the following features: women rarely received payment up front, men determined the amount of crack women received, women were often expected to take their payment in the form of individual 'hits' whilst performing sexual act, and they were frequently ripped off when men reneged on deals after sex. While the extent to which women were able to mobilize occupational norms to control sexwork transactions has been undermined by crack-induced market shifts, these women felt that sex-for-crack transactions rendered them even less able to control the terms or the outcome of the encounter.

There is also the issue of 'respect'—an important element in understanding inner city, urban cultures in general (Bourgois, 1995)—but an issue which assumes critical significance in relation to a population of devalued and disrespected street-level drug users. As many of the narratives presented here indicate, women were conscious of the multitude of ways they were continually disrespected, usually by men. Moreover, for a group of people who have reportedly plummeted to the depths of social degradation, they were concerned, not only with respectful treatment of themselves, but to extend respect to others, including myself and a male colleague.[8] Sex-for-crack transactions carry with them implications for women's sense of self-respect and gender relations more generally. As Keisha related,

I had a offer today. He say, 'Yo Keisha, come on over in da lot'. I say, 'I ain't goin' in no lot'. He say, 'We goin' arouna' corner'. I say, 'I ain' goin'

---

[8] Although women smoked crack without hesitation and at apparent ease in my presence, it was not until relatively late in the fieldwork that I was actually permitted to scrutinize the intravenous administration of drugs. Prior to this, while I would watch them prepare the shot, most women would ask me to momentarily turn my head while they inserted the needle. This, I was told on many occasions, was because they did not want to be 'disrepecting' me. In my experience, male injectors were somewhat less circumspect in this regard.

arouna' corner, I stayin' righ' here'. He say, 'Ya gotcha demo?' (crack stem). I say, 'Yeah I got my stuff'. Dis eight o'clock dis morning. An' nen niss nigger say, 'Here take dis half an' I'm gonna take de other half an' we'll go smoke dis, an' den we'll go aroun' de corner and den we'll do dis'. I say, 'Boy if you don' take ya half capsule back'. I say, 'I don' need it'. [What did he want you do to get the half?] He wanned to have sex. Sex for half a cap ($2.50 worth of crack). Homeboy mus' be buggin'.

Lady B. simply explained that she was not a 'crack prostitute'.

I'd rather not see those kind. Like, I don't want them to say 'Oh, here's two bottles. Give me a blow job.' I'd rather have the money. [Like what percentage want you to get high with them or do a trade?] Maybe 25 per cent cause I try not to see the ones that ask you to get high. Usually, the ones that get high want to do it in trade. I like the ones that pay. As I said, they got to pay first, and then mention that. If they mention the crack first, I don't like to do crack trades. I'm not a crack prostitute.

This reluctance on the part of the women to engage in non-cash exchanges may be specific to drug transactions and does not appear to violate any codes or strongly held beliefs in relation to bartering practices more generally. That is to say, it was common for women to exchange sexual services for other commodities. As Rachel told me,

I got back here about 4.30 (am). I caught one date. Oh, the, uh, the pastry man. He comes around here. And I got him this morning. And I got a couple of, uh, pies. I got a couple of pies for a blow job.

Women frequently and routinely exchanged sexual services for shelter or accommodation. Many women also exchanged sex for food, clothing, and material goods/consumer durables. Below, Sugar, a 36-year-old Latina, recalled having done a blow job in exchange for two watches and having exchanged sex for clothing on another occasion.

He gave me the watches to do a blow job. So I knew it was a good deal . . . we got at least twenty dollars here. [Is that unusual that a date would offer you goods rather than money?] No it's not. A date will do it all the time. [But you don't usually take advantage of that? You prefer the money?] Yeah, I usually do it if it's a good deal, you know. The watches I took cause I like the Citizen one. It looks pretty good. The Citizen is pretty good. I had this date that he sells one of the knitting factory, or sewing factory, or whatever it is clothes, and uh, I would exchange (sex) for clothes. And, uh, he'd give me like $200 worth of clothes. [You have any other dates that offer you stuff like that?] They offer drugs. But I, that I won't go for. I won't go for drugs. [Why?] It's because, uh, you just, uh, you lower yourself too much then, you know.

Notwithstanding her acknowledgement of sexual bartering and her sense that exchanging sex for commodities often resulted in a 'good deal', Sugar refused to engage in sex-for-drugs transactions.

Despite recent crack-induced shifts in the price, structure and nature of street-level sexwork, for the women, money still defines the nature of the interaction. While prices are clearly deflated and their work devalued, sex remains *work*. Although it is not excluded from bartering practices in the drug economy, the exchange of sex for drugs and, in particular, crack, is strongly contested. Like the accounts provided by Goldstein et al. (1992) of women who bartered sex for drugs, the accounts of these women provide a strong counter to the notion that women are passive victims of their crack use (1992:358).[9] Women had a strong sense that sex-for-crack exchanges compromised an already insecure position in an unstable market. They recognized that a willingness to engage in such exchanges undermined the commodity nature of the transaction by reducing the exchange to that of a 'gift' (Ouellet et al., 1993:91). Gift exchanges have traditionally been perceived as being embedded in on-going relations which obligate the receiver. While such exchanges may gratify the desire for drugs and obviate the need to convert cash to drugs, they clearly are not conducive to maintaining either occupational norms or professional integrity. They are also anathema to the market logic which sustains sexwork as a feature of commodity capitalism and one of the few avenues of income generation available to women within the drug economy. For good reasons then, the women in this study strongly resisted attempts by dates to mix 'business and pleasure'.

No Place for a Pimp

In her book on Milwaukee 'street women', Miller develops a continuum of types of male managers of street prostitutes: 'At one end is the pimp, a flamboyant male who manages a "stable" (group of pros-

---

[9] Although they do not document these strategies in detail, Goldstein et al. (1992) suggest that women who bartered sex for drugs employed a number of strategies to minimize the risk of victimization, some of which provided them with opportunities to victimize men.

titutes) in a fairly bureaucratic way. At the other extreme is the "man", who is the husband/lover of the woman' (1986:39). One of the consequences of recent changes in street-level sexwork has been the declining significance of the pimp.[10] A recent study of women crack users in Miami found that none of the women interviewed had pimps: 'All were "outlaws", whether they walked the streets or worked the crack houses' (Inciardi et el., 1993:85; see also Goldstein et al., 1992:360). Similarly, many of the women in this study also commented that '[c]rack the only pimp I got'. In many ways, this development can be seen as a logical response to changed market conditions. Given the decreased market value of street-level sex, the costs of drug consumption are too high and sexwork prices too low to support the functions traditionally associated with pimping structures. Although most women did not have a 'pimp' in the formal sense, some were involved in relationships whereby at least a proportion of their income was diverted to a man or men.

A total of eleven women (25 per cent) were 'turned out' or initiated into sexwork by a pimp. Eight of these women were African American, two were European American and one was a Latina. A further two women claimed to have been 'turned out' by other women. Of these eleven women, ten started out on street-level prostitution strolls and one was a mistress in an S&M club on the Upper East Side. All but one of the eleven women were members of the earlier cohort of 'professionals' and all had worked at least two other street-level prostitution strolls before coming to Bushwick. The remaining women (71 per cent) claimed to have 'turned themselves' out. These women were less likely to report having worked other prostitution strolls, with nine women having only ever worked the stroll in Bushwick. For the most part, their experience of street-level sexwork was limited to adjacent Brooklyn strolls.

Most of the women who were 'turned out' by pimps commenced prostitution at an early age. The youngest was Aiesha, an African American woman, now aged 24. At age 11, Aiesha ran away from a violent home in the midwest to New York City with a 39-year-old man. This man 'turned her out' at the age of 12. Similarly, Slim was only 14 when she met her 'old man', B, who was an experienced pimp

---

[10] As noted by File (1976) and Morningstar and Chitwood (1987), in some contexts this development may have been in train prior to the advent of crack.

with a large 'stable' of women workers.[11] As the following quotation suggests, Slim was both young and impressionable.

[Who turned you out?] Ma ol' man. [Well how did you meet?] Um I was livin' uptown . . . An' he had on his whole shit, jewellery hangin', droopin' like Mr T. An' I say, 'Yo wassup Mr B', an' nass 'is name, B—JB. An' I say, 'Yo wassup'. An' he say 'Ay, wass happenin'. An' I tol' ma girlfrien' an' ma cousin, 'Yeah, I'ma get that nigger. I like dat nigger'. [What did you like about him?] Cowboy guy. The way he looked, the way he was dressed. Livin' large—larger dan large.

Jonelle and Sissy were 15 and 16, respectively, when they were turned out by pimps. Jonelle met her pimp on the streets of Chicago, where she worked for many years before coming to New York. Sissy's old boyfriend from junior high school in Brooklyn already had one 'wife-in-law' working as a prostitute when he recruited Sissy. Dee Dee and her man Lamar came to Bushwick via several Manhattan strolls and Williamsburg's Southside. Dee Dee had started working the streets 11 years previously after meeting Lamar at a local discotheque in Bedford Stuyvesant. Similarly, Princess, also an African American woman, was 'turned out' by a guy from her old neighbourhood in East Flatbush. As she reflected,

[y]ou know, you don' know until you really get out that you don' really need a guy. [So you met a guy and he stuck you out there?] No, he didn't put me out there, I went willingly, but I didn't know it was gonna, y'know, I was gonna end up like that. I knew him for a long time, y'know from the neighbourhood where I grew up. And y'know he used to talk to me all the time y'know and then he'd say 'Oh you can have nice thing in life'. [Did he have other girls?] Yeah a few, more than three. He wasn't a bad guy. Well, he wound up, y'know getting twenty-six to life for murder.

Rosa, a Latina, was brought to Bushwick by an African American pimp who had 'turned her out' up in the Bronx. Rosa was the only Latina in this study who reported being turned out by a pimp.

[Who brought you down here?] Same guy, he know everything . . . he dead now . . . [What was your relationship with him?] Well, was my pimp and then we was started doin' relationship you know . . . [He was like your boyfriend or your ripping and running partner?] Both. First we was only rippin' people—friends right—but then you know, we start to do a little better.

---

[11] Some 15 years later, and although no longer part of a 'stable' of women, Slim remained with this man. Dee Dee was also still involved in a relationship with the man who originally turned her out, as was Jonelle.

[But he didn't start as your boyfriend, he started just as your partner?] Uh huh, then we came in bed, did boyfriend and everything together . . . about four years, and he's the one who show me everything, all the trick and everything, you know. I felt very sorry that he die.

Jenny, a 25-year-old European American woman, was turned out by a pimp she met in a welfare hotel after being made homeless.

I was being pimped. By this pimp, he had threatened me, you know . . . He conned me into staying with him, and I did, you know. I was vulnerable, hungry, you know. I lost my welfare . . . I was staying there because I had no other place to stay, and then he turned me out to the streets . . . He would say like, 'Hey bitch, get out on the stroll' and I would have to come up with $300 or $400 to get him a new package.

Eight women were in a relationship that involved redistributing some or all of their income to a pimp/man during the study period. Three of these women were in relationships with the same pimp/man who had originally turned them out. Repeated interviews and observations of this smaller group of women with pimps/men revealed little evidence that these relationships actually provided women with protection or benefit at any level. In fact, the drain such relationships placed on women's economic resources put them under greater pressure to generate income, as suggested below by Jonelle.

I feel like iss up to me. Homeboy be on my back all da time. An' shit changed out here. With the prices we be gettin' now, this muthafucka don' know what time it is. He be stressin' me—'Whatcha got? You got sometin' for me?'

The women's retrospective accounts of their initiation into sexwork, combined with their contemporary experiences, suggest that the 'pimp' and the 'man' are difficult to distinguish in this setting. For some women, Miller's (1986) 'intermediate type' is indeed part man/part pimp. However, recent changes in street-level sex markets suggest that a 'management' model may fail to account for the diversity of arrangements whereby individual women enter into understandings with various men (e.g. intimates, dates, users, dealers, police, and others). These arrangements may take the form of men either 'watching their backs' on the stroll as was most common in this study, or, within the context of the crack house scene described by Inciardi et al. (1993) and the Cleveland street-level sex markets described by J. Miller (1993), other types of relationships with men which enable women to procure drugs.

Women's 'independence' from exploitation by pimps/men has

come at the price of heightened vulnerability on the street. While women are 'free' from exploitation in one sense, they are also devoid of protection insofar as many potential victimizers correctly perceive that they no longer face consequences for 'messing' with these women. The exit of pimps from the stroll has created a physical site in which the risk of victimization is increased—both by dates and male drug users seeking money and drugs. The space vacated by pimps has created a kind of pseudo or 'situational pimping' whereby men enter into informal relationships with women to 'watch their backs' for a few dollars or shared drugs.[12] This has produced a new form of income generation for drug-using males. The emergence of the informal 'lookout' system, adopted from the occupational structure of street-level distribution, provides yet another way for men to 'get paid'. Below, Candy explained how this system typically worked.

[Who's your lookout?] Whatever guy I pick for the night. [You don't have a regular person] No. Yeah, well a lot of times I get stuck without any . . . These guys just sit there and wait for you to come back with the money and the drugs. They watch when you cop a date, and they sit there. When you come back, they take you down to cop, and it costs you five bucks each time. I mean shit. They're gettin' high. You know most of them are crack smokers, or some of them, you get, some of them the ones that are heroin users, that's a bitch because then you got to buy them heroin. [How do you find a lookout?] They come down here, most of them as tricks, and then you ask them, you know, if you got time to hang out why don't you just watch my back, and they like the idea, and they like the money they gettin' so they come back every night. I'd do the same thing if I had a car.

Like pimping, being a lookout is easy money for men. However, it carries few obligations and responsibilities and, in its current form, provides women with little in the way of protection, reassurance or material support. As Rachel put it, 'they're not really doing anything'.

[Who do you get to watch your back?] Uh, well, uh, if I want somebody to do that, I'll ask them for their work and pay them, you know, buy them a hit or something like that. [Do you generally do that or do you generally work alone?] I generally work alone because for the most part all you're doing is buying them a hit. They're not really doing anything. And for the

[12] In their study of the income-generating activities of heroin users, Johnson et al. also noted that prostitutes often hired men to 'watch their backs'. These men were usually 'nonsexual friends' of the woman (1985:59).

most part if something comes down they're gone, you know. It doesn't really pay.

And as Dee Dee, a 29-year-old African American woman, told me, even when 'lookouts' performed their lookout function, having a street drug user 'watch your back' could not really be effective given the conditions of street-level sexwork.

I don' really believe in havin' somebody out there watchin' ya back. Caus wen you get in a car wit' a guy, he's not gettin' in nere wit' you. If dat man wanna y'know take off speed an' take ya here an' dere, wherever, wass ya lookout gon' do? What can he do? There's nuttin' he could do.

Women in drug-using relationships were arguably further disadvantaged by the formal erosion of the pimping structure. Typically, the men/pimps were no longer expected to maintain a front of protective authority by looking out for 'their' women and warding off potential aggressors. Whatever semblance of protection was offered—or perceived to be on offer—by men/pimps in the past was no longer apparent. While women were cognisant of their increasing vulnerability, pimps/men more often presented a hindrance than a help. As Latisha explained,

[t]his dude I know, right, a walkin' date, wanted to go out. He gives me $15 and then he smokes with me. Then fuckin' Tre comes up the block and spoils it. Tre's stressin', right. I just bought two cracks. I'd caught a date before that, a quick blow job and I bought two cracks and I gave him one and a half and I took a half a one for myself. That was so he would be nice, be calm, that shit, you know, chillin' out, not on the stress.

The pimp/man ambiguity was especially evident where both partners in a relationship used drugs. Most of the women in such relationships exercised little control over their finances. Women in drug-using relationships with men were at an economic disadvantage compared to women who either were not in relationships or who were in relationships with men who did not use illegal drugs. Women in drug-using relationships were expected to pool their resources with their man—usually a heavy heroin and/or crack consumer—despite the fact that most of these men generated little income and/or refused to share whatever income or drugs they had. As Latisha told me,

[e]verybody told me Tre was in the doorway an' he had money, he was spendin' it, he bought ten cracks. He had smoked them by the time I'd seen

him. Just for the hell of it I said 'Oh you just got here?'. He said 'Yeah and guess what, I missed my boss and I didn't get paid'.

One might have expected that the decrease in formal surveillance as a result of the erosion of the pimping structure, would have provided women with greater freedom to earn and spend their money. This was the case for those women not in relationships with a pimp/man. For the eight women in relationships, the typical pattern involved a traditional surrender of autonomy over how they spent their money, but with little value in return. Men were ineffectual in their roles as protectors and most women saw them as 'just another habit to feed'. Male partners rarely accompanied 'their' woman while she was working, preferring instead to 'hang out' on the side streets which provided access to the principal drug market block. This enabled them to intercept the women as they left the stroll with their hard earned cash and headed towards the copping area. Women in relationships bore additional burdens as a consequence of male perceptions of shifting power relations. Constant conflict ensued between drug-using intimates over how much money women had generated and what it should be spent on: these factors which placed already vulnerable women at further risk of intimate assault. The earlier qoutation from Latisha bears repeating.

Last night I went up there you know, I tricked. Took me about an hour and I made money an' I have to tell him how much I made. I made forty-five dollars . . . He call me 'dope fiend' in front of everybody and 'lowlife bitch', 'bitch suckin' on white face dicks', you know, and this the same money I share with him. I mean, after I gave him twenty-five dollars, I took twenty and you know that he smoked it all up, right. I bought me a one-on-one (heroin and cocaine) an' a crack, right. I had to give him half of my one-on-one so he wouldn't jump on me an' beat me up—after I gave him twenty five dollars. Then I had my crack, right an' he want half my crack an' caus I didn't give it to him, he jumped on me an' beat me up and my sweater is all bloodied up from him beatin on me . . . He knows I got no place to go.

Compared to freelancers, women in relationships with pimps/men had it worse. They were no better off in terms of protection and safety than women without men/pimps but they had considerably less freedom over how they spent their money. As a freelancer, Keisha maintained that although she earned more, was 'treated better', and felt less exposed to violence working in Manhattan for a pimp, she preferred working in Bushwick where 'what's mines iss mines'.

Dere (Manhattan) ya don't get treated fucked up. Word. Ya get treated like a lady. But ya don't get ta keep the money. Ya gots to give it up. So ya can make less money and get to keep it yourself, or ya make mo' money and give it to a pimp caus in Ma'hattan you gots to have a pimp. If ya don't got one, ya gon' get taken by one of dem anyway. Iss less money here but *what's mines iss mines*, right.

Finally, the complexities inherent in drawing clear-cut distinctions concerning relations with males—be they husbands, boyfriends, pimps, dates, or dealers—are illustrated in the following quote from Kizzy, who took the view that all heterosexual relations were anchored in a form of prostitution.

You always sell your ass when you really look at it. OK, caus even with my man I sell my ass you know. Caus, um you buy me stuff, you know what I'm sayin', he gives me money you know, so the only thing different, they out here, you know what I'm sayin'- go with dis one dat one and I don't, I just go with one. I trick one man, you know, for five years. You know, that's the way, you still sells your ass. I tell 'em 'You all buy pussy. Realize it and face it—you buys it. You buy it from your damn wife muthafucka—every-time you pay that damn rent or you give her twenny and thirty dollars. You know what I'm sayin', you're pullin out ya pocket, you're payin' for pussy' . . . You know I hate when dey do that—'I don't pay for pussy, I could never'—'Yes you does. Wake up and smell that coffee baby.' I tell mine, 'You gon' pay for this pussy'. I ask Stanley, 'You think you ain't pay for no pussy—Din't you buy me those LA Gears (sneakers) punk?' You know and I show him and he be like, you know, uhuh, thinkin' bout it.

Market Conditions and the Victimization of Women

A girl gets raped everyday almost out here. Things down here are getting really bad. Bitches getting knocked off one by one. Dyin' or getting stabbed or beat up or something. A lot more people getting beat up because of the crack. Stressing bad and holding up people. (Candy)

During the three-year fieldwork period at least eight women drug users were killed. One woman was hurled into a parking meter from a van being chased by the police; another was murdered and her decapitated body, minus her breasts, was found over by the railway tracks. As Rosa told me about the latter incident,

they found one by the, you know, the railroad tracks, you heard about those? There's where the factories are, right? They found this girl with no head, no titties. Nobody knew her caus' nobody found her head. She was a Black girl. [And nobody noticed their friend was missing?] There was another girl missing though. You know sometimes we think they locked up in the lock-up. We don't know they be killed, you know.

Another woman, was beaten to death by a man Latisha believed was a date.

She was workin'. He was a crack head and he used to flip, used to go buy a bunch of crack right, give it to the girl and then, you know, do what you want, but then he would flip out and then he'd beat em up. That was her date.

One Sunday evening, Juanita was repeatedly stabbed and her breasts were mutilated. For several weeks she remained in intensive care in a local hospital. As Princess told me, early in the evening Juanita had been on the lot on Crack Row in the company of two white males, which was most unusual in this neighbourhood. The next we heard, she was in Woodhull Hospital.

I heard she got a hundred stitches. They cut her breasts off . . . They was hangin' out in the lot. I can't understand why would you take somebody (away) from the lot where everybody's there—you know, if he do something to you all you gotta do is scream—and bring them to some secluded area. [But they were white guys we heard?] That why she went. To Hispanic and Black people, it's white, is OK—that's bull.

Another woman, was found dead in an abandoned lot on the other side of a main thoroughfare where many of the women slept at night. She had two bullet holes in her head.

For more than half of these women, victimization on the street extended a continuum of violence that began at home. More than one third (38 per cent) grew up in abusive households where they were subjected to violence and 29 women (64 per cent) reported having been in a physically abusive relationship as an adult. These women, then, had extensive experience of victimization by males within familial or 'private' settings prior to their immersion in street life. Some women's experiences of domestic violence were ongoing, as Latisha's account attests.

I can imagine myself like waitin' til Tre go to sleep and killin' him cause I promise myself once I get grown, nobody was gonna beat on me no more. Caus' I can't take it. I don't wan' nobody beatin on me no more. I said when I get grown nobody's gone ever hit me again. Now, it's startin' to happen all over again [sobbing]. I'm scared, I'm gon' kill him, I can't take it . . . I be askin' him 'Why are you hittin' me?' and then he'll say the same thing my mother say, 'Just shut up' and I can't fuckin' take it. If there's a God, why, why is he makin' me suffer like this? I go in my pocket and give people my last, if I see people (dope) sick I share—I share with them. I sell my body and I give him. So, I can't take it . . . either I kill him or I kill me [sobbing].

Victimization on the street also takes place at the hands of men— male drug users, neighbourhood youth, and dates. Women were regularly robbed and beaten, routinely pushed or forced to jump from moving vehicles and, less frequently, shot at (Maher and Curtis, 1992). The following narratives indicate the multitude of ways violence manifests itself in heterosexual relations on the street.

They (two dates) wanted their money back after we finished—threw me off the van naked—then he hit me with a blackjack caus I jumped back onto the van because I wanted to get my clothes. It was freezing outside so I jumped back onto the van to try and get my clothes and he smacked me with a black-jack on my eye. (Cookie)

I got ripped off. I was ousside—standin' ousside and this guy came and took my jacket off me. I had a leather (jacket)—like up to here (indicates length) and they took it off me. And not only that, I got beat up by four guys too. I was standin' on the corner and they went up to my friend and they were bothering her and so I got scared and I started runnin' so I heard one of them say, 'Let's chase her caus she's runnin'. They chased me alright, and they got me. (Lorraine)

Robbery was regarded by many of the women as an occupational hazard. In addition to the loss of hard earned cash and/or drugs, robbery may also result in serious injury. Rosa related a recent experience where she was robbed by two male drug users on the stroll.

[What happened yesterday]? (She had a cut face and a black eye) Well, somebody tried to rip me off, two black guys, right there, they came from nowhere. I didn't give up the money, they hit me, police came in time (they were going past) but you know, hey I wasn't givin' the money so I told them, 'You can kill me.' They saw me gettin' out of the (date's) car . . . They hit me, cut me, with a ring or something. I went to the Precinct, I was bleeding.

Lady B., a 32-year-old Jewish woman, was a self-described former 'BS&M Queen' who had lived in California for nine years. She claimed to have several pornographic videos to her credit and reported freebasing at Hugh Hefner's Playboy mansion. Since coming to Bushwick, Lady B. had been robbed several times and raped twice: she also lost all her teeth as a result of a pistol whipping when two men tried to rob her and a friend for a dollar. Her experiences were not exceptional. Almost all the women reported having been raped in the context of sexwork, and all of them had been beaten as a consequence of their involvement in either sexwork or drug activity. As Boy told me,

I got raped twice. [Down here?] Yeah, down here, y'know. An' dat blew ma fuckin' mind. Cos' sometime you get somethin' dat jus' frightens you dat bad, y'know. [What happened?] The firs' one, right, met a guy, right, so he wanned ta. We wen', right, we headed ta da tracks. We were walkin' tagether, but when we got there, y'know the situation—he wanned ta do somethin' I din' wanna do. [What did he want to do?] Inna butt. I tol' 'im I wanned money on the bottom line. He didn' go for it.

Rape inevitably traumatizes women. However, as is the case in the larger population, reactions and strategies for coping with sexual assault varied widely. For some women—typically the few with a relatively intact support system and somewhere else to go—violent sexual assault may provide an impetus for re-evaluating or even leaving 'the life'. Debbie was one such woman. As she told me,

I was raped at gun point about six weeks ago by a Spanish kid. It changed my mind about a lot of things down here, in terms of working. Right on Flushing. It wasn't a car, it was a walking date, that's really what's crazy about it. It wasn't a car date. And 'til then I was almost actually enjoying it and you can imagine that. I feel like I should be embarrassed saying it, but I really didn't mind making money that way. If the guy was a jerk I wouldn't be with him much time and actually I meet a lot of neat guys. I was always meeting different guys and, you know, (now) things have changed.

For Kizzy, as for many women regardless of their individual situation, the physical violation may be less at issue than the complex relations of identity, reputation, power, and control invoked by the act of rape.

I got raped. A piece of pussy ain't nothin'. A Dominican muthafucka. I told him, I said 'Thas all right. Pussy ain't nothin' to me'. I said 'But you know somethin', I'm gonna see you again. I will though. Issa a small world' I said, and check this out, you know he gonna ask me, 'Did I like it?' I said 'What the fuck, you don't turn me on. You disgust me'. I wouldn't buy it. I'm gonna stick that fat muthafucka. I told him I said 'You know something, if I had a knife I'd cut your fuckin' ass up. I'm a bad bitch ain't I?' I was callin' him much shit. I was callin' him all kinds of muthafuckas.

Sometimes the response of others compounds the initial violation. Although many women are further traumatized by the reactions of others—including that of the legal system—the trauma is often exacerbated when the rape victim is a sexworker. As Candy related,

I was working and I got raped. And everybody laughed when I said to them I got raped. People feel that a hooker has no right to say she's been raped which is not so. OK, we're all still human and anything done by force or violence is rape to me. The people were laughing and they said 'How did you get raped?' You know, they laughed. You know, and I think it's, they're stupid. Because I'm going to sit here and lie? I work and do what I do but that doesn't mean that I can get abused and just beat up and people feel that's life for a hooker. I mean, this is a real life for me. I'm living it. People that don't live there, they're quick to talk about it but they're not quick to identify with me and try to really come, come to reality and say well, you know, this girl is going through all this.

As Candy's narrative illustrates, rapes of sexworkers are rarely reported and the perpetrators of these and other violent acts are unlikely to be brought to justice. In only two of the cases of rape identified by the women in this study were charges brought: both resulted in convictions. Jo-Beth told me of her experience.

One of the men got caught though, he's in jail now. I got him caught. I fought with him, and he went to pull away and I turned the steering wheel and he hit a wall. [Who, caught him, the cops?] Yep. They beat the shit out of him. [What, you watched that?] Yeah. [I guess that felt good, right?] It felt great, cause, you know, he had a gun and shit. I was very—I was real green at the time. And I really didn't, like now I would never have done the same thing that I did then, to tell you the truth. You see people die, you realize it's reality. But then I just, I wasn't, you know, I wasn't happening, I guess you can say.

In sum, the price deflation of sexual services has in turn spawned a self-selecting process of cheaper 'rougher' dates which has made the stroll a 'rougher' and more violent place to work. Despite the fact that they were more likely to be victimized, some women were reluctant to 'blame' either dates or male drug users. Rather, like the wider culture, they attributed increases in victimization to crack-induced carelessness or shortcomings on the part of individual women. As Jonelle saw it, '[a] lot of them be thirsty and dey ain't got no time to judge'. The earlier cohort of women were often able to secure a better price for sexual services through skilled negotiating or by doing the job 'well enough' to receive a 'tip'. Yet these 'negotiating tactics', such as the one Latisha talks about below, also ran the risk of violence.

I just get in the car. Princess taught me this—never turn down five dollars, cause if he got five, he got ten. I used to say 'Get outta here', then I started gettin in the car . . . Because if he gave me five, I touch their penis a little bit and then I go, 'What you want for five dollars?' and then get ready to get out and they go, 'Here, here'.

Given the intense competition for dates—especially ones prepared to pay the increasingly cheapened 'market rate', most women had few alternatives. As the following quotation from Dee Dee suggests, while they had limited resources at their disposal, many women prided themselves on their ability to discern dates who presented risks to personal safety and economic security. Women relied on a combination of past experience and cultivated intuition, or 'gut feelings', in attempting to discriminate among dates. As Dee Dee related,

I'm more leery so regardless to how much money dey offer me. Like the other day I got in a (red) van with a guy. It was a red van and I just remembered Anita. I don't know if you know Anita—but a little while ago she got beat real bad with a crowbar or somethin'. Dey told me it was a red van, and I started feelin' real funny, and he didn't want to park where I said either, you know. When he did park, I act like I had to pee and I said 'Let me get out, I got to go pee'. And I said, 'I'm not gettin' back in'. He said 'You sure you don't want to go? You sure?' And den he offered more money and dat really made me like 'Oh no, I'm not gettin' back in here.' I had the most ugliest feelin'.

However as Rosa suggested, often there was simply no way to tell.

As you know, the guy killin' the girls. [So you are careful?] Oh God, careful, I am pretty scared. That doesn't tell you if they being sick—you just bump into them or people stop. And then you don't realize until the thing happen, you know. They pull over, a guy—a knife or a gun.

And unfortunately—as the following accounts by Candy and Jo-Beth suggest—intuition alone offers women scant protection.

You can't always tell. That's why I was raped. That's how it was, see, cause I, I wasn't sure. I never thought this guy would do something like that. He was too straight, you know. Can't always be reading people right. I don't care how long you in business. You know what I'm saying? (Candy)

I was raped four times. Two Spanish guys and two Black guys—that's why I don't date black guys. [So, ah, what did you do behind all that?] What can you do? You get a little more careful about which cars you get into, that's about it. (Jo-Beth)

However, in practice, experience and intuition were bolstered by the existence of women-centred street networks which functioned as valuable conduits for information and the pooling of scarce resources. As street-level sexworkers, women interacted frequently—both on the stroll and off it—and considerable time was spent discussing the latest violent incidents and detailing narrow escapes. This, in turn, ensured the widespread circulation of information in relation to particular vehicles and suspect individuals. The ways in which women utilized this combination of experience, intuition and information in attempting to ward off potential victimization was illustrated by the earlier quotation from Dee Dee. Although the recollection of her friend's experience with the red van set off an alarm bell, Dee Dee got into the van. However, the subsequent behaviour of the occupant and his reluctance to park confirmed her initial suspicions, prompting her request to urinate as a ploy to leave the vehicle and place herself in a relatively safe position to decline the transaction. The fact that this date then offered her more money only served to affirm what she described as 'the most ugliest feelin'.

'Viccing' as a Form of Resistance

[R]acial prejudices and suspicions, sexual stereotypes and discrimination are also apparent in the hustling world. However, in many instances these otherwise negative conditions and attitudes are actively taken advantage of and turned around and used against society to the benefit of the hustler (Biernacki, 1979: 540–1).

The term 'viccing' has become as much a part of the lexicon of crack use as more familiar words and phrases such as 'beaming up', 'talking to Scotty', 'the mission', 'klingons', and 'nickelonians'. According to Hamid, viccing is a variation of the 'mission'—'the pilgrimage or mendicancy of multiple, high-risk tasks by which they [crack users] acquire money to buy crack' (Hamid, forthcoming:46). 'Vics' or 'victims of circumstance' are usually male. The distinguishing feature is that the 'vic' is encouraged to feel that he will receive sexual services, only to be denied them and relieved of whatever valuables or drugs are in his possession (Hamid, forthcoming). Viccing, although a new term in the crack argot, is not a new phenomenon, nor is it exclusive to crack use.[13] Some women had long histories of thieving or

[13] See for example Goldstein (1979).

'robbing' dates to generate income for drugs. For example, Rosa told me about her 'dope-fiend' days up in the Bronx.

Then I was like robbin' more people. [How would you do that—how do you rob somebody?] Well, I was goin' with guys, you know, maybe they want to go out (have sex) and we used to set 'em up and I used to take 'em to a place and de guys would take the guy off . . . I used to go on the street like, you know stand on the corner, guy come and say 'Hey you go out?' (Are you working?) and I say 'Yeah' and take him to a place . . . to rob them.

However, women clearly distinguished between conventional theft, sexwork, and viccing. As Rosa recalled,

[t]here I started doin', you know, startin' workin' like a hooker, you know. I mean I was doin' the job—I was gettin' paid. [When you were really working like a hooker, you weren't robbing or doing stuff?] No, no no—jus' doing job and gettin' paid, you know.

While, on face value, viccing dates appears to be nothing new, a further examination reveals that it is closely connected with crack-induced shifts in the contexts of street-level sexwork. Although the act itself appears similar to other instrumental thefts, the motivations undergirding it are more complex in that they are intimately linked with women's collective sense of the devaluation of their bodies and their work. Viccing provides a way of contesting this devaluation and, simultaneously, a means of adaptation to the changed conditions of street-level sexwork post-crack. As Candy told me,

I robbed a guy up here not too long ago. Five o'clock Sunday morning . . . a real cheek gonna tell me five dollars for a blowjob, and that pisses me off—arguing with them. I don't argue no more. Jus' get in the car sucker, he open his pants and do like this and I do like this, put my hand, money first. He give me the money I say 'See ya, hate to be ya. Next time muthafucka it cost you five dollars to get me to come to the window'. Ain't give 'em shit for five bucks, you can't get nothin' for five bucks . . . I rip off someone if he gonna be cute like that, but I don't (just) rip anybody off . . . I haven't done that often, making a habit, but that guy got me so pissed off. Sunday morning I'm hungry, I'm stressin' like a son of a bitch, I got my ride here stressed with me because he ain't done a blast and here come a sucker offer me five bucks an' got pocket full of money . . . That's the guy that's insulting you and I don't like that. Like sorry, if I'm hungry or I'm stressin' and I want a blast bad enough. I'll get in the car for two dollars if I'm short, don' mean you gon' get your dick sucked.

Women viewed these conditions as exacerbating already strained gender relations, as illustrated in the following quotation from Boy.

I had a guy yesterday come and say 'You suck my dick I'll give you fi' dollar'. I said 'If you suck my pussy I'll give you ten.' Bitch. I'll kill somebody out here. Because I'm not going to get played out by no guy. I didn' get played out by my kids' father and I'll be damned if I'm going to get played out by any guy out here.

Viccing dates is not without consequences however—not the least of which are 'cutting your own throat' and the everpresent threat of retaliation. As Candy recalled,

[l]ike I lost a steady, he was a $30 blow job, used to come once a week and I was so ill this one day I took him in the bathroom and he paid me and I said 'Not this day baby, I'm sorry' and I just took the money and ran down the stairs and he said 'Where you goin?' and I said 'I'm sorry I'm not in the mood today—later' . . . Now I lost that customer but at that point I didn't give a fuck, I was that sick . . . I just wanted to get mine, get straight and that all I cared about. Now I hurt because I miss that thirty bucks on that Wednesday morning you know.

Viccing is a high-risk activity which carries strong potential for violent retaliation. Viccing perpetuates a destructive market cycle whereby theft begets violence. Rosa explained this process.

Some girls they, you know some girls they been playin' dirty, try to take the money out of the people, you know, in the night. The other night it was raining a lot right. I was standing right there on Flushing right. And this guy came and he put off the car right. So the girl was ready to get out of the car, and he pull her back. He pull her back and start beating the shit out of her. And she start to run and he grab her by the dress, and her dress fell down, and she was running naked out the car. And he was following her saying you know, 'Give me my money, give me my money.' [Because she tried to take his money?] Exactly. Some guy they don't go for that. That's no good though, 'cause you know she make it bad for everybody.

Within the drug economy, the practice of viccing represents a particularly gendered innovative 'solution', albeit one that is deeply entrenched in the most traditional gender relations—those of prostitution. The practice of viccing reflects the conditions of crack-saturated sex markets and the positioning of women in the street-level drug economy. In a context where blow jobs could be had for as little as two or three dollars, these forms of robbery, theft and assault were common events. They were committed primarily against dates but sometimes against other 'vics' and even other women, but always because street-level sexwork was the only major form of income generation for women drug users. While viccing appears to represent women's extended criminality and excursions into the male domain, in fact it reflects women's continued subjugation: their marginalization within prostitution and cheapened sex markets and a greater vulnerability to violent victimization (Maher and Curtis, 1992).

Viccing has emerged as a response to these conditions and in this sense, the victimization of others provides a way for women to 'recoup their own status as victims' (Simone, 1989:159). Rendered peripheral by the sex segmented labour markets of the drug economy and the crack-accelerated commodification and devaluation of their bodies, these women make the most of the limited opportunities that come their way. While viccing may achieve a temporary 'penetration' of their condition (Willis, 1977), ultimately it becomes a limitation insofar as it serves both to exacerbate the deteriorating conditions of street-level sexwork and to intensify the victimization of women. Rather than providing a way out, viccing binds women back into the oppressive structure of street-level sexwork, reinscribes their marginal status as labourers within the drug economy, and reproduces them as 'criminal women'.

Conclusion

[T]he major trends in cocaine-era prostitution appear to be a more mono-maniacal fixation on procuring the drug of choice, an increase in the trading of sex for drugs, perhaps an increase in sexual activity in return for drugs or money for drugs, and a greater desperation that is reflected at the least in decreased prices for sex. These trends, while pronounced in those who inject cocaine, appear even more extreme in rock smokers (Ouellet et al., 1993:91).

The advent of crack cocaine has had a profound impact on street-level sex markets in New York City. Crucial to understanding these changes and addressing their implications is the gradual undermining of an institutionalized set of norms governing transactions, behaviours, and relations within the context of street-level sexwork. While previous drug eras have also spawned myths surrounding the lack of normative values among drug users (Faupel, 1991), a particularly potent brand of mythology has developed in relation to the 'thirsty crackhead'. This mythology posits the crack user as a pharmacologically driven, impulsive, desperate criminal who responds randomly to opportunities for income generation. Both media and some social science accounts are responsible for perpetuating an image of crack users as so desperate and amoral that they are prepared to steal 'the gold from their grandmother's teeth' (e.g. see Anderson, 1988:88). Women crack users are portrayed as being even worse. They will truly do 'anything' for a hit, as the caricature used by Rosenbaum and her colleagues to illustrate this point suggests: 'we "know" from reading the paper and watching TV that after one hit of crack, women take off their clothes and have sex with anyone, including the family pet . . . To make a long story short, women crack users are amoral animals, lacking a conscience' (1990:2).

While recent research is attempting to specify more carefully who these women are and what they do, highly sexualized images of women crack users continue to dominate the literature. For example, Inciardi et al. (1993) suggest that 'many crack addicted women engage in any manner of sexual activity, under any circumstances, in private or in public, and with multiple partners of either sex (or both sexes simultaneously)' (1993:95). With pervasive images of women crack users as 'hypersexual' and unable to adhere to even basic normative values, it is not surprising that these women have been constructed as bereft of occupational norms. I have endeavoured to offer a more accurate, nuanced, and sympathetic reading of these women, the occupational norms which govern their behaviour, and the difficulties they face in maintaining compliance to these norms.

The gradual erosion of occupational norms in relation to street-level sexwork is not the result of the pharmacology of crack, but rather, of broader social and economic shifts in street-level sex markets in the wake of crack cocaine. Changes in the drug economy produced by the widespread consumption of crack in low-income minority neighbourhoods have been constitutive of changes in the contexts of street-level sexwork. In impoverished urban neighbourhoods where crack has become the de facto 'currency of the realm' (Inciardi et al., 1990), it is not surprising that its possession facilitates the exercise of power. As Jody Miller (1993) has suggested in relation to women's 'liberation' from traditional pimping structures, crack-induced shifts in the character of street-level sexwork provide a graphic illustration of 'how gender regimes change over time and are reconstituted in new ways with changing environments' (J. Miller, 1993:23). Neither these regimes nor the relations that constitute them are fixed or immutable. In examining the conditions of women drug users' labour as commercial sexworkers, I have sought to illustrate the gaps, contradictions, and resistances that appear in these regimes and to contest the excessively sexual scripts which reference both popular and scientific discourse on women crack users.

Street-level sexwork cannot be viewed in isolation from the informal drug economy. In the drug economy, the advent of crack cocaine has served to reproduce, rather than rupture, existing gender relations. Women have not been 'liberated' from the oppressive confines of sexwork nor have they challenged the hegemonic masculinity of male-dominated street networks. Apart from their roles as consumers, the position of women within the drug economy remains marginal at best. The exception is clearly street-level sexwork which often provides the only opportunity for women in this system of constricted choices. Lorraine, a 27-year-old Latina, spoke about the lack of opportunity for women.

I don't think that most of the girls out here could do anything else except sell themselves. I think once you're here, you're stuck, it's a rut. I don't think you can get out until you do something. If you're drug addicted, you have to do something about that. That's the only way you're ever going to get out. But the girls are luckier than the guys. Guys have a hard time, they're limited. Girls got something that everybody wants. That's all they can do, but that's all they have to do.

While many women agreed that their options were limited, some felt that women were fortunate to have steady work: 'Girls got something that everybody wants'. However, they also recognized the centrality of sex/gender to this division of labour, as Candy's comments on gender and work reveal.

[So you think it's harder for women or harder for men in terms of getting money?] Men always make money if he's any kind of a man . . . I feel sorry for these guys stop to eat if they don't make money. That's why a guy like that, I'll turn a guy on before a girl because we can make it but a guy can't. So it's harder to deal with. You know, but, you live the street, you play the street, you get your money. [But it's divided like guys will do the scrapping and stuff like that and girls have the stroll.] Yeah, you know, you do what you do best, that's it. Two different systems.

Like contributions to the formal economy, contributions to the drug economy are gendered. As such, they are subject to contestation, as differently situated social actors struggle to impose the greatest value on the positions they occupy. Some of the women and all of the men thought that women 'had it easier' because they could always sell their bodies. Both Lorraine's and Candy's use of broader cultural ideas about sex/gender are the logical outcome of a desire to elevate the status of their work. And yet in doing so, they illustrate how men and women in the drug economy work to reproduce existing sex/gender relations.

7

Intersectionalities: Gender–Race–Class

Issa Spanish neighbourhood, you know, and Black girls be gettin' dogged
(Boy)

Opportunities for labour-market participation in the informal economy are not empty slots waiting to be filled by those with the requisite skill. As we have seen, who fills these slots and how certain slots
come to be associated with a particular status influences the creation
and maintenance of employment hierarchies and social hierarchies
more generally. But little is known about the ways in which multiple
dimensions of identity[1] interact to produce divisions of labour and,
in particular, how convergences of race/ethnicity and sex/gender contribute to labour-market segmentation.

Labour-market segmentation and labour process theories have typically focused on class. The economic determinism inherent in these
analyses has tended to eclipse the role of other dimensions of social
stratification such as sex/gender, race/ethnicity, age, and immigrant
status in accounting for the over-representation of certain groups
among the ranks of what has been described as an 'industrial reserve
army of labor' (Bravermann, 1975). For the most part, explanations
of labour-market segmentation remain entrenched in the labour
process, and sex/gender and race/ethnicity continue to be viewed as
functional aspects of underlying class relations: they tell us little

[1] Following Coombs (1996), I use the term 'identity' here to refer to socially produced categories such as gender, race, age, immigrant status, religion, sexual orienta-
tion, and the like. These categories do not simply reflect pre-existing social, cultural
or biological realities: 'one's identity is always contingent and contextual . . . determined by particular persons for particular purposes at particular times in a process in
which the person identified participates with varying degrees of freedom' (1996:223).
In relation to labour markets, identity-based phenomena such as race are clearly implicated in the processes by which particular people are classified as suitable for particular slots and how these slots themselves come to be associated with particular
identities.

about why particular people fill particular places (Hartmann, 1979). Since the 1980s, analyses of the informal sector have underscored the declining significance of class as a determinant of social stratification. For example, Castells and Portes argue that the expansion of the informal sector and the increasing heterogeneity of work situations have led to a blurring of the class structure.

[T]he process of informalization tends to reinforce some specific social groupings that differ markedly from those associated with stable class lines . . . The combination of an expanded informal economy and of segmented labor markets specified by gender, ethnicity, or age creates fundamental changes in the class structure (1989:32).

Their recognition is part of a more general move away from primarily class-based explanations towards acknowledgement of a more complex set of cross-cutting influences—race/ethnicity, sex/gender, age, immigrant status, and other social relations. While connected to more general trends in social theory, this shift has been shaped by political struggles on the part of feminists and racial/ethnic minorities and, in particular, by Black feminists who have sought to specify the interactive terms that constitute social, cultural, and economic relations in particular sites (e.g. hooks, 1984, 1990; Lorde, 1984; King, 1988; Crenshaw, 1989, 1991; Collins, 1990). But if sex/gender and race/ethnicity have their own logics and can no longer be viewed as derivative of class, how does one go about analyzing these relations?

In analyzing the failure of legal discourse to register the dual positioning of Black women, Crenshaw (1989) coined the concept of 'intersectionality' to refer to 'the various ways in which race and gender intersect to shape the multiple dimensions of Black women's (legal) employment experiences' (1991:1244). While pluralist accounts are increasingly common in both legal and social theory (feminist and otherwise), social science offers little guidance for those grappling with empirical data. 'Intersectionality' thus poses something of a dilemma for social science. How do we map these intersections of identity and chart their implications for social life?

[W]e may be able to imagine the simultaneous expression of multiple social relations, but to transform those imagined terms into an explanation of the patterning of social phenomena is a different matter. While it is possible to describe the subjectivity of individuals within a nexus of multiple relations, it is more difficult to describe patterned subjectivities and group-based behavior (Daly, 1994:433).

Daly argues that the class-race-gender construct reveals how social science '(1) flattens and depoliticizes social relations as "variables" and (2) views social relations as independent and discrete rather than interdependent and multiple' (1993:65). Within Black feminist criticism, class-race-gender has had a productive history as a referent of subjectivity and politics, but within the social sciences it has tended to be reduced to group comparisons or confined to the statistical analysis of interaction effects (Daly and Stephens, 1995).

There have been few attempts to understand the interactive effects of inequality in influencing participation in the informal drug economy (e.g. Bourgois, 1989; Padilla, 1992). None has specifically addressed women's involvement. Ironically, most research which examines racial/ethnic differences among women drug users tends to affirm the salience of class. As Murphy and Rosenbaum have recently argued, among women, '[p]overty is the crucial variable framing the context of crack use' (1992:382). Similarly, using data collected in Miami and New York during the early 1980s (see Inciardi and Pottieger, 1986), Logio-Rau found that the strongest statistical predictors of women drug users' involvement in crime and prostitution were economic—the presence or absence of a partner, a legal job, an education, and government assistance.[2] Although these findings indicate little direct influence of race/ethnicity, it is well known from other sources that race/ethnicity has an important bearing on economic standing. But quantitative analyses reveal little about the actual operation of gender, race, and class and even less about participants' understandings of them. In the absence of detailed qualitative information on the nature and structure of particular informal economies and the everyday lives of participants, quantitative research is unable to account for those factors which serve to differentiate access to illegal opportunities for income generation.

This chapter suggests that privileging class—or indeed race or gender—fails to provide an adequately nuanced explanation of the operation of systems of social stratification in the drug economy. While social class may well act as a crucial determinant of pathways to and from the drug economy, it fails to elucidate relations among people who ostensibly share a class position. In this chapter, I focus on

---

[2] Age and education also emerged as significant predictors of whether women ranked prostitution as one of their top three money-making offences, with both older women and better educated women less likely to report reliance on prostitution as a principal means of income generation (Logio-Rau, 1994:48).

racial/ethnic differences among women to illustrate how the inter-sectionality of gender and race structures women's participation in the drug economy and the particular forms it takes. I explore how sex/gender and race/ethnicity move in and out of women's under-standings of themselves, structure their relationships to various 'others', and underpin the organization of labour markets in the street-level drug economy. Beginning with an excerpt from my field-notes and drawing on examples from three areas—social networks, drug distribution and sales, and sexwork—I examine the expression and reproduction of these intersectionalities.

Race-gender and Social Networks

A warm afternoon and a very pregnant Candy and I are hanging out on Knickerbocker. I had bought her an 89-cent Kohl pencil and had given her some of my lipsticks. We are sitting in the sun playing with the makeup and I'm trying to fix her hair when Slim comes by pushing a baby stroller piled high with her worldly possessions. She parks the stroller, hits me up for a cigarette, climbs atop her chariot and proceeds to take over the conversa-tion. Slim says she is glad to see Candy has finally gotten hold of a pair of flat shoes for her swollen abscessed legs. Candy's half-hearted response that 'dates prefer heels' prompts a dramatic display of street theatre from Slim as she runs down what a 'real ho' should look like. We are joined by Star (usually distinctly cool to me) who surprises me—and Candy—by bending down to rub and coo at Candy's swollen belly. A long conversation on kids, motherhood, and BCW (Bureau of Child Welfare) ensues . . . Shelly arrives and asks to borrow some lipstick. Soon we are joined by a Spanish woman I don't know—wearing a man's shirt belted as a short dress—something our resident style consultant Slim takes great delight in dissing her about. (field-notes)

Here we are—two white women, two Black women and two Latinas, ranging in age from 19 to 41 years—a picture of ethnic diversity hanging out on a sunny day in the middle of Brooklyn's busiest drug supermarket. Yet, as my fieldnotes go on to describe, Candy and Slim are only speaking to each other because I am there (and in fact they go on to have an argument), Star continues to 'diss' me despite my obvious attempts to cultivate her as a research subject (and I suspect her interest in Candy has more to do with her love of pregnancy and babies than any affection towards Candy per se), Shelley is looking for a hit (of crack), and the unknown Spanish woman is after condoms. Within a few hours, they have gone their separate ways, and I am on the train back to Manhattan.

At first glance, and particularly to outsiders, the social networks of women drug users in Bushwick appear racially and ethnically heterogeneous. On closer examination, they are for the most part, biracial with European American women moving between loosely formed associations with African American women and Latinas. European American women occupy an odd position in this world whereby they are simultaneously both advantaged and disadvantaged. Initially at least, most European American women were seen as 'easy marks' and potential victims. Both African American women and Latinas tried to 'get over' on white girls by intimidating them, particularly if they were new to the neighbourhood. Lady B., a European American woman, related an experience which occurred not long after she arrived in Bushwick.

OK, so she (an African American woman) put her arm around me and said, 'You want me to cop for you?' And I said, 'No I don't'. And she said, 'Why you don't let me cop for you?' You know, she was saying it in a very persuasive manner. And the whole thing was, no I didn't want her to. And she said, 'Well if you don't let me then, then we gonna have to take it from you.' And I said, 'No, you're not gonna take it from me.' I said, 'The last person that took from me, I put in jail, caus I don't like getting robbed. And if you let someone rob you once, they goin' do it again and again and again. And if I let you do it, the same thing will happen with you.' She says, 'Oh what, are you threatening me?' And I said, 'No I am just letting you know.' Anyway, to make a long story short you know she tried to take me off, and thank God the cops were at the corner . . . I guess that got her mad, so whenever she sees me you know, that thought or anything around it, is what goes through her mind. And that makes me very uncomfortable.

As a highly visible minority in a neighbourhood where, as Holly put it, 'kindness is taken for weakness', European American women were constructed as potential victims. They were presented with two choices for survival—either learn to fight back or forge inter-racial associations. Those women who were unable or chose not to fight back were viewed as 'pussies' (see Chapter 4) and inevitably victimized further. As the following quotation from Jenny indicates, survival meant overcoming one's fears and standing up for oneself.

She robs them. She takes them off. She's known for that. She thinks that white girls won't fight back. Because Black girls are supposed to be tough—

which they are. I'm not a fighter. I don't want to fight. I'm very scared to fight you know. [So you would give it up to a Black girl?] No, she'd have to fight me for it, or find it. I don't give up my shit to nobody. I'll get stabbed first, you know, caus I work hard for it. [So it's not true that white girls are an easy mark round here?] No, not really. They're just not fighters.

There was ample evidence to suggest that many European American women did not fight back, preferring instead to form instrumental inter-racial associations. Often, as can be seen in the case of Jo-Beth, a 23-year-old European American woman, these were with powerful neighbourhood males.

I was accepted, you know caus he's the kind that no one messes with, you know. He got juice. Everybody looks out for me because of him. [So, how did you meet?] Just hangin' out. [But what attracted you to him?] I don't know, we just started talking, started getting high together and I just liked him. [So you just hit it off?] Exactly, you know what it's like out here. It's a convenient arrangement, caus he's got a lot of heart. He's got a good rep out here. And when he's not around, I don't got to worry about anything because no one will do anything to me. . . . I hang out with guys that are like that, because you know, I have to be protected.

'New girls' like Jo-Beth were perceived as 'meal tickets' by male drug users, and individual men often fought over who got 'first dibs' on these newcomers. As described earlier, both Rachel and Jenny were recruited as wives-in-law by an African American male, within weeks of their respective arrivals in Bushwick. Their vulnerability or amenability to this kind of arrangement was in part a product of racial/ethnic stratification in the neighbourhood. Below, Maria, a 19-year-old Latina, suggests that Latinas, and especially those who grew up in Bushwick, may experience different relations with neighbourhood males.

A lot of the girls, especially like the new white girls that I see, when they come around, right away you got all kinds of guys trying to make them girlfriend, you know. [Do they try and hustle you like that too?] You see baby, there is difference when there is new girls coming in, (to) when you grow up with them. I grew up with all these guys. Is like the guys is rapping to me. You know all these muthafuckas, we went to school together. We smoke reefer. Come on, I don't wanna fuck with none of these kids, forget about it . . . You know, and I would be telling the girls say, 'Baby watch it.' They don't want to hear it, fuck it. Then they see for themselves.

Other researchers have emphasized that urban crack users inhabit a 'dog eat dog' world (e.g. Dunlap, 1991). The women in this study were initially reluctant to characterize their associations in anything more than the most instrumental terms and I certainly tired of hearing the 'there's no friends only associates' line. As Debbie, a 31-year-old European American woman, told me about her relationships with other women,

I have never seen anything like it, like it is here. The most cut, cut throat, stab in the back type girls that I have ever seen. You know, the rule out here, we are all being used and victimized the same way and rather than watching each other, helping each other, these girls fight and steal . . . [Do you have any friends out here?] I don't really think so, not because I don't wanna be friends but because they all turn out to be the same way. Ah, they're buddy buddy when they're gonna get something. And when they're not they can't be bothered with you.

However, it became clear over the course of the research that women formed both instrumental and affective bonds with each other. Latisha explained:

[n]obody really lets nobody stay sick over here. I mean, somebody that might just know you from seeing you once on the Avenue, you know, and they know you sick. They might pass you three or four times that day, but they'll say 'Listen, come on, I'm goin' get you straight.' [These are the girls helping each other?] These are girls. Oh the guys, we don't even, you know, we don' deal with them, we don' know what they do with each other.

Among the women, Latinas and African American women appeared to maintain dense but largely separate social and support networks. When contact occurred between Latinas and African American women, it was frequently minimal and instrumental, as in the case of sharing drugs or injecting equipment. Given the different cultural, historical, and economic circumstances that have shaped their lives and identities, it is not surprising that these differences manifest themselves among women who are street-level drug users. African American women especially tended to have particularly strong affective and emotional bonds among themselves. As they put it, they 'go back further'—some having grown up in the same neighbourhood and two of the African American women in this study having met twelve years previously when they had been in hospital giving birth. As the following quotation from Jonelle suggests, these bonds transferred to the workplace where African American women tended to 'watch each other's backs'.

[So, do the black girls stick together more out here?] In a sense. Like we might not hang together, after all we workin'. Like I'm a loner I like to—I can' hang aroun' wid no girlfriends really too much caus after one tried to stab me inna back, it's always bin like dat y'know. But, if there trouble, summin' like dat, we'll stick together. Even in situations where two might not even like each other, when it comes to one o' them bein' in trouble, especially with a trick or somethin' we stick together.

This may also be partly attributable to the fact that some of the African American women were involved in long term relationships with a man/pimp, and as such, were part of what appeared to be a loosely structured pseudo-kin network. As Dee Dee, a 29-year-old African American woman, described this network,

[It's a kind of friendship thing—it's a bit more than associates you were saying.] Yeah. It's jus' a handful, not even a handful, jus' a couple, maybe four people that me an' ma man feel that way about but we know the whole neighbourhood jus' about.

This particular network consisted of three couples—Dream and Moo, Dee Dee and Lamar, and Jonelle and Toby—although another two couples, Slim and B. and Duke and Jeneane could be described as peripheral members. Other African American women in the neighbourhood—some of whom were also in relationships with African American males (e.g. Latisha and Tre) and some of whom had longstanding relations with individual women in this network (e.g. Princess's relationship with Dee Dee)—were not part of the network. As Dee Dee explained, obligations within this particular network involved 'looking out' for the men as well.

We look out for each other. Say if one o' the girls is in jail, her boyfrien', y'know, me an' ma man will look out for him caus we know he got a dope habit or somethin'. An' we know thas how he makin' his money, from her, but if she's in jail, there's no money so we buy 'im a bag o' dope and make sure eats. Smoke with 'im and look out like dat. We try an' keep it like dat caus ev'ybody needs somebody sometime.

As indicated in Chapter 2, women drug users' networks primarily revolved around exchanges designed to promote income generation, drug use, personal safety, shelter, and companionship. These exchanges involved a combination of economic motives and social incentives. While they were primarily women-centred, networks were differentiated by race/ethnicity with the strongest and most enduring networks being those of African American women. European American women and African American women appeared to have more in common with each other than either group had with Latinas.

As I will explain, the relative isolation of Latinas may be a product both of their identity as 'neighbourhood girls' and a unique sex-work/drug use trajectory. In contrast, the drug use/sexwork trajectories of African American and European American women, while not identical, were similar in many respects. Latinas were the 'other' in this context: identified as price cutters and sexual barterers, they provided a 'common enemy' and an additional point of convergence for African American and European American women.

The day-to-day frictions and tensions that exist between women on the street were especially apparent in relations between African American women and Latinas. African American women felt that Latinas consistently undercut the market rate for sexual services whereas Latinas believed that African American women were more likely to 'vic' dates. These (not unreasonable) beliefs were deeply implicated in both ascribed and experienced race/gender identities in the neighbourhood, as indicated in the following quotation from Dee Dee.

[Is there much friction or competition between say Black girls and Spanish girls here?] Yeah. Y'know iss like the Black girls, for some reason, seem like we bin bad-mouthed. But in a sense iss true caus a lotta the Black girls aren't from New York—a lotta dem are from outta town. An' all o' them they steal. I steal too, but a Puerto Rican girls don'. Say one trick mighta picked a Black girl an' she took 'is money an' the word goes on an' on. It makes it harder for us. Iss like dey jus' see us like—wassa word—like stereotype.

As Dee Dee's comments illustrate, identity was also structured by an insider/outsider dimension whereby African American and European American women were seen as 'outsiders' by Latinas who both self-identified and were identified by others as 'neighbourhood girls'. That some Latinas were to some extent integrated into the broader community is evident in the following excerpt from my fieldnotes.

About two o'clock I was walking along Knickerbocker towards Crack Row when I saw Yolanda sitting in the sun on a milk crate. She wasn't doing so good and told me she was unable to walk because she had frost-bitten feet. I told her she really needed to see her doctor as she could lose her feet. She said she wasn't interested and started getting annoyed when I pushed it so I figured I'd check back later.[3] As I moved off the block, a young Spanish girl

---

[3] I found out later that Yolanda did not have frostbite. She had in fact been shot in the foot by the managers of White Top crack for tapping their vials during a recent work stint.

came down from a nearby apartment and handed Yolanda a hot-dog on a paper plate. (fieldnotes)

While such incidents were not routine and, for the most part, non-drug-using residents expressed considerable animus towards drug users as a collective entity, some Latinas were clearly involved in community life in the neighbourhood in ways which differentiated them from both African American and European American women. Many of the Latinas in this study were also forced to confront the reality that at any moment they could come face to face with their kin or their children on the streets of Bushwick.[4] Despite the often tangential nature of their positioning within the non-drug-using Latino community, the identification of Latinas as neighbourhood girls served to demarcate them from both African American and European American women.

Race-gender and the Drug Business

This section examines how sex/gender and race/ethnicity intersect to underpin the organization of labour in the drug business. African American women felt that being a 'neighbourhood girl' granted Latinas, if not immunity, then at least leniency where the police were concerned. In contrast, African American women clearly suffered in their dealings with police—something they attributed to both their 'badass' identity and their non-neighbourhood status. As Jonelle told me,

[y]'know the Puerto Rican girls aroun' here, like bein' in this neighbourhood is like a majority of Puerto Rican. Like even when we get picked up by da police, a lotta the police pass right by (them) because they look jus' one 'o the girls from the neighbourhood. We know, the other regular girls know, dat girl is workin' too. But dey might pass 'em by. An' dey're out dere jus'— y'know dey makin' it harder too because dey'll take a fi' dollar date. Dey jus' supporting dere habit, y'know. [But the police won't pass you by?] No way. Like da black girls—caus y'know you could be carryin' out sometin'. We look more like we workin' ta tell ya the truth. An' we be the firs' ones dey go for.

    [4] During the first half of the study period, Cherrie's three-year-old son resided with his paternal grandmother Mena and her extended family in a small rundown house situated on Crack Row. The house was located directly opposite the lot where women congregated to smoke crack. From behind the mesh of the high wire fence, the children were well acquainted with street life and Cherrie's son could often be heard calling to his mother.

Similarly, Boy felt that African American women were more likely to be harassed by the police.

The pol-eece, dey be bad out here. Specially if you Black, you had better watch your ass. Issa racial thing. If you Black you don't belong inna neighbourhood and the pol-eece know. Dem Spanish girls be doin' like we do, but if we on the block then the pol-eece gon' go for us. Issa Spanish neighbourhood, you know, and Black girls be gettin' dogged.

While Latinas—to the extent that they actually were seen by residents and police as 'neighbourhood girls'—may be afforded some degree of advantage in street life, they were caught in a different bind. Family remains an integral aspect of economic relations and social networks among Latinos, and among Puerto Ricans in particular (Rogler and Santana-Cooney, 1984), including drug users (Fitzpatrick, 1990) and adolescent male gang members (Padilla, 1992). For example, in relation to low-income Puerto Ricans in New York City, Fitzpatrick has noted that,

neither the community nor the peer groups reject their heavy drug users or addicts to the extent that rejection occurs among middle-class and upper-class Americans . . . [T]he traditional, isolated drug subculture was not found to any great extent among the Puerto Ricans of this study. They remain within their neighbourhoods, in close relationship with family and friends. The degree of tolerance by the community in general is noticeably high (1990:120).

Previous research suggests that ethnic and kin ties work to the advantage of men in the drug economy and Latinos in particular (e.g. Waterston, 1993) by providing them with access to higher levels of the business where members are usually recruited from pre-existing social and kinship networks. The exploitation of personal ties and obligations works to ensure a measure of trust and reliability which extends beyond that usually encountered in employer-employee relationships—something which assumes critical import to those without recourse to formal legal mechanisms. In Bushwick, where ownership and control of the drug business was dominated by Dominicans, the preferred source of labour was clearly the Dominican community. However, workers and sellers were also recruited from friendship or kin networks among local Latino populations, most notably Puerto Ricans. Many Latinas appeared to fit the criteria for street-level drug distribution roles, such as 'looking the part' in terms of being relatively inconspicuous in the neighbourhood setting and having a broad circle of friends and social contacts (Maher et al., 1997). In fact one young Latina, Cherrie, saw the fact that she 'looked the part' as the reason why, after numerous rejections of her offers to work, a local Dominican manager allowed her to work a shift. As she told me, '[t]hey just came up to me and said, "You want work?". I say "Yes". I guess I was just like a Dominican to him. Big baggy pants'.

Within this context, 'looking the part' is not limited to looking male or looking Latino but much more specifically, involves 'looking Dominican'. Cherrie's comment is evocative of the significant cultural differences between Puerto Ricans and Dominicans. These differences are magnified in the drug business and were manifest in Bushwick, where the control of drug distribution activity by Dominicans was viewed with resentment, not only by African Americans and European Americans, but also by Puerto Ricans, who had previously dominated the trade during the 1970s and early 1980s (Curtis and Maher, 1993). Relegated to the ranks of street-level functionaries during the late 1980s and early 1990s, Puerto Ricans became an increasingly disaffected labour force. The gulf between Dominican management and the Puerto Rican labour force sharpened the traditional rivalry between the two groups. Although non-Dominican Latinos were increasingly marginalized with respect to ownership and control (and to a lesser extent management) of drug distribution businesses, they were clearly preferred over non-Latino labour. The growing attrition in the ranks of trusted Dominican operatives due to law enforcement activity during the study period created additional opportunities for Puerto Ricans to participate in lower levels of the drug business. As the policing onslaught continued, some Latinos moved up the ladder into managerial positions, and opportunities in the lowest paid, high-risk jobs were increasingly made available to African American and, in some instances, European American males.

While this process confirms the importance of race/ethnicity in facilitating access to the drug business, the more significant and unspoken criterion was undoubtedly that of being male. For example, the only female manager I encountered in Bushwick was part of a successful and diverse family drug business, as described by Connie, a 25-year-old Latina, in the following excerpt.

[And the owner, was he a Dominican or a Puerto Rican guy?] Dominican. Dominican woman. She was old. She was the owner of the Brown (Brown Top crack). Her brother was the owner of the coke and her sister owned the dope. She was in her forties maybe. See there might have been somebody bigger than her, but from what I was told she was the owner.

This successful woman manager was not a drug user and clearly acquired access to the drug business through kin ties rather than an intimate relationship with a male. The criteria used to determine access to selling and distribution roles produced by race/ethnicity highlight the importance of kinship networks and cultural ascriptions of gender-appropriate behaviour (see below). The gender and ethnic exclusivity of these criteria were compounded by the highly structured nature of drug markets in Bushwick, which worked to preclude sexual relationships between higher-level (male) operatives such as managers or distributors, and women drug users, which in other contexts have been seen to facilitate women's access to drug sales and distribution roles (e.g. Koester and Schwartz, 1993).

In contrast to recent commentary,[5] the paucity of women at any level within the local drug business suggests that the same associations that work for Latinos appear to work against Latinas insofar as Latin cultures prescribe fairly narrow roles for women.[6] Within some Latin cultures, notably Puerto Rican and Chicano, women who use drugs are typically viewed as fallen (una mujer caida) and many are estranged from their families. Latinas who deviate from the normative pattern of good mothers, wives, and daughters are not rewarded in the drug economy, where Latinos who hold traditional cultural beliefs continue to regard them as fallen. As Glick has argued, a double standard exists whereby drug use and dealing activity are regarded as,

behavior that is in keeping with traditional role expectations for men that allows street activity and drinking . . . The behavior of the female Puerto Rican involved in street activity—in gangs, abusing and dealing drugs— is antithetical to the traditional role expectations for the Puerto Rican woman, who is expected to serve as wife and mother and be homebound (1990:89).

---

[5] Steffensmeier and Streifel argue that, '[s]ince Hispanic groups are prone to include female co-offenders in their crime networks, we can expect the continued influx of Hispanics into the large urban areas to increase somewhat the overall involvement of females in delinquent gangs and drug distribution groups' (1993:98).

[6] For example, research conducted by Soto (1983) suggests that Puerto Rican women display greater traditional sex-role socialization than non-Puerto Ricans and that even controlling for age, generation, and education, Puerto Rican women are more 'traditional' than non-Puerto Rican women.

Moore (1990) also found that while Chicano families in Los Angeles communities where heroin use was endemic did not generally ostracize heroin users, this may only apply to male users. That women heroin users were more likely to be rejected by their families suggests that drug use, like many other forms of 'deviant' behaviour, is not tolerated (even in communities and cultural groups with a long history of exposure to such behaviours) when the actors are women (Moore, 1990). Indeed, it was clear that the increased access to dealing and selling opportunities for Latinos during the study period was effectively denied to Latinas. While such a finding does not suggest the existence of a universally accepted or blanket cultural prohibition, it may help account for the relative under-representation of Latinas (cf. Latinos) in the drug business. However, culturally specific perceptions of gender-appropriate behaviour and roles only provide part of the explanation.

This can be seen more clearly in relation to European American women. In the neighbourhoods I studied, culture-specific prohibitions clearly could not be mobilized directly by European American ethnic groups in such a way as to deny women access to the drug business. While the fact that they are women is crucial to understanding their marginalization within this labour market, the intersectionality of race-gender is clearly an important factor in accounting for, and indeed justifying, the nature of this exclusion. Rachel was one European American woman who clearly possessed 'savvy' and street credibility. A drug user and sexworker for many years, Rachel had a reputation for having an unusual amount of 'juice' for a white girl— no doubt enhanced by a long ugly scar down one side of her face. Ironically, being white and female may work to position European American women like Rachel as doubly disadvantaged in relation to the drug business. As she told me,

[Do they ever ask you to sell anything for them?] No. [How come?] Well, the most obvious thing is I'm a white girl with blonde hair. I stand out like a sore thumb. I would be busted in two days. You know, I make a spot hot, you know. Just comin' to cop I make a spot hot. For me to have a package, I, you know . . .[If you were Spanish or Black, you could probably go down there and find a job right now?] Uh-huh. But they're very chauvinistic. They would much rather give jobs to a guy. Yeah, a Spanish guy at that.

Rachel's comments suggest that race differentially affects incongruity. Within this complex social geography, there is a clear hierarchy of acontextuality. While African American women may be regarded as out of place and, as a consequence, are more likely to be harassed and arrested by the police, European American women may be even more so. And, as Rachel notes, while gender is seen by some women to be the crucial consideration, it is the intersection of gender with race/ethnicity that mediates suitability for employment. My examination of the intersectionality of race-gender suggests that such intersectionalities work to differentially position women with respect to opportunities for income generation in the drug economy. The ways in which sex/gender and race/ethnicity intersect are not consistent or coherent across sites: intersectionality may be a marker of inequality in some situations but not in others. The intersection of being a European American and a woman may work to produce 'advantage' in one site and 'disadvantage' in another. Latin-ness may be more salient than gender in determining labour-market positioning in some contexts. The multiple dimensions of identity produced by particular intersectionalities resist simplistic explications of identity as an either/or proposition (see also Crenshaw, 1991:1242). These shifting configurations of intersectionality are perhaps most graphically illustrated in relation to sexwork. Within this 'secondary' secondary labour-market, gendered opportunities are clearly structured by race/ethnicity.

Race-gender and Sexwork

Both European American and African American women were more likely than their Latina counterparts to have been turned out by a pimp. European American and African American women were also more likely to be involved in a current relationship with a pimp/man and more likely to have a history as a professional prostitute. European American women were also the only women in the sample with professional sexwork experience at other than the street-level. For example, Lady B. had considerable experience in the X-rated film circuit, upmarket escort agencies, and bondage parlours prior to becoming involved in street-level prostitution. By contrast, Latinas were more likely to be 'local' girls from either Bushwick or Williamsburg's Southside who initiated street level sexwork subsequent to their use of crack. Latinas were less likely to have been officially 'turned out', less likely to have a history of professional sexwork, and less likely to have had prior experience of other prostitution strolls. Just as their drug-use careers were more often initiated with non-pimp boyfriends (Maher, 1995a), their careers in sexwork were more likely to have commenced through boyfriends, informal connections, and neighbourhood associations. Below, Maria, a 19-year-old Latina, discussed how she 'broke the ice'.

[Let me ask you, how did you first start getting money when you started using?] I started goin' out with a friend and his friend started to give me money. [What for?] For sex. [When did you start working the stroll?] I was not out there like the way these girls do. I was like more or less one of the quiet ones on the down low. Maybe I know a neighbour of mine, and I tell him, 'Hey you want to fool around and you can give me a couple of dollars' or whatever. That was about me breaking the ice before I go to the Avenue.

Maria's comments suggest that women are differentially situated by and within the neighbourhood contexts, relations, and opportunities in which particular drug markets are located, as much as by race/ethnicity itself. Both Latinas and European American women were more likely to have had a history of regular support by men—either husbands, boyfriends or 'sugar daddies'—than African American women, many of whom were more likely to have been supporting their boyfriends (see also Pettiway, 1987). Yolanda, a 38-year-old Latina, spoke of her pre-stroll activities:

I had about six regulars. I would get at least um, $35 or $40. Cash, that's cash. That's not talking about when I go meet them, take me to dinner. You know, to the movies, you know, if I need something for my kids or for myself, they buy it for me.

These associations were part of a trajectory which exposed Latinas to sexual bartering and flexible pricing structures long before they hit the streets. As crack initiates, many Latinas did not have opportunities to learn other hustling skills. Confronted with a need for money and drugs in low-income minority neighbourhoods devastated by crack use, many Latinas initially drew on existing kinship and social networks. Within these informal networks, barter was an established practice which encouraged the circulation of goods and services among those with little or no cash income. Influenced by broader patterns of sex segmentation in the drug economy and the restrictive conditioning of Latino cultures, the reliance of Latinas on non-cash payments was compounded by the deteriorated conditions of street-level sexwork. This relative lack of opportunity, coupled with how and when they entered street-level sexwork, placed Latinas at a

distinct disadvantage in relation to opportunities for income generation. It may also have worked to render Latinas more likely to engage
in sex-for-crack exchanges compared to European American and
African American women. Many of the European American and
African American women who identified as professional prostitutes
viewed Latinas with contempt. For example, Jo-Beth, a 23-year-old
European American woman who started working the stroll on
Williamsburg's Southside when her dealer boyfriend was imprisoned,
looked down on these 'neighbourhood girls'.

I started prostituting when he got arrested. [Why did you do that?] Shit,
money. I wasn't going to depend on, like, I'd rather go out and get mine, and
be with someone for fifteen minutes, than hang out with one of those spics,
you know what I'm saying. Suck their dicks, excuse the—you know—suck
their dick all night for the same amount. You know what I'm sayin? I'm not
down. I'd rather do it the way I do it, than like do all the neighbourhood
guys.

In making distinctions between themselves and Latinas, African
American and European American women invoked a discourse of
professional sexwork. This discourse informed perceptions of Latinas
as novices who capitalized on their status as neighbourhood girls and
their local knowledge to conduct low-level, high-volume sexual transactions without attracting police attention. Latinas were resented by
the other women both for their informality, or lack of professional-
ism, and their links to the neighbourhood. In contrast, the shared
occupational identity and drug use history of many European
American and African American women meant that while their histories were not identical, there were points of convergence, most
notably around street-level sexwork as an occupation. I asked Jenny,
a 25-year-old European American woman, about relations between
the two groups:

Well, once they get high and work (with us) they're usually cool with us, you
know, if we know them . . . It depends, I think of a Black girl as a girl. You
know what I mean. I don't go by race or nothing. I take a person as a person no matter what colour they are caus I'm not prejudiced at all, but there
are a lot of them that are around here. Especially the Spanish girls. They
think they got it like that [snaps fingers] around here.

African American and European American women felt strongly
that the entry of neighbourhood Latinas into street-level sexwork was
responsible for the current state of the sex market. Latinas were
identified as more likely to engage in price cutting and sex-for-crack

exchanges. As such, they were resented by non-Latinas who blamed them for the decreased prices and declining standards of the Bushwick stroll. An economist might argue that these African American and European American women—many of whom had long histories as professional sexworkers—had a higher reservation wage than Latinas. Alternatively, African American and European American women's longer histories of drug use in combination with their sexwork careers may simply have meant that they knew what it cost to support a poly-drug habit, causing them to resent the declining cash value of their services. As Dee Dee told me,

[a]nd tricks dey wanna pay us fi' dollar because of it, like I said, y'know. An' mos' o' dem [girls] are Puerto Rican too, I'm not prejudiced or nothin'. But y'know the ones that are supportin' (their habit) dey got to take care deyself. Dem ones dere just ta get high (only use crack), dat'll take fi' dollars. So now the trick know he can get it for fi' dollars, so of course he's gonna try an' jus' spen' fi' dollars.

Overall, European American women were better placed than either African American women or Latinas in relation to income generation from sexwork. Sometimes this was a product of a long, steady, and geographically stable career as a sexworker. Candy had had such a career and, when she found herself pregnant at the age of 41 and unable to generate much income, she was able to rely on some of her 'steadies' to see her through this period.

Some guys seem to have a, even though I am a hooker, they still have respect for me and they feel like they're taking advantage of woman or something like that. You know, I have a few clients like that. You'd be surprised. They're not all dirty old men out there. They're just men with needs.

European American women also appeared more likely to possess particular skills such as S&M or to be prepared to engage in anal sex which was regarded by many of the African American women and Latinas as 'non-normative' (see Chapter 6). This may partly account for their relative advantage. As Lady B. told me,

[s]ometimes, like on my birthday, I saw this guy that gave me thirty dollars for me to pee on him real quick. And I like that kind of thing caus I'm a domini-trix at heart. Well, I like doing things out of the ordinary. [Are there a lot of guys out here that ask you to do things out of the ordinary?] Not a lot, but there are some. A lot more than I thought. [Really?] Yeah, caus I like to let people know that I do like to be a domini-trix. To me, OK, when they

ask for something kinky or crazy, to be honest with you, that's what I'd prefer. Caus I was a domini-trix, I like doing things out of the ordinary. So the crazier the better for me.

More often however, the increased earning potential of European American women was the product of racism. Although some European American dates clearly eroticized the ethnic 'other', many were fearful of African American and Latina prostitutes. In all likelihood these men have internalized the broader racial stereotypes in relation to African American women and, to a lesser extent, Latinas, that Dee Dee elaborated earlier. Jenny, a 25-year-old European American woman, first came to Bushwick to escape a violent and exploitative relationship with her pimp. The combination of her whiteness, youth, and physical attractiveness meant that when Jenny first arrived she could command more than the market rate.

[So when you say that you could make a lot of money in the beginning, how much money could you make say in a night?] I used to make like $200 or $300 a day. [Wow, and how many dates would that involve?] About ten, fifteen. I used to charge $20 a blowjob, and $40 for half and half (blowjob and sex).

Although her earnings declined over time, Jenny suggests that European American women retain a relative advantage in that their skin colour allows them to cater to the racial prejudices of clients which devalue the sexual services of minority women. Thus while the market sets the prices for sexwork (i.e. exchange values fluctuate according to general economic conditions in the street-level sex market and the availability of sexwork labour) it is ultimately the dates, and not the market, who discriminate. Even though she could no longer demand in excess of the market rate, Jenny—and other European American women—were, for the most part, the consumer preference. Sexwork then, just as much as the drug business itself, is a 'race thing'.

[You said that being a white girl down here some people think you make more money.] Yeah. [Why?] I don't know. It's just that I used to—when I was heavier and I first came around, I made a lot of money. You know, but now it's slowed down, and I'm known. You know when you're new around here you make money. But they—the Spanish girls around here they think that white girls make more money. And it's true in a sort of sense, because white guys like to go with white girls, and a lot of white guys don't like to go with Spanish or Black girls. You know, they like white girls. They like their own type I guess, you know. But it is true a lot of white girls make more money than the Black girls. (Jenny)

Pervasive images about the proclivity of minority males for violence and crime also permeate the consciousness of women sexworkers, regardless of their race/ethnicity. These images, coupled with actual experiences of violence at the hands of minority men, made many women extremely wary of African American and Latino dates. European American women were able to take advantage of their position in the market to avoid minority males as dates. As Lady B. told me,

I don't go with any Blacks or Puerto Ricans professionally. [Oh, you don't?] No. I had enough bad experiences that I said 'No'. And I don't just see any-one that wants to give me money. I have to have good vibes from them. And I do go by my vibes, caus usually they're good.

Or as Rachel put it,

I don't go out with Blacks or Puerto Ricans. [Why not?] I had too many bad experiences. Yeah. You know the Blacks and Puerto Ricans thing is, you act good and they'll hold on to you. And then have you do what you don't want to do. And not pay you. And if you have money on you, they even take what you have. So that I don't like. [You just go with the white guys?] White or something as similar to that as possible. You know, not because I am preju-dice but because I have had bad experiences and so have a lot of the other girls.

Most Latinas expressed a strong preference for white dates, in part because they tended to pay more, but they nonetheless accepted clients of all races. Many African American women also sought to avoid Black men as clients and many also couched their reasons in terms of the risk of violence. However, for some African American women, the desire to avoid Black men as dates rested on a complex of factors which, in their eyes, indicated a fundamental lack of respect towards Black women who used drugs. While Black men were seen by many Black women as 'cheap', money was only part of the story. As Dream, a 39-year-old African American woman told me,

[u]h uh. I don't date Blacks. No. [Why not?] Because they're slobs. [You know all the girls say that. A lot of the girls say that they don't date Black guys but I could never really figure out why that's the case.] Because a Black man, they consider a Black woman if she smoke crack, 'Here gimme a blow job, let me fuck you for five', and I'm not with that five dollar shit. You gonna pay me fifteen dollars or more.

European American men were identified by all of the women as the 'easiest' kind of dates. Their desirability was typically couched in terms of a perceived lack of potential for violence, an ability and will-ingness to pay, and, in some cases, perceptions of white men as 'soft touches' which provided women with opportunities to 'get over'. While my observations confirmed that many dates appeared to be white men or light-skinned Latinos, some of the women also drew distinctions between white dates based on ethnicity. Here, Latisha, an African American woman, compares 'them Polaks' with 'Jewish dates' whom she calls 'creeps'.

I'm used to white guy dates, these guys are soft, you know . . . Polaks always go cheap. They sell cheap. They ain't going over ten dollars. And they always wanna argue. They ain't coming out here unless they drunk anyway. [The girls avoid them for the most part, right?] Them girls that got pimps rob all them Polaks . . . I hate Jewish dates. They're creeps. They never want to pay no money . . . Once you get in their car door you can get any money you want. All you gotta do is be smart and say, 'Look, I'm not getting out until you give me twenty, thirty dollars'. They'll, they'll give it to you, if they got it. But now you got the tough ones (Jews) that say, 'I don't give a damn. Come with me to my house.' You know, you got those too.

Despite the women's acknowledged preference for white dates and their avoidance (when they could) of non-white men, it is not only Black men and Latinos who present a threat to women sexworkers. While Black men and Latinos were widely believed to be more capa-ble of, and more likely to use, violence, white men were also a source of coercion and danger. As Lady B. acknowledged, despite the fact that women felt safer with them, white men could also mean 'h-u-u-ge trouble'.

Oooh it's bin bad. [What do you mean it's been bad?] Whad do I mean—so bad? Girls have been gettin' killed. That's what I mean—not bad. Horrible—murder. I mean torture, murder. A whore an' her baby gettin killed, getting burned. I mean, c'mon, ya can't get much worse. [Are you scared when you go out there now?] Am I scared? Of course I'm scared. I don't go in any cars with any Black men. I don't go in any cars with any Puerto Rican men. But it doesn't mean that there aren't white men that don't do this or that or the other thing. I feel a lot safer not goin' with Black or Puerto Rican men because that is where you do have the most trouble. As I say, it doesn't mean that you don't have h-u-u-ge trouble with white men. OK, I did go with this one white guy, he said he's a cop, I dunno if what he said was bullshit. What it came down to was he said that he didn't wanna pay me ahead a time. I said 'Well, that's nice . . . when I spend ma time with you, I will take care of you accordingly, you take care a me an' I'll take care a you like there's no tomorrow. But you don' give me nothing, don't expect anything'. An' he took me by my hair and slapped and started choking me an' I got scared shitless. I din' know what was gonna happen. I din' wanna find out, so I did it. I didn't want to, but I did. I don't know how far he woulda went, you don't know. The guy was drinkin, beer, I din' wanna find out. Man, he scared the hell outta me.

That Lady B. and the other women in this study were, regardless of their race/ethnicity, unable to find steady alternative means of income-generating activities in the face of death, rape, and disfigurement, suggests that overall these women have few choices indeed. Within the drug economy, the advent of crack cocaine has clearly served to reproduce, rather than rupture, existing race-gender relations. Regardless of race/ethnicity, women have neither been 'liberated' from the oppressive confines of sexwork nor have they challenged, in any meaningful way, the hegemonic masculinity of a Latino-controlled drug market and male-dominated street networks. Within the context of an increasingly heterogeneous drug using population, an extremely fluid street scene, and a deteriorating street-level sex market, inter-racial tensions, and intra-gender conflicts work together to foster the social isolation and occupational segregation of women drug users.

Conclusion

As we have seen, opportunities for income generation within the drug economy are both colour-bound and gender-bound. Refracting gender through the lens of race illustrates how culturally and situationally-specific dimensions of identity intersect to produce divisions of labour in the street-level economy. While these divisions are also distinguished by other statuses such as age, immigrant and neighbourhood status, and kin ties, it is the intersectionality of race-gender that primarily determines labour-force positioning. Together, race/ethnicity and sex/gender hold significant implications for the organization of work and the generation of income in the drug economy. An employment system built around clearly-defined notions of race/ethnicity and sex/gender holds considerable advantages for owners, managers, and male workers in maintaining a demand for labour which is vulnerable. The distinctive legal vulnerability imposed on workers in the drug economy serves to foster the isolation of participants and to promote the street-level drug market as an enclave for minorities and immigrants. However, while the maintenance and reproduction of non-market statuses provides drug business owners with important advantages, employers do not create these statuses.

Race-gender segmentation within the drug economy also involves the reaction of participants to the gendered identification of occupations in which 'the other' is concentrated. For example, the social and economic construction of sexwork as a gender-specific enclave of production acts to discourage the participation of men as sexworkers. Like most occupations characterized by high concentrations of women (e.g. secretarial work), over time, the occupation comes to reflect the status of its occupants as opposed to the skills or aptitudes required of the work itself (i.e. feminization). There is nothing inherently feminine (or 'white') about sexwork or anything inherently masculine (or 'coloured') about drug distribution, although most participants in the drug economy insist that women, and white women in particular, are better placed in relation to sexwork, and men, particularly Latinos, are the preferred source of labour for drug distribution and sales activities. Owners and employers, workers and employees both shape, and are shaped by, the gendered and raced status of occupants and internalize this status as a condition of employment.

Within the drug economy, men and women take an active part in constructing their work as both sexed and raced. While minority males draw on race/ethnicity and kinship in order to monopolize access to drug distribution and sales, they also organize around their gender. As one male informant told me,

[i]ss not that we don't aks women to work or say that women shoudn' be hired. Iss just that we like to have it all men. Iss safer that way. A man can protec' hisself—he knows what to do. There be less trouble.

The identity of this particular labour force has been constructed around the intersectional identities of minority men, and in particular, Latinos. The earlier quotation from Candy in Chapter 6 confirmed the centrality of sex/gender to this division of labour. There, Candy suggested that men's ability to make money was strongly tied to dominant conceptions of masculinity: 'Men always make money if he's any kind of man' (see p. 166).

Contributions to the drug economy, like contributions to the formal economy, are both raced and gendered, and as such, are subject to contestation as distinct groups of participants struggle to assign greatest value to the positions they occupy and least value to those positions occupied by 'others'. This chapter has sought to demonstrate how the confluence of categories of identity constructed external to the labour process organizes opportunities for income generation in the drug economy. It has attempted to show how the use of broader cultural ideas about sex/gender and race/ethnicity by women and men within the drug economy work to reproduce existing social and economic relations. I have used the concept of intersectionality to illustrate how sex/gender, race/ethnicity, and other dimensions of identity (e.g. insider/outsider in the neighbourhood context) interact to shape women's informal sector employment experiences.

In mapping some of these intersectionalities, I have attempted to problematize the tendency to view race and gender as mutually exclusive dimensions of identity operating on diverse and isolated terrains. I have also suggested that, while they may be central to our understanding of systems of domination, sex/gender, race/ethnicity, and the like cannot be viewed simply as categories of inequality. The stratificatory implications of particular intersectionalities are contingent and context-specific: they may structure inequality to the benefit of some as much as to the detriment of others. For example, in this context, the intersectional identity of Dominican males works to position them as the preferred source of labour. Treating complex social identities as synonymous with categories of inequality invokes a deficit discourse in which certain identities are constructed as a priori evidence of domination. Such negative frameworks undermine the potential for delineations of difference to empower, shape, and subvert negative categorization (Crenshaw, 1991).

This is not to say that identity is not implicated in the production of inequality. As I have demonstrated, race and gender can and do converge to (re)produce experiences of oppression and marginality for particular groups in particular locations. While Crenshaw's (1989) pioneering analysis revealed the many ways in which the experiences of Black women were missing from legal discourse, and indeed, how Black women could not be apprehended by legal discourse, this analysis has attempted to broaden the concept of intersectionality by suggesting how it can be applied to social and occupational life on the street. In adopting a more fluid and nuanced approach, the analysis presented here shows how sex/gender and race/ethnicity move in and out of women's understandings of themselves, structure their relationships to various 'others', and underpin the organization of labour markets in the street-level drug economy.

8

The Reproduction of Inequalities

The women portrayed in this book are part of a highly visible and heavily stigmatized population. They are among the poorest and most exploited of workers in the drug economy. Their lives are anchored in a complex geography which to outsiders presents as a 'stark tableau of pathology and vice' (Stansell, 1982:321). These women live and labour by their wits in a world marked by violence, victimization, and mutual exploitation. While they have 'chosen' sex-work, they have not done so under conditions of their own choosing. Their choices are neither those of 'equal competitors in an open market with equal opportunities to invest in human capital and advance in the labour market' nor those of 'deranged isolated individuals' (Sullivan, 1989:247). Rather, they are choices shaped by a collective consciousness in which gendered and raced meanings of 'crime as work' form an integral part of the habitus (Bourdieu, 1977) of street-level drug users.[1] These schemata of 'perception, appreciation and action' (Wacquant, 1992:16) serve both to condition and to contextualize their criminal agencies.

The women who participated in this study neither strip cars nor fight turf battles. Men still very much control the streets and the drug economies which increasingly dominate social and economic life in low-income minority communities. Drug economies take complex and multiple forms, but cultural practices within them remain embedded in broader relations and structures of gender, race, and class. These relations and structures, in turn, inform drug users' understandings of, and opportunities for, work in the local level drug

[1] Habitus is 'a system of lasting transposable dispositions which, integrating past experiences, functions at every moment as a matrix of perceptions, appreciations and action' (Bourdieu, 1977:82–3). While habitus operates from within individuals, 'it is neither strictly individual nor in itself fully determinative of conduct' (Wacquant, 1992:18).

economy. While, within this context, women help create the repertoires of social action, it is not incidental that their experiences are
confined to the margins. As workers at the intersection of race and
gender, they are positioned by a specific set of cultural, social, and
economic practices which regulate and normalize the material and
symbolic spaces which constitute the street-level drug economy.

Here, the organization of the labour process and divisions of labour
are profoundly influenced by external structures, processes, and discourses which shape the construction of identity at both the individual
and the collective level. In demarcating itself from all that is 'feminine',
the street-level drug economy (re)produces a form of hegemonic masculinity (Connell, 1987; Messerschmidt, 1993) whereby economically
marginal males 'reconstruct their notions of masculine dignity around
interpersonal violence, economic parasitism and sexual domination'
(Bourgois, 1996:414). These cultural narratives influence the formation
of identities which in turn structure the organization of work. Women
are defined as external or incidental and are positioned, in varying
ways, as peripheral others to a (minority) male core.

I began this study concerned to challenge media representations of
women crack users. The media traffic in lurid images of women drug
users has been an enduring legacy of the crack epidemic. Corrupted
and polluted by their passions for the 'glass dick', women crack users
have been depicted as prone to violence, immorality, and sexual
depravity. As the research progressed, it became clear that the
vilification of women crack users was not confined to media representations but extended to social science. Determined to seek out and
register their 'voices', I came away from this research with a much
deeper understanding, not only of the women themselves, but also of
the neighbourhoods and the street-level drug and sex markets in
which their experiences were situated. Much previous research has
focused on women crack users as individuals, with researchers failing to locate women within any kind of broader social and economic
context. Combined with the inability of some researchers to read
drug use beyond the boundaries of the psycho-pharmacological
script, these features have served to distort and obscure critical
aspects of women crack users' lives. These omissions on the part of
the research community have helped to effect the demonization of
women crack users. This book takes issue with a number of claims
which have been made about women drug users, and crack users in
particular. I recapitulate three key themes here.

First, I would challenge the highly sexualized images of women crack users that dominate the social science literature. The claim that women crack users are desperate, depraved creatures without historical parallel is inaccurate and irresponsible (cf. Inciardi et al. 1993). Drugs have long provided a vehicle for articulating profound social anxieties, and historical accounts are replete with the prototypes of contemporary drug iconography—among them the 'polluted' or despoiled woman (e.g. Kane, 1881; Terry and Pellens, 1928), the 'hypersexual' female (e.g. Fischer and Dubois, 1937; Kalant, 1987) and the 'unfit' mother. All are familiar narratives which have been used to signify a highly sexualized and often racialized menace. Similarly, notions of women's bodies as dangerous, diseased, and polluted have long occupied a prominent place in legal, medical, and criminological discourse (Douglas, 1966; Walkowitz, 1980; Smart, 1989; Mahood, 1990; Zedner, 1991). However, women's sexualized status within contemporary drug discourse warrants special consideration. The spectre of the AIDS virus renders women crack users' sexual practices extremely vulnerable to what Foucault (1985) called 'moral problematization'.

The demonization of women crack users has been effected through the deployment of the 'hypersexuality hypothesis' (Inciardi et al., 1993:39) which, in providing a convenient explanation for the visible presence of large numbers of women on inner-city streets, simultaneously obscures the broader social, cultural, and economic contexts in which these women are situated. This hypothesis is ultimately secured by reference to pharmacology: crack use has been graphically equated with chemically-induced sexual slavery. Women crack users have been portrayed as desperate, pharmacologically driven criminals who respond indiscriminately to opportunities for income generation (e.g. Anderson, 1990:89; Inciardi et al., 1993:95). Overdetermined by their 'addictions', women crack users are inscribed in a discourse of risk and contagion and readily positioned as vectors of AIDS, drug use, and moral contamination.

In contrast, my research suggests that, while the advent of crack had a profound effect on street-level sex markets, it did not produce a cohort of hypersexual 'others'. The women I studied were not women who would 'do anything' for a 'hit'. My research identified the existence of a set of occupational norms which cohere around the concept of discrimination as a central organizing principle in street-level prostitution. These norms—in relation to price, sexual acts,

clients and bartering practices—governed commercial sex transactions at the street level and regulated both individual and collective
conduct. When women exchanged sex for crack, they did so reluc-
tantly and recognized the compromise of principle this entailed. Sex-
for-crack transactions served to jeopardize an already insecure
position in an unstable market. By placing the women's sexual practices within this framework, I have endeavoured to contest the exces-
sive sexual scripts which characterize discursive constructions of
women crack users and to refute claims that women who use crack
are prepared to do anything, and at any price, for the drug.

Secondly, these women's experiences within a highly gender-
stratified labour market provide a counter to the romantic notion of
the informal drug economy as an 'equal opportunity employer'
(Bourgois, 1989:630). It has always struck me as somewhat bizarre
that one could claim to have found, within the drug economy, a
haven of equal opportunity and affirmative action. Such a position
suggests that the drug economy—which is free from formal legal
regulation and uses violence as its principal enforcement mechanism—has managed to achieve something which the formal economy
either cannot or will not achieve, despite decades of commissions,
judicial rulings, compliance monitoring, and regulatory enforcement
strategies.

Claims that '[s]igns of the changing status of women in drug markets are evident in the relatively high incomes some achieve, and the
relatively insignificant role of prostitution in generating income'
(Fagan, 1994:210) were not substantiated by this study. Rather, my
findings suggest that women remain marginalized with respect to
most opportunities for income generation in the street-level drug
economy. The major exception was sexwork which was integral to
women's economic survival. Indeed, it cannot be emphasized enough
that the advent of crack cocaine and the concomitant expansion of
the drug economy can in no way be read as 'emancipatory' for
women drug users. The conditions of street-level sexwork have been
adversely affected by shifts in social and economic relations produced by widespread crack use in low-income minority neighbourhoods like Bushwick. The sex market became flooded with
novitiates, the going rates for sexual transactions plummeted, and
deviant sexual expectations by dates increased, as did levels of violence and victimization.

Within the drug economy, women have neither been 'masculinized' nor have their opportunities for illicit income generation expanded. Women remain confined to an increasingly harsh economic periphery. Their experiences contradict the conventional wisdom, shaped by studies of the labour market experiences of minority group men (e.g. Bourgois, 1989, 1995; Williams, 1989; Anderson, 1990; C. Taylor, 1990; Padilla, 1992; Hagedorn, 1994) that the drug economy acts as a compensatory mechanism, offering paid employment that is not available in the formal labour force. The 'new opportunities' said to have emerged with the crack-propelled expansion of street-level drug markets were not empty slots waiting to be filled by those with the requisite skill. Rather, they were slots requiring certain masculine qualities and capacities. These qualities, while presented as 'human', are deeply gendered and, in many instances, highly racialized.

Thirdly, this study takes issue with the claim that, in the wake of crack cocaine, we are witnessing the emergence of a 'new' violent female criminal. While concern in relation to 'rising tides' of female criminality has been evident since at least the mid-nineteenth century (e.g. see Morris, 1987:36–7), the confluence of women, crime, and crack added a new dimension to discourses on women's lawbreaking. From the mid-1980s onwards, 'drugs' were increasingly implicated in claims that women had 'gone beyond the traditional limits of prostitution and shoplifting into major-league drug trafficking, extortion, auto-theft, loan sharking and highjacking' (Inciardi, 1986:137). By the early 1990s, claims that '[t]here are more girls in gangs, more girls in the drug trade, more girls carrying guns and knives, more girls in trouble' (*New York Times*, 25 November 1991) signalled the purported arrival of a 'new' and violent 'criminal woman'—the female urban 'gangsta' (Maher and Curtis, 1995).

My research found little evidence to support such claims (cf. Baskin and Sommers, 1991). The women who participated in this study did not become more violent over time, even as their reliance upon commercial sexwork increased and their use of crack and other drugs became more pronounced. Extensive ethnographic research conducted in Brooklyn over a period of two decades suggests that increases in crack-related violence can be attributed to the collapse of formal and informal social controls, the depletion of economic and human capital necessary to sustain a formal economy, and the resultant increased participation in the drug economy (Hamid, 1990). The advent of crack cocaine clearly intensified the social processes that facilitate violence. In Bushwick, many women were involved in violent events, but usually as victims rather than perpetrators (see also *New York Times*, 23 July 1990). Violent acts committed by the women were usually initiated in response to intimated or actual harms perpetrated against them, the antecedents of which can be located in changing social and economic relations at the local level. It is the everyday contexts in which these women live and work that are conducive to violence, rather than the women themselves. These findings suggest that the debate about whether women are becoming more violent is a historically recurrent rhetorical exercise, which, in ignoring structural and contextual influences, contributes little to understanding the ways in which violence impacts on women's lives.

In taking issue with the claims of others, I have sought to draw attention to the deficits of previous research, and, in particular, the absence of agency and the lack of attention to shared social, cultural, and occupational practices which has made possible the demonization of women crack users. I have chosen these examples because they highlight the representational problems involved in making claims about women drug users. In particular, the traffic in derogatory images of women is central to the historical continuity between women crack users and their opium, heroin, and cocaine using sisters of previous drug eras. Like those of the media, the accounts of some social scientists reproduce the victimization/volition dichotomy; whether they take the form of the chemical slavery of the debased crack 'ho', the economic opportunism of women dealers, or the instrumental violence of the new female gangsta. This dualism does women drug users grave injustices. On the one hand, the desire to demonstrate that women are active subjects often degenerates into accounts which can be 'misread as evidence of women having power and control equivalent to that of men' (Okely, 1996:230). On the other hand, accounts in which women are viewed as passive objects not only reinscribe their victimhood, but in so doing may actually harm them (McClintock, 1993). The claims highlighted here minimize the impact of any enduring structural influences on these women's lives; crack or the women themselves are held responsible and questions of inequality and subordination are evaded.

Now it is necessary to make some claims of my own. The findings presented in this book can be summarized in terms of their implications for three distinct but inter-related theoretical domains. First, my research has implications for how we 'read' women's lawbreaking and, in particular, the thorny issue of women's agency. The wide-

spread use of crack in low-income minority neighbourhoods pro-
pelled women into the drug economy. The experiences of these
women, though varied, are distinct from those of men. In Bushwick,
increased opportunities for participation in drug distribution and
sales were available to non-Latino males, but women remained a
reserve army of labour. They were confined to street-level sex markets where relations between genders, among women, and across
ethnicities were extremely competitive and marked by increasing hostility. Such relations—informed as they are by broader cultural
understandings of gender and race—served to exacerbate racial tensions and to increase the atomization and social isolation of women
drug users. In light of these conditions, it is important to describe the
tactics women use to resist and contest the constraints that shape
their occupational lives.

James Scott (1985:292) suggests that those who study the working
class have tended to employ a restricted concept of resistance which
is based on action that is formally organized, collective, and selfless.
Such a definition eclipses the informal, fragmented, less visible, and
certainly less dramatic 'garden variety' resistances which characterize
the history of oppressed groups (Scott, 1985:241). By largely exclud-
ing the opportunistic and everyday resistances of women, it casts
them as passive and indifferent to their condition. The strategies of
resistance employed by the women in this study rarely involved con-
certed cooperative action, nor can their actions be viewed as consistent with a cohesive 'street culture of resistance' (cf. Bourgois, 1995).
Yet within the limited avenues available to them, these women developed creative ways to circumvent and subvert, at least in the short
term, some of the constraints of a sex- and race-segmented labour
market.

These women were not merely the passive casualties of occupational hardships: they refused to play with the hand they were dealt.
Many women, and especially younger women without histories of
sexwork pre-crack, substituted investment in viccing for allegiance to
the occupational norms of an industry which increasingly failed to
provide for their needs. Tactics such as viccing can be seen as an
attempt both to 'recoup their own status as victims' (Simone,
1989:159) and to moderate the exploitative elements of sexwork
while continuing to utilize the limited opportunities available to them
for 'getting paid'. The victimization of others represents a crude cultural adaptation both to their own victimization, and to poor work

prospects and increasingly restricted opportunities for income generation.

But while viccing represents a short-term solution which achieves a temporary 'penetration' of their condition, ultimately it becomes a 'limitation' (Willis, 1977) insofar as it serves both to exacerbate the deteriorating conditions of street-level sexwork and to intensify the victimization of women. Rather than providing a way out, viccing binds women back into the oppressive structure of street-level sexwork, reinscribes their marginal status as labourers within the drug economy, and reproduces them as 'criminal women'. By interpreting these resistances solely as lawbreaking and responding to them solely within the confines of the criminal justice system, we neglect the conditions of their existence and criminalize what are, in effect, women's survival strategies.

Within criminology, feminist attempts to focus on the economic conditions of women's lawbreaking—through the concept of 'criminalizing survival'—have attracted criticism for their tendency to essentialize both the experience of women (as victims) and the meanings of lawbreaking (as crime). In ignoring the different experiences of women and the diversity of pathways to lawbreaking, some feminist research has tended to characterize women lawbreakers as victims of social structures, pharmacology, oppressive relationships, or some combination thereof. Women's lawbreaking is presented as symptomatic of their victimization. On the other hand, non-feminist research continues to interpret the agency of women lawbreakers within the confines of a western cultural logic anchored in individualism and free choice. For the women in this study, the framing of agency solely in terms of individual choice erases the complex and contradictory ways in which agency is negotiated in interaction with dealers, dates, and others within the context of the street-level drug economy.

The relationship between structure and agency, while poorly understood, is not an ontological binary opposition. Anthropological studies of the survival strategies of the urban poor (e.g. Stack, 1974a; Valentine, 1978, Susser, 1982) suggest that we can recognize the conditions that criminalize survival without reducing individual lives to a discourse on victimization. Ethnographic work on low-income communities has sought to blend economy and culture. Economic constraints are understood to be imbued with cultural meanings and culture is shaped by economic conditions; both are the product of patterned interaction among individuals (Sullivan, 1989:242; see also Willis, 1977).[2] By analyzing how patterns of economic activity, forms of social action, and cultural meanings are related to structures of opportunity in the street-level drug economy, I have tried to strike a balance between dichotomous readings of women's lawbreaking as either denying women criminal agency or over-endowing them with it. I have tried to create a space between the twin discourses of victimization and volition that inform current understandings of women's drug-related lawbreaking. While this space must be large enough to include the constraints of sexism, racism, and poverty that structure women's lives, it cannot be so big as to overwhelm the active, creative, and often contradictory choices, adaptations, and resistances that constitute women's criminal agencies.[3]

Throughout this book, I have critiqued both feminist and non-feminist representations that view women lawbreakers as driven by forces beyond their control. Working from the lives of women drug users, I have tried to explore the tension between agency and victimization and how this reflects power relations and practices within the street-level drug economy. In doing so, I have tried to avoid reifying the women's experiences into categories of helpless victim or volitional agent. In order to transcend this duality, future research efforts should attempt to chart the middle ground identified here as spaces of action, ingenuity, sensibility, and rationality. However, in order to illustrate the pre-emptive strikes, points of consciousness, and moments of resistance that rupture this dualism, we must first get close enough to see. The impoverished set of characterizations which dominate the literature stem in part from a reliance on other methods. The ethnographic approach used in this study reveals that, in the absence of a temporal frame and observational data, interviews may yield an inaccurate and incomplete picture. In particular, the one-time interview misses the changing and fluid nature of relations in the

---

[2] Sullivan's (1989) comparative ethnography of inner city youth across three low-income Brooklyn neighbourhoods is an excellent example of this kind of work insofar as it illustrates both the economic rationality of certain types of crime and the cultural meanings which attach to lawbreaking in particular contexts.

[3] Scheper-Hughes provides an eloquent summation of a related point: '[I]n granting power, agency, choice and efficacy to the oppressed subject, one must begin to hold the oppressed morally accountable for their collusions, collaborations, rationalizations, "false consciousness," and more than occasional paralyses of will. With agency begin responsibility and accountability' (1992:533).

drug economy and is unable to provide the dynamic, contextualized picture that is the promise of ethnography.

But ethnography brings a different set of problems and challenges, central to which are those which inhere in the politics of representation. On the one `hand, the use of ethnography is no guarantee of active subjects, especially in situations where participants may not recognize and articulate their agency. Here we must be careful not to mistake *existence* for *resistance* and, in so doing, to romanticize human suffering (Scheper-Huges, 1992:533). On the other hand, while indigenous interpretations are important, participants may not always recognize their subordination. The fact that people do not necessarily see themselves as victims of domination does not in itself constitute proof of its absence (Okely, 1996:211). While it remains important to contest the casting of women as pawns and objects, as Okely suggests, sometimes even well-intentioned accounts may 'charm' the audience 'into the comfortable conclusion that women are equal but different' (1996:207). The desire to focus on women as active subjects can 'conflate lack of subservience with absence of subordination' (Okely, 1996:21). Activity cannot be equated with equality and, as we have seen with respect to the drug economy, presence is not synonymous with participation.

Secondly, I have endeavoured to expand Crenshaw's pioneering analysis of intersectionality by moving beyond the black/white dualism to explore intersectionalities across a range of ethnic groupings, including the dominant white/European American category. I have suggested how this concept can be applied to social and economic life on the street and have attempted to illustrate how the convergence of raced and gendered dimensions of identity influence the labour-market structure of the street-level drug economy. In doing so, I have sought to demonstrate that, notwithstanding the proliferation of transgressive sexual agency and dance-floor difference, it actually *does* make a difference if 'you're black or you're white [or] if you're a boy or a girl' (Madonna, 1990), and to reveal the ways in which such differences are constituted within a particular social space.

The confluence of race/ethnicity and sex/gender has a direct effect on selection, tenure, and earnings. As illustrated in relation to drug distribution and sales, street crime, and sexwork, the intersectionality of race-gender not only distinguishes participants but also determines where they work, how often they work and how much they earn. Race and gender then are not merely labels assigned to individual workers but have a material basis external to the labour process and are deeply rooted in cultural processes beyond the workplace. These cultural processes provide the raw materials with which men and women construct their work as sexed and raced. The drug economy neither creates nor produces the distinguishing statuses of sex/gender and race/ethnicity but, rather, seeks to utilize them to individual, organizational, and economic advantage.

The construction of men's and women's work in the drug economy involves agency on the part of both management and employers and the individual men and women who seek to generate income at the street-level. In this context, production is organized not only in reference to the labour that is actually performed but in accordance with the 'human qualities' that owners, managers, and workers perceive as integral to the job. Opportunities for income generation are at least partially defined by the qualities believed necessary to perform them. These qualities, whether grounded in cultural perceptions of biology and physiology (e.g. strength and the capacity for violence), mental states (e.g. courage and aggressiveness), or even kinship itself (e.g. loyalty and trustworthiness), are infused with sexed and raced dimensions of identity. Women are not as 'strong' as men. Men, and minority men in particular, are more 'bad'. Kin ties among non-white ethnic groups serve to secure allegiance and trust. The gendered displays of violence that men incorporate into their work practices not only cement their solidarity as men (Messerschmidt, 1993), but reinscribe the occupational salience of these traits and, in so doing, work to justify the exclusion of women.

The significance of these gender- and race-based qualities and the symbolism used to convey them were evident in the examination in Chapter 4 of women's use of instrumental aggression. Boy's discussion of how to 'dress for success' on the streets reveals that, much like the formal labour force, power dressing is 'dressing like a man' or 'dressing down'. It is anything but 'dressing dainty'. Both on the street and in the boardroom, it appears that a combination of clothing and attitude makes the woman (Kanter, 1981 citing Hennig, 1970). In the drug economy, conveying the message 'don't mess with me' is integral to nurturing and maintaining a reputation for 'craziness' that women perceive as affording some measure of protection.

The tactics women use to defend their positioning in this particular labour market, the strategies they adopt in an attempt to resist it (e.g. viccing), and the criteria which men use to justify their exclusion are all part of the way in which drug users as economic actors interpret, defend, resist, and reproduce the cultural meanings that organize work within the drug economy. As we have seen, the drug economy does not simply reproduce the bifurcated labour market of the formal economy whereby white males dominate the top of the hierarchy and minorities, women, and immigrants constitute the most exploited sections of the labour force. Within the street-level drug economy, where, for the most part, European American males are excluded, both immigrant and minority males manage to fare better than women.

However, while race/ethnicity serves to mediate the positioning of Latinos in the drug business, perceptions of Latinas are also influenced by gendered conceptions of women workers and culturally specific understandings of Latina drug users as 'fallen' women. Similarly, while participation in street crime is also structured by sex/gender, European American women may have a relative advantage over minority group women in relation to their ability to manipulate stereotypes concerning trustworthiness. Finally, within the sphere of sexwork, where the labour force is composed of women, distinctions between women on the basis of race/ethnicity are central, and in general, European American women tend to fare better than minority group women.

The labour of street-level drug users is, then, deeply implicated within over-lapping systems of race-gender stratification and the forms they take at the neighbourhood level. Gender and race are related to, but not determined by, class inequalities. Together, they constitute an intersectionality which ensures that cultural understandings of sex/gender and race/ethnicity continue to shape the desirability of women as potential bosses, employees, and colleagues in the drug economy.

Thirdly, this study offers insights for cultural reproduction theory. The blurring of class boundaries in the wake of expanded informal sector economic activity holds significant implications for analyses of cultural reproduction.[4] Traditionally, theories of cultural reproduction have sought to determine the role of social institutions in sustaining existing relations of production in advanced capitalist

[4] For example, Portes, Castells and Benton have argued that, '[t]o the extent that informal relations persist and expand, their most general consequence is to blur the profile of the class structure and alter expected patterns of class relations and class struggle (1989:308).

societies. However, in doing so, many theorists have either ignored non-class dimensions of social stratification (particularly sex/gender and race/ethnicity) or else insisted upon economic determinism 'in the final instance'. Concentrated in studies of education and schooling, cultural reproduction theory has tended to posit individual human agents as passive subjects shaped by the logic of class domination. For the most part, it has relied on a deficit model of social stratification whereby race and gender have been treated as a priori evidence of domination, and subsumed as non-class categories of inequality.

Rather than view the disadvantaged status of women drug users as a product of either pharmacology, class relations under capitalism, or patriarchal relations of reproduction, this study has shown how the division of labour within the street-level drug economy and broader systems of social stratification external to the (illegal) workplace work together to produce and maintain that status. Put simply, drug users are not merely a medium for the expression of forces inherent to particular pharmacologies or systems of (re)production. Explanations of the operation of systems of social stratification in the drug economy were sought in the way that participants defined and interpreted their situations and acted accordingly. By examining the role of non-market statuses in the drug economy in light of these meanings, I have attempted to illustrate how they serve to sustain not only divisions of labour, but gendered and raced forms of social organization more generally. However, the organization of the labour process and divisions of labour are also intimately linked to the form that particular drug markets take. Forms such as the highly structured, vertically differentiated drug markets evident in this study are clearly determined by extra-market forces. These include the disadvantaged status of particular groups in the formal economy, neighbourhood-level manifestations of, and responses to, broader structural changes, the history of particular drug markets, the degree of local shelter and tolerance for illicit activities, and the nature and extent of external regulation (e.g. Curtis and Maher, 1993).

By examining the relationship between structure and the deeply internalized values, beliefs, attitudes, and experiences shared by members of a particular social world, this book has sought to render rational and intelligible the cultural, social, and especially, the economic practices of women drug users. The ethnographic method, in providing for the expression of women's subjective interpretations, understandings, and responses to their positioning in the drug

economy, allows us to understand the dialectical and mutually constitutive relations between structure and agency. Indeed, their experiences cannot be separated from the structure their actions help to
produce. As social and cultural agents, workers in the street-level
drug economy are actively involved in demarcating the boundaries of
economic life. But while their lives are shaped by broader systems of
social stratification, it is the actions of women drug users themselves—in negotiating, interpreting, defining, and contesting these
systems of meaning—and not the practices of owners, managers, and
male employees, that ultimately facilitate cultural reproduction.

In reproducing inequalities, workers in the street-level drug economy draw on the same markers of identity apparent in conventional
cultural formations. The street-level drug economy is not an anomaly. It is not an exotic oppositional subculture which takes the values
and beliefs of the dominant culture and inverts them. Nor can it be
understood as a peculiar bastion of racialization and male domination; a product of cultural values unique to a particular group, system, or way of life. The production of inequalities in the street-level
drug economy mirrors the production of inequalities in the formal
economy. It is in this sense that the margins serve to reproduce the
mainstream.

This study has illustrated the role of the drug economy as a site of
cultural reproduction by demonstrating how gender and race are conceived and structured within broader social, cultural, and economic
spaces. By drawing attention to the specific practices by which gendered and raced dimensions of identity are constituted, contested,
and reproduced in street-level drug and sex markets, I have attempted
to specify the economic lives of women far removed from, but no less
influenced by, the cultural understandings that continue to shape the
legitimate world of glass ceilings, affirmative action, and 'equal
employment opportunity'.

Appendix

On Reflexivity, Reciprocity, and Ethnographic Research

Few attempts have been made outside anthropology to address the processes by which a field presence is established and maintained, access is continually negotiated, sample selection and construction are ongoing, and repeated interviews are conducted with individual informants. Despite some discussion about 'research-as-a-process', the conventional social science literature maintains a series of artificial distinctions by dividing the research endeavour into discrete areas such as gaining access, selecting a sample, conducting *the* interview, and analyzing the data. The nature of the ethnographic encounter dictates that not only are these events recurrent, but that they are concurrent. As opposed to the process of 'retrospective' construction typically assumed by most research methodologies, ethnography involves the active construction of an (ongoing) story. A dialogue—the product of developing and shifting relations between the researcher and the researched—is generated. The process involved in this particular research entailed the active discursive construction both of women's past lives and of these lives in the ethnographic present. These narratives were neither in a final form nor independent of the interactional process involved in their collection (Shostak, 1981, 1989:231–2).

This appendix provides an account of the construction of a research project. It attempts to elucidate the 'messy business' involved in 'doing' and 'writing' this particular ethnography. In presenting this set of 'tales from the field', I also raise substantive issues about process: about the relationship between the researcher and the researched, the cultural silences that haunt particular lives, questions of subjectivity, reflexivity, and the responsibilities of authorship, and how power/knowledge relations are implicated in the construction of ethnographic texts. While these issues continue to plague anthropology, in some quarters they have been cast as a crisis of representation, provoking what Edward Said has described as an 'aesthetic response' in the form of a retreat to literary solutions and 'ingenious textual strategies'(1989:211).

But textual cleverness side-steps power relations. By privileging the polyphonic and prioritizing the playful, discursive ethnographers evade issues of power, politics, and participation; the use of representational devices does little to alleviate the unequal relations that exist between ethnographers and those they study. Yet ethnographic observation is increasingly viewed as a hostile act tainted by a colonial past. Indeed, current challenges to ethnographic authority appear to threaten the very existence of fieldwork as an empirical undertaking. But a retreat from fieldwork will not resolve the contradictions that inhere in the politics of representation. In relation to domestic cultural formations, we need *more*, not *less* ethnographic work, especially among those who live at the margins of our own societies. For some of these groups, participant observation may be the only way to obtain accurate information. It is, after all, somewhat naïve to expect that those involved in underground or illegal activities will politely provide full and accurate disclosure of their income-generating strategies to a stranger with a survey form.[1]

There is another, less pessimistic, way of looking at the ethnographer and the role of fieldwork. The ethnographer can also be, as Scheper-Hughes suggests, a kind of 'record keeper'; 'a minor historian of ordinary lives of people often presumed to have no history' (1992:29). While it has been argued that in 'post-modern America, the natives are now writing their own ethnography' (Frank, 1990:146), for whole groups of 'others'—and the women in this study in particular—'access to autobiography' (Spivak, 1986:229) continues to be mediated by researchers, journalists, and other 'outsiders'. In writing this book, I have endeavoured to construct a record (of sorts) of a group of people whose principal record-keepers to date have been AIDS researchers, the tabloid media, and the criminal justice system. And while this account ultimately represents *my* interpretation of *their* lives, I have tried to portray, fairly and accurately, events as I have observed them, and people as I have known them.

Getting There: an Assisted Passage

Fieldwork is situated between autobiography and anthropology. It connects an important personal experience with a general field of knowledge (Hastrup, 1992:117).

Within anthropology, there is growing recognition that the privileging of 'being there' (Geertz, 1988) begs the question as to how the ethnographer actually got there. Although Geertz provides an analysis of various entrance scenarios, his overwhelming concern is with their textuality—the displays of 'Dickensian exuberance and Conradian fatality' on the part of ethnographers (1988:13). I am concerned here to acknowledge the fact that every passage is

---

[1] According to Bourgois, 'most of the criminologists and sociologists who painstakingly undertake epidemiological surveys on crime and substance abuse collect fabrications' (1995:12).

in some ways an 'assisted' one and, indeed, the fact that the ethnographic journey itself—the preconditions necessary in order to get from 'here' to 'there'—often traverses a familiar, but rarely discussed, road. Critical dimensions are left unexamined by the way in which Geertz deals with this question of ethnographic arrivals. On one level 'being there' necessitates an acknowledgement of the politics of domination and the power relations that inhere in ethnographic encounters. Anthropology is not easily separated from the 'process of empire' (Said, 1989:214) and, as Said has pointed out, the anthropologist was 'there' simply because 'he could be there' (1979:7). By drawing attention to the historical conjuncture that made possible the appropriation of Asia, Said problematizes the physicality of 'being there' and the necessary impact of the ethnographer's arrival, presence, and exit on the ethnographic 'there'. These problems cannot be evaded by abandoning the study of 'primitive' or colonized peoples in favour of marginalized or exotic groups closer to home. Indeed, in some instances, the study of local cultural formations may exacerbate these dilemmas. In this instance, the very different social, cultural, and economic histories that position the ethnographic self in relation to 'the other' and 'the other' in relation to the ethnographic self— even within the same society—not only meant that I 'could be there' but, moreover, that the likelihood of resistance to my presence was low.

On another level, 'being there' requires an acknowledgement of practical assistance and in this instance, personal tutelage. I was fortunate enough to cut my ethnographic teeth under the supervision and guidance of two experienced anthropologists, Ansley Hamid and Richard Curtis. Between them Hamid and Curtis have more than twenty-five years of ethnographic experience in researching illicit drug use. Better teachers could not have been found. Although the three of us often spent time in the 'field' together, most days were spent with Curtis, getting to know him and the neighbourhoods. Long evenings were spent up in Harlem with the Hamid family, cementing personal and professional ties while going over the day's events. During the first twelve months, a field presence was established and maintained in three Brooklyn neighbourhoods (Williamsburg, Flatbush, and Bushwick). Both Williamsburg and Flatbush constituted well-established fields in which Curtis and Hamid had been working for several years. Without any signs of the territoriality for which anthropologists are famous, they generously allowed me to share these fields. In addition to introducing me to the lesser-known pleasures of dining in Brooklyn, their tutelage allowed me to expose my naïveté without serious consequences, to learn how to listen and what to listen for, and to practice my interviewing skills. Perhaps more importantly, these crucial early months provided me with the opportunity to overcome my own anxieties and fears about researching 'the other' in potentially dangerous settings. Working as part of a team also reduced the risk of violence and victimization and enabled me to develop at least some measure of the much needed 'street smarts'—essential if one is to avoid being 'got over on' too much. As fieldwork progressed, additional benefits of team work, such as facilitating the interpretation of information and the exploration of questions and concepts, became apparent.

Being 'There': Establishing and Maintaining a Field Presence

The anthropological literature is replete with what di Leonardo has described as 'fables of rapport'—narratives describing the process of 'acceptance' which are 'intended to convince the reader of our hard-earned expertise' (1991:23). In particular, retrospective accounts of fieldwork often suggest that a particular incident precipitates the transition from 'outsider' to 'insider'. Such incidents typically involve a common experience and appear to be most effective when they involve an 'external' threat. Perhaps the best known example is Geertz's encounter with the police at a Balinese cockfight (Geertz, 1973). As my fieldnotes indicate, a similar experience occurred shortly after our arrival in the principal study site—a new field for both Richard Curtis and me.

Winter on Crack Row. Wind whips the neighbourhood and solitary rays of sunlight struggle to find their way through the concrete. A motley collection of crack smokers and dope fiends slouch at various angles against the brick wall, its fading murals a testament to the particularly short and brutish quality of life in Bushwick. As usual, Princess is in the middle of it all, holding court. Cherrie, Boy, and Francine provide the few friendly faces I am looking for and I zoom in. Boy and Francine are both pregnant—always a good topic of conversation. As we talk, this African American guy from the Projects starts on a morality play about how when he and his friends dealt, they would never sell to pregnant women. Suddenly four of NYPD's finest appear out of nowhere on the next block. Conversations halt in mid-sentence and all eyes divert towards the oncoming traffic. As they approach, guns are drawn and one of them shouts 'No one move'. As they close in on a Black man two bodies removed from me, it dawns on me that there are two types of shooting gallery in Bushwick. Spinning him round, they slam his face against the wall and start to do their thing . . . A fat white cop tells the rest of us to take a 'long slow walk'. As we walk away, I fall in with a small group of women and we begin exchanging our reactions and perceptions of the event—already beginning to embellish the incident. By the time we reach Troutman, yet another tale of police brutality has been added to the annals of urban folklore. (fieldnotes)

These accounts are always subjective, inevitably constructed in hindsight and, as my own example suggests, often influenced by previous writing. However, while such accounts illustrate that common experience may assist in establishing 'rapport' and facilitate a sense of 'acceptance' on the part of the researcher, actual acceptance—in the form of de facto membership of the group or network or the conferral of some legitimate status or role—is not automatic and usually has to be worked at. In this instance, establishing a legitimate field presence as a researcher required honesty, persistence, and, at least initially, a very 'thick skin'.

As many researchers have pointed out, covert research methodologies are patently unacceptable in the world of illicit drug use. In addition to ethical concerns, there are practical problems.[2] As Avril Taylor notes, in attempting to interview women heroin injectors, 'unless one is or has been an intravenous drug user, it would be extremely difficult to pass as one' (1993:11). Ironically, after making this very point, Taylor goes on to describe how she was 'mistaken' for a 'junkie' on several occasions. Unlike Taylor, I was not mistaken for a drug user—a fact that probably has much to do with the relative rarity of 'white girls' in the study neighbourhoods.[3] I was conscious of both my 'colour' and my gender during fieldwork and deliberately dressed in oversize coats, baggy overalls, and tee shirts. Most of all, I adopted what I thought was the slick strategy of wearing a favoured baseball cap to cover my blonde hair. Halfway through the research one of my informants kindly told me that I should stop wearing the hat; my taste in headgear apparently corresponded to that of many undercover police. Small wonder this choice of attire had initially made some people suspicious of me.

My informant's explanation may also help account for the hostile reception I received from some neighbourhood youths during the study. One young man in particular, a part time dealer and crack smoker whom I called 'Nasty Boy', took an intense personal dislike to me. Perhaps sensing my uncertainty and fear, Nasty took to hassling me in the street, often calling out in a loud voice 'there's that lady cop from the 9-0 (precinct)'. Nor does gender guarantee sisterhood.[4] Initially some of the minority women also gave me a hard time. This was strongly related to my whiteness and their negative perceptions and experiences of white people. A favourite refrain was 'white girls got no business down here'. Boy, a 26-year-old African American woman, was one of the first women I met in the Bushwick 'field'. Although we liked each other's company, our relationship was based on a mutual recognition of shared interests; a kind of mutual exploitation. Boy very quickly became my 'friend'. This meant that I could hang out with her and

---

[2] For example, Rosenbaum notes, in relation to her study of women heroin users, that, 'regardless of how much we tried to pass as the hippest of nonaddicts, we were still taken as straights' (1981:141). More recently, Hagedorn has pointed out in the context of his research on gangs that, '[t]rying to act like an insider . . . is phony, and the data reported will inevitably be phony' (1990:253).

[3] I am assuming here that the women in Taylor's (1993) Glasgow ethnography were all white. She does not specify race/ethnicity.

[4] The notion that membership of a particular class, race, gender, etc. offers a unique or even privileged understanding of the 'other' informs much feminist research (e.g. Oakley, 1981) as well as 'halfie' and indigenous ethnographies (e.g. Fahim, 1982; Ohnuki-Tierney, 1984; Abu-Lughod, 1988; Limon, 1991). However, while gender clearly inflects women's lives, one is never 'just a woman' (Grimshaw, 1986:85), nor, I would argue, just an African American or a white person etc. (see Chapter 7).

the other women smokers on Crack Row, facilitating my access to women's street networks. Boy was also a valuable source of information about what was going on in the neighbourhood. In addition, her tactile manner meant that I was the subject of public displays of affection whenever we met. In exchange, Boy secured a dependable source of 'change' (small amounts of money), food, and cigarettes.

Despite the absence of any one 'protector' or 'key' informant, as the fieldwork progressed, I found that some of the women began to 'watch my back' and to act as a 'lookout' for me on the streets. One incident in particular took place as I sat with Latisha, a 32-year-old African American woman, conducting an interview in Ric's car. It was a hot sunny day and, despite the noise from traffic and booming car radios, we had the windows down. Suddenly Latisha threw herself across my lap, jerking my head and shoulders back against the seat. I noticed the hand out of the corner of my eye as Latisha shouted to 'do the windows quick'. A man had been an instant away from ripping the gold hoops from my ears. That some of the women came to 'watch my back' was more likely the product not so much of my particular vulnerabilities, but the intensive nature of the fieldwork, involving a sustained street presence and daily contact with the women. As fieldwork progressed, relationships with individual women inevitably shifted, some for the worse, but most for the better.[5] Not unlike the selection process by which one includes and excludes people from personal friendship networks, we began to establish more durable relations. The following excerpt from my fieldnotes serves to illustrate the nature of the relationship between myself and Slim, a 29-year-old African American woman.

Bumped into Slim and her main man B. down on Troutman this morning. They were sitting on upturned milk crates selling used works. I asked Slim if she had seen Candy. She wanted to know why I was looking. I told her that Candy was supposed to have met me up in Harlem at 7.00am this morning to see about getting into a program for pregnant women. This seemed to infuriate her and she really dogged Candy out, to wit: 'She don't want no program, she ain't serious, I'm gonna beat her ass caus she be taking advantage—and you is good people—it's not right'. A few minutes later the police came by. I asked Slim if, given the police presence and the fact that they had works on them, I should leave. Slim surprised me by responding in no uncertain terms with 'Lisa, I don' care—you can hang out wit' me anytime caus we friends, you know that. I don' care if it attract attention from the po-leece or these people be wantin' to get in my business. You might be white but we friends, right?' (fieldnotes).

---

[5] Some of these shifts were the result of individual personality differences while others were externally induced by factors such as death and arrest. However, in some instances arrest served to cement deep ongoing ties, as was the case with Rosa, a 31-year-old Latina, arrested and subsequently imprisoned during the study period. At the time of writing Rosa and I continue to correspond and I stay overnight with her during my annual visit to New York.

From Slim's perspective, our relationship was qualified by my whiteness. As many of the women told me on different occasions, I was alright—'for a white girl'. I may have been 'good people' but I remained white people, something which serves to illustrate the partiality of much ethnographic contact. For many of the women in this study, and for minority women in particular, my 'otherness' was shaped not only by what I was not (e.g. drug user, American, 'down'), but by what I was (white, middle class, 'square'). 'Otherness' on the part of both ethnographer and informant is 'not an ineffable essence, but rather the sum of different historical experiences' (Rabinow, 1977:162). Informants do not have a monopoly on otherness. The relationship between the ethnographer and her informant(s) is a relationship in which each party draws on her own historical experiences to make sense of 'the other'.

Such partiality does not mean, however, that the emotions and feelings exchanged within such relationships are inevitably shallow or superficial. Some of my relationships with women who participated in the research, and particularly those which continued after fieldwork, attest to the intimacy which can develop as very different women in very different circumstances come to like and trust one another through the sharing of time, space, and personal confidences. These fleeting moments—the small incidents, unequal exchanges, and often sad snippets of conversation—could also be seen as conveying my gradual 'acceptance' in the field. However, it is a simplistic reading of the ethnographic encounter that merely repositions the 'outsider' in the frame of 'insider'. Such a reading ignores the effect of a dual transition on the part of both researcher and researched as they struggle to create and continually re-negotiate the space or 'between-ness' opened up by the ethnographic encounter. Establishing and maintaining a field presence is not about gaining a season's, or even a lifetime, pass to the exotic world of the 'other'. It is about creating and sustaining a world 'between' ourselves and those we study (Hastrup, 1992:117). Ideally, the knowledge that emerges from this encounter is dialogic rather than monologic: it is knowledge 'produced in human interaction' (Scheper-Hughes, 1993:25). A truly reflexive approach to fieldwork involves talking about how we create these worlds—about how the 'there' we study does not exist prior to, and independent of, the shared worlds we create with our informants. Such approaches remain rare.

Hunting and Gathering

As Clifford has noted, ethnography can be viewed as a form of 'cultural collecting' in which 'diverse experiences and facts are selected, gathered, detached from their original temporal occasions, and given enduring value in a new arrangement' (1988:231). In the course of this research, I observed and recorded details of the lives of 211 women drug users in three Brooklyn neighbourhoods. All of these women were active cocaine and/or heroin users recruited at the street-level. The ethnographic net for the study was initially cast wide in order to fulfil three basic goals: to address the day-to-day variability which drug use phenomena exhibit; to represent the diversity of contexts in which women use drugs at the street level; and to allow the basic social, cultural, and economic processes common to women's drug use in low-income street settings to emerge. Intensive preliminary fieldwork and prolonged contact with these informants, including the construction of networks (Mitchell, 1969; Boissevain, 1972), enabled me to reach a wide variety of women.[6]

Detailed fieldnotes which described daily events in the lives of participants in the street-level drug economy were collected over the duration of the study.[7] This rich descriptive repository yielded details both of individual women's lives and the shifting local social and economic conditions in which these lives were situated. In addition to daily fieldnotes, tape-recorded interviews were conducted with individual women.[8] Also, a small number of interviews were undertaken in the primary study site with both female kin and male partners of the women in the study. The final data set consisted of more than five thousand pages of transcribed interview narrative, several hundred pages of typed fieldnotes, a field diary, and photographs, as well as personal letters, poems, and drawings provided by individual women.

Initial interviews were conducted as 'life history' interviews (Frank, 1979) designed to elicit a core of basic demographic information and to reflect the significance assigned by individual women to a range of areas: childhood, adolescence, schooling and employment history, pathways to drug use, current use, social network composition, income generation and involvement in lawbreaking, health and risk-taking behaviours, and experiences of pregnancy and mothering. These initial and, by comparison, 'formal' interviews were crucial

---

[6] Because it is impossible to select a random sample from this population (the parameters being unknown), initial neighbourhood samples were selected using a combination of techniques including self-identification and snowballing (Weppner, 1977; Biernacki and Waldorf, 1981), chains of referral (McCall, 1978), and theoretical sampling (Glaser and Strauss, 1970).

[7] Most standard research methods texts suggest that at the outset of a research project, field notes will be copious and abundant but will then reduce. Initially my fieldnotes were very scanty and only as the research progressed did these notes begin to provide a detailed and focused source of data. I suspect this was because, as I became more familiar with both methods and techniques and the research sites and the people in them, I both 'saw' more and was better able to read and comprehend actions, relationships and situations.

[8] The research was described in detail and women were informed of the goals and purposes of the study, and the uses to which their accounts would be put, prior to their decision to participate in the study. Once agreement to proceed was secured, the tape-recorder was turned on and formal agreement or 'informed consent' was recorded prior to commencement of the interview.

insofar as they familiarized me with the broader contexts of women's lives. While ethnographic interviews were checked for internal consistency against field observations, the technique of triangulation (Denzin, 1970; Spradley, 1979; Hammersley and Atkinson, 1983) was used in order to examine the 'validity' of the data. This meant that the accuracy of field observations and the veracity of ethnographic interviews were, wherever possible, confirmed by multiple sources. As most of the respondents who participated in ethnographic interviews knew each other, typically as members of local drug using networks, they were often able to confirm or refute claims made by others. In the case of field observations, triangulation was assisted by close collaboration with a male ethnographer (Richard Curtis) who was engaged in a different project but was familiar with both the research participants and the study site.

The interviews for this study took place in a variety of locations[9] and ranged in duration from twenty minutes to three hours. For some women, interviews involved considerable emotional pain as they divulged details of their childhoods, intimate relationships with men and, of course, their children. Some interviews were suspended in order to comfort visibly distressed women or simply to talk off the tape about particular incidents and to discuss appropriate agencies from which they could seek further help. Some interviews could not be completed. A number of women became distracted or fidgety during long interviews and quality sometimes suffered as a result. Some were in the throes of heroin withdrawal while others merely wanted to get back to the streets; understandable given the considerable drain on their time and resources for small recompense. Many heroin users fell asleep or 'nodded out' at repeated intervals (see also Rosenbaum, 1981c:144). Most women, however, spoke freely and at great length and some women expressed appreciation at my interest and the opportunity to talk about their lives.

Each woman was paid $10 or equivalent for her initial interview. I felt strongly that women should be compensated for their time—time they could have spent 'getting paid' in other ways—and to do otherwise would have been highly exploitative. Payment is also consistent with established practice in the field of drug research.[10] However, while the women in this study

[9] Interviews were conducted in private houses and apartments, drug-consumption sites, cars, restaurants and fast food places, abandoned buildings, parks, public bathrooms, and on the street. Sometimes the locations contributed considerable background noise which made tape-recording and/or subsequent transcription difficult and, in some cases, impossible. Three interviews—conducted on the subway, in a local shooting gallery, and in a local Dominican restaurant—were excluded for this reason.

[10] For example, Rosenbaum notes that 'the paid interview made the women feel important; they were being paid to share some of their knowledge and expertise rather than being "therapized" and they appreciated this . . . [However] most of the women interviewed were poor; all other reasons aside, they came to be interviewed because they needed the money' (Rosenbaum, 1981c:144).

certainly needed the money, the fieldwork phase of the research was not officially funded and my own relative poverty meant I was not always in a position to provide women with cash reimbursement beyond the initial interview. Many subsequent interviews were obtained in return for cash, food, clothing, makeup, cigarettes, subway tokens and, most often, a combination thereof. Throughout the study period, many women and some men who were not part of the formal sample also ate and drank with me, smoked my cigarettes, wore my clothes, and hustled a few dollars out of me.

Unless otherwise stated, the data presented here consist of repeated interviews and multiple field observations with 45 women in Bushwick, the primary study site. These 45 women represent the range of ages, racial/ethnic backgrounds,[11] life experiences and diversity of drug use histories evident among the larger population. Once selected, these women were the subject of intensive and repeated observations and interviews. While this does not mean that women never 'lied' to me, the sustained nature of the ethnographic dialogue between myself and these women meant that 'lies' and 'cultural silences' could be discussed, explored, and subsequently addressed as a crucial part of the analysis (see below on 'Sex, Lies and Tape-recordings'). Contact with these 45 women was extensive and the number of tape-recorded interviews conducted with individual women ranged from a minimum of three to a maximum of fifteen.

For the most part, given the frequency of contact (which in most cases was daily—arrests and imprisonment permitting), subsequent interviews tended to be shorter in duration than the initial interview and often focused on specific topics—either discussions or concerns individual women initiated and indicated that they wished to 'do' an interview about—or areas that were of specific interest to me. For example, many of the interviews in the later stages of fieldwork focused in detail on women's income-generating activities over the previous twenty-four hour period. Sometimes these interviews took place in the context of a conversation with a woman during which I would ask if I could turn the tape on. Sometimes we would arrange a mutually agreed upon time and place to conduct an interview. On other occasions I turned on the tape at the woman's insistence that I 'should be getting this down'. In one situation, I was an observer in Kizzy's 'gallery' when she insisted I turn on the tape covertly. After a great deal of hesitation, I overcame my reluctance, only to find out later that the noise level was so high and distorted that the recording was of little value.

This process of repeated interviews at regular intervals (or as regular as 'regular' could be in this context) also suited the women better by intruding less on their lives and providing an opportunity for extended discussion and reflection at mutually convenient times. The busy lives of these women and

[11] Twenty women identified themselves as Latinas (Spanish), sixteen as African American (Black), and nine women identified as European American (white).

the wide range of activities in which they were involved (e.g. generating income, avoiding police, purchasing drugs, consuming drugs, seeking shelter) meant that care had to be taken in relation to the timing of interviews. Patience on my part and careful attention to the timing of interviews also reduced the incidence of 'nodding' and alleviated the desire to 'race through' the interview, frequently experienced in conducting research with active street-level drug users. To summarize, the process of interviewing and observing a smaller sample of women in the primary study site over a prolonged period of time revealed a great deal about women's everyday lives and, in particular, about their social relations and income-generating activities, that could not have been obtained by any other research methodology. Such data surpass one-off interviews (even within the ethnographic context) in ways that extend beyond the rich detailed accounts and minute attention to everyday life, by providing a unique source of information about the changing contexts and shifting relations in which both the research project and these women's lives were situated.

High-risk Activities

In her ethnography of a community of female intravenous drug users in Glasgow, Avril Taylor (1993) has usefully identified three elements of risk which may confront the drug ethnographer: legal, health, and personal. These are discussed in turn.

Legal risks

Despite the obvious potential, there appear to be few recorded incidents where drug researchers have actually been arrested during fieldwork.[12] Legal risks were particularly salient in the context of an intensive police presence in the principal study site for most of the fieldwork phase. Participant observation placed me in a situation where I was a constant witness to lawbreaking, and thus potentially the object of police enquiry. In contrast to the protections offered institutional researchers working on large grants (e.g. see Williams et al., 1992), I began this project as an unaffiliated researcher without institutional support. I did not seek, nor was I offered, police protection or immunity from arrest and possible conviction during the course of the research. In doing this, I took a chance that, if I were arrested, I might not have been able to establish my credibility as a researcher. The only identification I carried was my student card. In hindsight, this was a somewhat irresponsible approach and inevitably, had I been arrested, the burden of establishing my credibility would have fallen on Curtis or Hamid.

---

[12] Ethnographers are, however, frequently subject to questioning by the police about their presence in particular locations (e.g. see Inciardi et al., 1993:151–2).

With some notable exceptions, the police seemed as keen to avoid me as I was them. Regular patrol officers, especially the community policing officers deployed in the neighbourhood, associated me with the AIDS research store-front where Curtis worked. As such I was no doubt afforded some 'spill-over' protection from arrest by virtue of this association. However, such protec-tion did not extend to freedom from harassment on occasions such as on weekends when I came down to the neighbourhood alone or where I was confronted by officers from other precincts. At a general level, beat police or the 'foot patrol' appeared to work on a policy best described as 'guilt by association'. Some police officers took the view that drug researchers were akin to social workers. As one officer commented, he had 'heard that there were a couple of do-gooders in the neighbourhood'. Police consistently referred to women drug users in explicitly moral terms. Women were fre-quently addressed as 'girls', 'ho's' (prostitutes), and 'bitches'. Despite the fact that the sidewalks were teaming with (male) drug sellers and those in vari-ous distribution roles, whenever two or more of the women (including myself) congregated on the sidewalk, the police would tell us 'you can't be hanging out here' or 'you girls better move on up the ho stroll'. With the exception of the prostitution stroll, the presence of women drug users on the streets was not well tolerated by the police. Whether local police merely per-ceived women as easier to intimidate or interpreted their presence as a sex-ualized threat to public order, women tended to be rapidly dispersed while (male) drug dealers were left to continue their business.

For the most part, policing in the neighbourhood was highly sexualized. Police treated women drug users very badly, subjecting them to physical assaults, thefts, verbal harassment, and extreme forms of humiliation.[13] As a woman who hung out with women drug users, I was perhaps seen by those police who were aware of my role as 'weird' and certainly in violation of gender role expectations. The police were not alone in this view. For exam-ple, despite frequent attempts on my part to explain the research and my presence in the neighbourhood, both Johnny, the owner of a local restaurant, and his wife, and Chick, a neighbourhood 'slumlord' (all white) repeatedly came back to one question: 'What's a nice (white) girl like you doing in a place like this?' This type of challenge was not extended to Curtis who was

---

[13] For example, a common practice of police was to relieve women of whatever cash they were holding under threat of arrest. Police also routinely forced women to throw both money and drugs down the drain. Of particular concern was the practice (upon finding out that women were being given free condoms by health workers) of confiscat-ing condoms and destroying them in the women's presence. Less routinely, individual police engaged in both paid and unpaid sex with women drug users and subjected them to violence and other forms of degradation. One particular officer with a reputation for vindictiveness appeared to enjoy forcing emaciated women to do push-ups on the stroll in full view of their co-workers and potential dates.

never asked to explain either his presence in the neighbourhood, or his research, in such gendered terms.

Health risks

The most obvious risk to personal health encountered during the course of this study was the potential for contracting blood-borne viruses such as Hepatitis B, Hepatitis C, and HIV. In practice this risk is very small if one does not use intravenous drugs, share injecting equipment, or engage in unprotected sexual practices with one's informants. One risk factor which I was unable to eliminate arose from the possibility of contamination through contact with blood or other bodily products. On several occasions I assisted women in cleaning and dressing ulcerated and weeping body parts and on one occasion I received a needlestick injury while attempting to retrieve my cigarette lighter from a woman's bag. The owner of the needle in question, a European American woman, was HIV positive. I was adamant that I did not want her or any of the women to know about the incident. Despite my anxiety, I did not want to appear self-indulgent. For many women, the risk of contracting the HIV virus was no longer; infection was a reality. For those not already infected, the HIV virus represented either a fate to which they were resigned, an occupational hazard to be avoided (where possible), or simply something they dealt with as part of a much larger set of constraints on their lives. For many of these women, AIDS simply wasn't the 'biggest problem on the block'. Placed in the broader perspective of the risks they faced on a daily basis, I worried that it might appear precious to indulge my need to 'deal' with this incident by discussing it with them. However, the personal experience of exposure to risk certainly served to increase my awareness of the devastation that this largely preventable epidemic has wrought, and continues to wreak, on injecting drug users in the United States.

Another potential threat to health was the possibility of contracting tuberculosis, which was endemic in the study population, given the cramped and poorly ventilated conditions in most shooting galleries and makeshift accommodations. Of course this risk can be ameliorated by vaccination and although I was not inoculated against Hepatitis B, I had received the BCG (TB) vaccine as a child. Another risk factor, which did not occur to me during the study but is discussed by Avril Taylor (1993:18) as something she could not do, involved the sharing of drinks from cans or bottles. This practice was uncommon in the study site, as was the use of alcohol generally. I did however, share 'drags' of cigarettes with women and often engaged in close physical contact in the form of hugs and kisses. It is my belief that such fears are exaggerated and, depending on the actual risks involved, need to be balanced against the fact that many intravenous drug users are acutely aware of their broader cultural inscription as sources of physical (and moral) contamination. I firmly believe that, in such a context, *not* to touch can be 'the hostile act, the act of indifference and of turning away' (Scheper-Hughes, 1992:28).

Minor health concerns included the constant risk of colds and viruses given the poor general health of the study population. Summer brought a different set of health hazards given the unsanitary conditions of life on the street and one summer I was badly bitten by fleas. An additional health-related risk for cigarette smokers is that ethnographic research with illicit drug users occurs in what can only be described as a smoke-friendly environment. This, in addition to a certain amount of stress produced by the research process, may serve to exacerbate a nicotine habit. Finally, as Taylor (1993) has noted, stress is a very real health concern for ethnographers and is produced by multiple sources, including the need to maintain a sociological vigil while conducting 'natural' conversations, the complex mental book-keeping entailed in protecting confidences, and the difficulties of 'coping' with particular 'pieces' of information (A. Taylor, 1993:19). I would add only that it is not merely individual 'pieces' of information that present difficulties for the researcher's emotional well-being but, perhaps more importantly, the picture that emerges when one considers these 'pieces' as part of a whole. In this context, a pervasive sense of the everyday violence that marked these women's lives was inescapable.

Personal risks

I was warned against doing this study by many people at the outset, some of whom I had expected to be more supportive. Most, but not all, of these people were men. Justifications and rationales were less often couched in terms of my (and their) relative lack of familiarity with ethnographic methods and techniques than they were in individual perceptions of the dangers that I—as a (white) woman—would face in such a situation. I was told on several occasions that I could reasonably be expected to be raped and robbed—perhaps worse. However, despite the everyday violence witnessed in the study site I was fortunate enough not to have been seriously assaulted 'in the field'. Although I found myself in several 'delicate' situations while conducting fieldwork, the only 'dangerous' situation occurred one evening on the train returning to Manhattan. This is not to say that I was, or even felt 'safe' in the field, only that sometimes the risk of victimization may be reduced in a context where one is known and seen to be involved.

Contrary to Taylor's experience, there was little evidence to suggest that the fact that I was a woman afforded me 'a degree of protection and acceptance from the men I encountered which might not have been given to a male researcher' (A. Taylor, 1993:23). Rather, I think the fact that I was a researcher was salient in affording me a degree of protection from the men that was not extended to women drug users (see also Williams et al., 1992).

Both my own experiences and those of the women in this study serve to illustrate that within this context at least, while all women are vulnerable, some are more so than others. Once in the field, the issue then becomes the strategies adopted and steps taken to minimize the risk of victimization. For example, despite the fact that women offered to guarantee my safety, I never conducted fieldwork on my own late at night.[14] I also decided after an initial visit that I would never again enter the 'tyre shop'—a shooting gallery frequented by local males that could only be accessed by crawling through a hole in the wall. Although Curtis continued to visit this site without incident, I decided to go with my 'sixth sense' (Williams et al., 1992) and avoid this particular location. There were several other indoor consumption sites or shooting galleries in the neighbourhood that I would not have contemplated visiting without Curtis, among them the notorious Pappy's place (see Chapter 2). These settings were run by men and my strongest contacts— women—had little control or say over what went on inside. They were often located in structurally precarious sites such as abandoned or, worse still, burnt out buildings. These sites rarely ran to electricity and usually had only one entrance/exit. I simply felt too vulnerable on my own in these settings. The one indoor gallery that I regularly visited on my own was run by Kizzy, a woman with whom I had a strong relationship.

Thus the general thrust of Rosenbaum's point (in giving her reasons for not doing an ethnographic study) is correct when she argues that, '[a]lthough several male ethnographers have done field work with addicts in urban centres as part of their research, we found that as women we were limited. We felt especially vulnerable, since we were less equipped to defend ourselves physically than a man might be' (1981c:147). However, as Taylor has pointed out, prior to her research, no participant observation/ethnographic studies of inner-city illicit drug users had been done by women (1993:21–2). While this is a serious omission, the risks identified by Taylor in the context of her Glasgow research are exacerbated within the context of impoverished low-income urban communities in the United States. This is not to argue that this type of research is 'too dangerous' for women, nor do I concur with Taylor that it is a 'highly suitable job for a woman' (1993:23). Rather, it is the communities and the conditions under which such research is undertaken, and the nature and degree of training, assistance, and supervision extended to the researcher that can make the difference between a successful and responsibly-executed project and one which risks serious injury and possibly death. My assisted passage into the field and the expert tutelage and careful guidance I received were crucial to the success of this project. The question, then,

---

[14] This contrasts sharply with current fieldwork among heroin users in a street-level drug market setting in South West Sydney, where I frequently conduct interviews and observations on my own until the early hours of the morning.

is not whether this kind of ethnography is a suitable job for a woman, but rather a question of which women and under what conditions.[15]

Pregnant Fields

I was pregnant with twins during the fieldwork phase of this study. Within the literature there exists an implicit assumption that pregnancy on the part of the researcher holds special implications for researching women. These implications were perhaps not so apparent in the current context given that my own pregnancy occurred during the final stages of fieldwork when I was well acquainted with the women and the principal study site. Rosenbaum notes in relation to the visibly pregnant status of herself and her research assistant during their interview study of women heroin users that,

[our pregnancies] perhaps made us appear less imposing—somehow more vulnerable and thus easier to relate to. (The women treated us quite gently when we were in this condition, being careful to ask us whether their smoking would bother us). In short, pregnancy seemed to indicate to the women that we were real people, like them, and that we shared female concerns (1981c:142).

The implicit assumption that an essential humanity or authenticity is located in the pregnant body—that the state of pregnancy conveys a universal image of gentility, honesty, and all things good—is problematic. While pregnancy may well hold those meanings for the researchers, they cannot simply be imposed on women subjects. The notion that the pregnant self conveys a cross-cultural message of authenticity—i.e. 'real people'—resembles the kind of eco-feminism that suggests racism and cultural conflict would not be a problem in a woman-centric world. While experiences of pregnancy and mothering may provide some basis for establishing common ground, they are not cultural universals, and individual women's experiences of pregnancy are both ontologically fractured and far removed from each other according to the social, economic, and cultural sites in which particular pregnancies are situated.[16] Because of both the ethnographic nature and the advanced stage of the research, my own experiences of being pregnant in the field did not extend to the need to indicate myself as a 'real person' or to convey shared female concerns. I was, however, acutely aware of the fact that my experience of pregnancy differed in a number of substantive ways to the experiences of the women in this study. Any assumptions of mutuality or shared

[15] For example, although some minority women appear particularly well-equipped to undertake this kind of research (e.g. see Bourgois and Dunlap, 1993:99), minority women may also need assisted passages to and through these fields.

[16] Moore and Devitt note that the fact that both Rosenbaum and her research assistant were visibly pregnant may have influenced the women's accounts of drug use during pregnancy and may account for both the relatively small number of women who admitted using drugs during pregnancy (2–3 per cent) and the contempt these women reportedly held for others who used drugs while pregnant (1989:68).

experience would have been delusory on my part—something that became increasingly difficult to ignore. For example, I had to leave 'work' early once a fortnight to attend an appointment with my obstetrician/gynaecologist on the Upper East Side—visits which cost me $150 each. The contrast between 'the field' and this doctor's surgery was stark and dramatic. Each fortnight as I waited with other (mostly white middle class) women to see the doctor, I was forced to reflect on my own position in relation to that of the women I studied—and the fact that the very different conditions of their past and current pregnancies had helped constitute my data.

Further differences were highlighted in conversations with individual women. For example, many of the women expressed their opinion that I would be a 'good mother' because I had a 'good man' (some of the women had met my long-distance partner and most had seen his photograph). They also knew that I would be keeping my babies; that there were no clouds hanging over their heads in relation to maternal drug use. And although they were always telling me what I should be eating and drinking, none of the women chided me for continuing to smoke cigarettes while pregnant. For the most part, women seemed either unaware of the potential risks of cigarette smoking, or—in the context of their and my behaviour—simply chose to ignore them (cf. Rosenbaum, 1981c:142).

Sex, Lies, and Tape-recordings

Knowledge about a particular culture—and especially its closed or hidden aspects—does not engulf the ethnographer merely by virtue of 'being there' (Clifford, 1988:67). The ethnographer must work to 'extract' information and the right of informants to remain silent is rarely respected. Most ethnographies involve the interrogation and violation of 'cultural silences' (Rabinow, 1977:129). However, these cultural silences—which sometimes take the form of 'lies' or partial truths—are at minimum revealing and, in some instances, critical both to understanding and writing about particular cultures.[17] In the context of this study, women drug users' cultural silences spoke volumes about the relationship between the researcher and the researched, the positioning of women in the drug economy, and the meanings of sex/gender and race/ethnicity.

Despite the stereotypical images of drug users, there is little evidence to suggest that they lie or avoid the truth to a greater extent than anyone else.

---

[17] I find that the concept of 'cultural silences' better illuminates the process identified in this research although it could be argued that the women were merely 'faking' (Duelli-Klein, 1983)—i.e. giving socially desirable, or as Hale has argued, '"politically correct" responses (what the narrator thinks the listener wants to hear)—rather than "honest" ones' (1991:125). However, as suggested in Chapter 6, there is more at stake here than 'the truth'.

While drug users, like most people, desire to present a favourable image of themselves while maintaining boundaries of privacy, the production of invalid or misleading data can be mediated by an ongoing and socially significant relationship between the ethnographer and her informants (Taylor, 1993:23–4). While this issue was discussed using specific examples in Chapter 6, a brief comment is warranted here. Initially many of the women were prepared to point to 'others' as being responsible for the price deflation of sexual services in the principal study site and as being willing to engage in sex-for-crack exchanges. Despite the fact that almost everyone spoke about these unspecified 'others', I was initially unable to find any women who fell into this 'other' category. In the absence of this 'other', I was confronted with a collective cultural silence by the women in relation to these activities.

As the research progressed and relations with the women developed, I began to probe this silence. Of course, it emerged that this 'other' (who engaged in sex-for-crack exchanges and cut-rate blowjobs) was often the 'self'. Women found it very difficult to talk about this in the context of their own experiences. This was exacerbated by occupational norms surrounding street-level sexwork which held such practices to be in violation of strongly held principles. Women's reluctance to talk about their own involvement was also linked to the symbolic significance of admitting that one had engaged in the equivalent of a 50-cent blowjob—hardly conducive to conveying a desirable image or maintaining a positive self-identity. It also meant confronting the image of women crack users as so desperate they would do 'anything' for a hit—an image which, for the most part, the women in this study strongly resisted. For some women, acknowledging their participation in price cutting and sex-for-crack exchanges also meant surrendering one of the few remaining criteria on which they both prided themselves and used to distinguish themselves from 'others'—the ability or belief that they were in fact able to control their drug use.

Word Up!

According to Blauner (1989), 'language symbolizes as well as expresses the distinctiveness of our personal identity and our most important group memberships and identifications: family, ethnicity, class, peer group, and lifestyle enclave' (1989:328). The narratives selected for presentation here remain in a 'raw' and, for the most part, un-edited form and are sometimes repetitive and confusing. Most of the women encountered during the course of this study adopted a non-standard English vernacular reflecting a combination of Black English (Abrahams, 1976), Spanglish, street slang, and a rich drug lexicon (Folb, 1980). Women shifted back and forth between these different linguistic codes (Painter, 1979).[18] Although the tape-recorded interview format preserves the accuracy of what was said, the spoken word is different to the written word. Many of the women's oral presentations were characterized by what I can only describe as a particular 'street style' which included a specialized vocabulary,[19] creative expressions, rapid and rhythmic delivery, rich textured sounds, dynamic variations of pitch, the use of dialect, register, and intonation to convey shifts in meaning and emphasis, the playful use of metaphor, in-group references, informal systems of punctuation characterized by the use of pauses, qualifiers, and key phrases or 'crutch words' (e.g. 'you know', 'right', and 'word'),[20] accentuation of certain syllables (e.g. 'po-leece'), and extensive use of satire. Although the interview material presented here has been transcribed verbatim in an attempt to preserve its original oral character,[21] including syntax and speech rhythms, the orality of many these voices has inevitably been lost in the process.

Few of these accounts display evidence of the features typically associated with women's narratives which socio-linguists suggest are characterized by an absence of the first person, frequent understatements and the playing down of individual achievements or accomplishments (Hoffman and Culley, 1985; Brodzki and Schenck, 1988; Etter-Lewis, 1991).[22] This may be a function of racial/ethnic differences or generational differences evident between this sample and the findings of other researchers. However, I suspect that it is more likely to do with the street vernacular and style which these women adopt in oral presentation. The form and content of what is said (stylin') provides a measure of status within the inner city (Black) street culture (Kochman, 1972). While stylin' has traditionally been believed to be the prerogative of Black males, the speaking styles and choice of words, as well as the use of innuendo or 'signifying' (Mitchell-Kerman, 1972), by the women in this sample suggests that, within the inner-city drug-use culture, women

[18] This is reflected in inconsistencies in pronunciation where individual women spoke in dialect in one sentence or phrase and not in another. These inconsistencies have been maintained in the transcribed material in an attempt to convey the meanings which shifts in dialect, register, and intonation connote in terms of emphasis, topic, and the presence of others.

[19] The rich, specialized vocabulary of street drug use (e.g. see Fiddle, 1967; Folb, 1980) expanded dramatically with the linguistic codes and conventions spawned by inner-city crack users during the 1980s (Williams, 1992:35–39).

[20] Despite advice that the persistence of these words and phrases may irritate the reader, they have been preserved in the text. This decision is based in part on Devault's (1990) discussion of the use of 'you know' in women's speech as a 'request for understanding' where language is wanting (Devault, 1990:103 cf. Blauner, 1987).

[21] This has also meant that some material contains comments or remarks which could be described as sexist or racist. However, these opinions—with some of which I strongly disagree—are their own and as such are preserved here. For a discussion of the problems in editing 'first person' sociology, see Blauner (1987).

[22] Much feminist linguistic research has been concerned to implicate the use of language and patterns of speech in the subordination of women (Devault, 1990).

too, manipulate words and phrases in a creative way in order to convey style and seek status.[23]

In comparison with some researchers (e.g. Miller, 1986) I did not attempt to emulate this vernacular, either consciously or unconsciously. Miller reports that her use of a 'street vocabulary' of 'Black English' both enabled her to fit in and improved the quality of her data over time. In fact, one of her subjects was prompted to ask if she had ever been a hooker because 'you sure sound like a hooker' (Miller, 1986:31). Although my speech now has a tendency to shift between a number of different dialects, I suspect that this has more to do with my own nomadic existence and exposure to a wide range of linguistic patterns rather than taking on the specific vernacular or pattern of any particular cultural group. While my vocabulary was certainly enriched as a result of the fieldwork experience, I never felt the need, nor I suspect would it have been considered appropriate, to take on or imitate the 'voices' of the women in this study. Moreover, perhaps the fact that I was a linguistic 'foreigner', as well as an 'outsider' in other ways, had its own advantages and many of the women were as interested in my speech as I was in theirs. My ability to comprehend women's words was facilitated by the extended nature of the fieldwork and, perhaps more importantly, through personal friendship networks and, in particular, contact with young minority group women and girls who were not part of this study. These young women accepted my interest in youth cultures and gladly obliged in keeping me up to date with shifts in fashion, music, and the lexicon of the street—despite the fact that I never did manage to achieve conversational fluency in pig latin.[24]

Finally, it is necessary to recall that interviews are socially-defined speech events with their own conventions for behaviour (Frank, 1979:87). Initially, I had planned to use a semi-structured interview protocol to guide the life history interviews. The results of the pilot of this protocol clearly indicated that the accounts elicited in response took the form of 'interview speech' (Wolfson, 1976), forcing me to abandon the protocol. In contrast, accounts gleaned from repeated unstructured interviews were more reminiscent of conversational narrative. This is not to privilege these accounts by suggesting that they represent some form of unmediated 'cultural truth'. Rather, women's narratives, as part of the ethnographic dialogue, are always already the product of a cultural encounter. Within this intersubjective world of fieldwork, both the ethnographer and her informants are engaged in spinning the 'webs of signification' by which particular ethnographic realities are constructed (Rabinow, 1977:151). Neither the 'utopia of plural authorship' nor repeated acknowledgements of the mediated nature of informants' voices can solve this 'authenticity trap' (Hastrup, 1992:122).[25]

---

[23] See also hooks (1989) on African American women's creative use of speech.

[24] Thanks Alecia, Deshana, Esme, Emily, Candace, Sara, Jessica, Nem and Africa!

[25] Hastrup has framed this dilemma nicely: '[h]owever many the direct quotations, the informant's voices cannot penetrate the discursive speech of the ethnographer. We

Analyzing the Data/Writing the Culture

Ethnography allows the other to speak [but] only through text it controls (Powell, 1993:174)

Consistent with the dynamic and interactive nature of ethnographic research, a systematic 'data sort' was conducted during the final year of fieldwork. This assisted in elucidating analytical and conceptual categories and served to reveal a number of 'gaps' and issues in need of clarification in relation to both the sample as a whole and individual informants. This procedure also provided the opportunity to reflect on the data that had already been collected and enabled me to seek the women's responses to several emerging theoretical constructs. The data were sorted manually using a standard word-processing program. Each individual woman's transcripts were assigned to a separate computer file. These transcripts were printed out and read many times over.

I developed a rough coding scheme by assigning numbers to specific portions of narrative which eventually reflected 22 loosely defined themes or constructs. Many sections of narrative were assigned to multiple categories. Once coded, I then extracted each section of narrative from the individual woman's interview file, marked it with an informant identifier and transferred it to one or more thematic files. These 22 theme files were then printed and, through the process of reading and re-reading, finally sorted into ten principal 'umbrella' constructs. A similar process was conducted for the fieldnote data base and the field diary in order to incorporate relevant material into the construct files. The complete construct files were subsequently printed and read over many times before proceeding to individual analysis of each substantive construct.

The analysis presented here is therefore guided by theoretical constructs as they emerged from the data; from women's own narratives and my recordings of the ethnographic encounters that produced them. These constructs are not merely 'abstractions' but, rather, categories constructed on the basis of days and hours of ethnographic observations, interactions, and interviews. They are *empirical* but not *empiricist*. For within this context, as Scheper-Hughes reminds us, some events remain 'factual' (1992:23). For example, there is no denying the fact that five of the women who participated in this study died violent deaths during the fieldwork. But while ethnographers are obliged to gather the 'facts' as scrupulously as possible, 'all facts are necessarily selected and interpreted from the moment we decide to count one thing and ignore another, or attend this ritual but not another . . . understanding

can cite them verbatim and record their speeches as acts made by people who are subjects in their own plot-space . . . The displacement from "I saw it myself" to "this is what I actually heard" reframes the problem of authenticity, but does not solve it' (1992:121–2).

is necessarily partial and is always hermeneutic' (Scheper-Hughes, 1992:23). As the product of a series of encounters and a historically specific set of relations, ethnography is always mediated by the subjectivity of the ethnographer. My own subjectivity has influenced the collection of these data, as well as the analysis and the concepts used to frame them. The account that emerges is necessarily partial and incomplete.

However, it is ironic that while within anthropology, ethnography is moving towards the 'textual' and is increasingly characterized by rampant self-reflexivity, other disciplines are beginning to applaud ethnography's potential to capture 'the real'. Both drug research and criminological study, as well as feminist inquiry, increasingly seek to utilize ethnographic methods and techniques in order to access 'real' people and 'lived experience'. Within anthropology, the 'post-modern turn' has been caricatured as the 'production of texts by means of texts, rather than by means of fieldwork' (Fardon, 1990:5 cited in Okely, 1992:3) and as the tendency to treat fieldwork as the 'poor relation' by reducing it to the process of data collection. This feature is perhaps exemplified by Geertz (1988) for whom, as Carrithers sees it, 'research seems only a frustrating and solipsistic appendage of the supreme act itself, writing' (1988:20). While this kind of privileging of theory sets up an artificial distinction between doing and writing ethnography, drawing attention to the conditions under which ethnographic texts are constructed highlights the agency of the author.

It is our choice to encompass their stories in a narrative of a different order. We select the quotations and edit the statements. We must not blur this major responsibility of ours by rhetorics of 'many voices' and 'multiple authorship' in ethnographic writing (Hastrup, 1992:122; emphasis in original).

As Geertz has argued, while both post-modern anthropologists and feminist researchers increasingly advocate the construction of 'poly-phonic' texts, the responsibility of authorship cannot be evaded by the invocation of 'method' or 'language' or 'the people themselves' (1988:140). In anthropology at least, the author remains alive and well and 'it still very much matters who speaks' (Geertz, 1988:7). Despite the many instances of sustained collaborative and reciprocal effort that went into this research, its presentation as the product of a democratized process would be deceptive. No amount of verbatim transcripts or rhetoric proclaiming 'their voices', or even the presentation of the text as one which 'allows them to tell their stories' can mitigate the ethnographic effect at the level of both interview/observation (see Frank, 1979; Hale, 1991) and cultural construction, or 'writing culture' (Clifford, 1988).[26]

---

[26] According to Clifford, '[e]thnographic writing is determined in at least six ways: (1) contextually (it draws from and creates meaningful social milieux); (2) rhetorically (it uses and is used by expressive conventions); (3) institutionally (one writes within, and against, specific traditions, disciplines, audiences); (4) generically (an ethnography is usually distinguishable from a novel or a travel account); (5) politically (the

Ultimately it is the ethnographic 'I' who is the author of this text. It is 'I' and not 'they' or even 'us' who has taken hundreds of hours of women's narratives, interpreted them, coded them, and (re)framed them. While a number of preliminary constructs were generated in the field in concert with women, some of which elicited discussion and debate, and tentative interpretations discussed with some women during the final phase of fieldwork, only three women read papers arising out of this research.[27] The unfortunate reality is that many of the women who participated in this research were not (either then or now) in a position to read the final product and most had little inclination to do so.

Power/Knowledge and 'Feminist' Ethnography

[T]he exploitative aspect of ethnographic process seems unavoidable. The lives, loves and tragedies that fieldwork informants share with a researcher are ultimately data— grist for the ethnographic mill, a mill that has a truly grinding power (Stacey, 1991:113).

The use of qualitative research techniques, and in particular, the life history method or ethnography, has often been seen as a natural or logical choice for (Western) feminist research. For some feminist researchers, '[t]he model of a distant, controlled, and ostensibly neutral interviewer has, as a result, been replaced with that of a sisterhood—an engaged and sympathetic interaction between two individuals united by the fact of gender oppression' (Patai, 1991:143). However, as recent feminist critics have pointed out, there is nothing inherently feminist about the use of such methods (e.g. see McRobbie, 1982; Gluck and Patai, 1991; Stacey, 1988, 1991). While the opportunity for women to 'tell their own stories in their own words' is often welcomed by women and indeed in some situations may serve to empower individual women,[28] informants are never equal participants in the research

authority to represent cultural realities is unequally shared and at times contested); (6) historically (all the above conventions and constraints are changing). These determinations govern the inscription of coherent ethnographic fictions' (1986:6).

[27] Two women read and commented on papers which were in a more conversational or 'talk' format for presentation at professional meetings, as opposed to a print format for publication in an academic journal. One woman requested and was sent a set of offprints from published research arising out of the study and was also sent this manuscript. Interestingly, several participants in my current research in Sydney have requested and read articles arising out of my work in New York.

[28] For example, Patai has argued, 'of the frequent claim that the interview process, as conducted by feminists, is empowering in that it "gives a voice" to those who might otherwise remain silent, one may well ask: is it empowerment or is it appropriation? When is the purported empowerment or affirmation just another psychological surrogate, a "feel good" measure, a means by which researchers console themselves for the real imbalances in power that they know—despite all the talk of sisterhood—exist?' (1991:146).

process: 'For no matter how welcome, even enjoyable, the field-worker's presence may appear to "natives", fieldwork represents an intrusion and intervention into a system of relationships, a system of relationships that the researcher is far freer than the researched to leave' (Stacey, 1991:113).

While seductive, sometimes it is simply inappropriate to adopt the inter-actional shared experience/woman-stance approach which characterizes some feminist interpretations of research methodology (Hale, 1991). In con-texts where the researcher and the researched occupy different cultural, class and race positions, sharing a gender is simply not enough, nor as Hale argues is it 'appropriate for the interviewer to want "equal time," or expect to be equally affirmed' (1991:133). To paraphrase Hale, it would have been futile for me to expect personal validation or reinforcement of my work—to 'be addressed as I see myself'—when to these women I represented so many other categories (e.g. white, middle class, square, foreigner etc.). Another way of framing this apparent dilemma is to ask whether it is appropriate to expect that women who have a difficult time just surviving—who face so many problems, risks, and dangers in their everyday lives—should be as involved and invested in this project as one whose future academic career rests on it.[29] Certainly, they were interested—but to a point. To expect any-thing more would amount to little more than the imposition of my own needs for reinforcement and affirmation on my informants. This is a burden that the women who agreed to participate in my study did not undertake to carry.

In the process of fieldwork, the ethnographer also takes away much more than the interview, or what is initially negotiated (and sometimes paid for). The impressions gleaned from ethnographic observations—even prior to negotiations with individual informants—can be just as powerful and inva-sive as transcribed interview material. Patai's account of her initial meeting with a poor Brazilian woman, who died shortly after the initial interview, raises interesting and rarely discussed issues (Patai, 1991:141). Indeed, Patai's questions forced me to confront and, in some instances, to reconsider the use of some of the material I collected. This involved observations and impres-sions gleaned when women were not 'at their best' and hardly in a position to object to, contest or remember—either then or now—my characterizations of them or my descriptions of particular situations. Nowhere was this more apparent than in relation to the use of the deaths of individual women as data. Some of the sad and tragic events that took place within the context of

---

[29] This point is conveyed with acerbic accuracy by Hobbs who writes: '[t]hose they leave behind on the streets, who experience "real life" every day of their existence, find heroic status eluding them in the daily grind of survival, while the ethnographer, who was nearly arrested, almost beaten up, and didn't quite go crazy, builds a career on a youthful flirtation with the terrible immediacy of life amongst the lower orders (1993:62).

the everyday violence in the study site—while they were experienced as painful then and continue to evoke a sense of loss and sorrow—have been constructed here as data.

As I have already noted, five women were killed during the study period. All of them suffered horrible, violent, deaths. Doing research in this context often placed me in a position where I was torn between my own feelings of shock, and in some cases, grief, the feelings of the women as they expressed their pain as well as their anxieties and the very real fear that 'next time it could be me' (i.e. 'them'), and the inevitable realization—not always at the time—that such incidents provided me with research 'opportunities'.[30] This was perhaps most apparent in those instances where collective anguish facilitated the suspension of barriers between the researcher and researched. Watching the news one Sunday night I was distressed to learn that a woman had been raped and subsequently burnt to death in Brooklyn the previous day. She was seven months pregnant. I was sure that it was one of my informants. The next morning Curtis and I met in Manhattan, briefly comforting each other before departing for the field. On our arrival, the women quickly converged on us to share their grief. One woman, Latisha, had been taken by the police to identify the body and she confirmed that it was indeed the woman I had feared for. Later that afternoon, Latisha and I began to organize a collection among the women to provide for a proper funeral. The coming together of the women around this terrible 'tragedy'[31] provided a unique opportunity for me as an ethnographer to gain a number of important insights into their lives.

As feminist researchers, and particularly as those researching relatively powerless or dispossessed women, it is imperative that we do not impose additional burdens or expectations on the women we research. Indeed, ethnographic research, by its very nature, 'exposes subjects to far greater dangers and exploitation than do more positivist, abstract and "masculinist" research methods' (Stacey, 1991:115). The greater the intimacy, the greater the potential dangers and the risk of exploitation. Moreover, such practices may also serve to raise the expectations of 'positive intervention' on the part of women who, by comparison with the researcher, are relatively powerless. As Patai has elaborated, the 'misuse of sentiment as a research tool' poses real dangers (1991:144–5). Neither feminist principles nor a commitment to feminist practices such as 'empowering' or 'dialogic' research can override

[30] Some of these conflicts were akin to the dilemma expressed by Bohannan (aka Bowen) in writing of the death of her Tiv friend in childbirth: 'A cool, objective approach to Amara's death? . . . Was I to stand aloof, observing the course of events? There could be no professional hesitation. Otherwise I might never see the ceremonies connected with death in childbirth' (Bowen, 1954:38).

[31] As it turned out, the deceased was not my informant but another woman who, while known to me, was not a formal participant in the study. Prior to her death, this woman had been staying at Pappy's place, a notorious shooting gallery in the neighbourhood.

the inequities and hierarchical ordering which inhere in researching dispossessed women.

Conclusion

There are no shortcuts to or through women's lives. Ethnography is a 'messy business' and nowhere more so than when it seeks to traverse race, class, and cultural boundaries. It would be less messy if we could just 'cut to the quick' (Fuss, 1989)—get in, get the information and get out—avoid entering the lives of our informants and avoid having them enter ours. The daily field presence, repeated interviews, and sustained observations which constitute this particular ethnography entailed tenuous and often painful human interaction. Despite the everyday violence in which these women's lives are situated—violence from which I have since walked away—being 'there' enriched my life. By forcing me to locate my own history and to confront my own privilege, this ethnographic encounter—its moments of genuine intimacy, powerful emotions, and fragments of inspiration—has left its imprint on my lived experience. I began this project with the firm belief that, in the face of widespread antipathy towards women drug users, and crack users in particular, this research was necessary in order to provide an alternative set of representations. I maintain that belief and have tried to achieve this modest goal without harming my informants or subjecting them to further violence.

Bibliography

Abrahams, R. D. (1976). *Talking Black*, Rowley, MA: Newbury House Publishers.

Abu-Lughod, L. (1988). Fieldwork of a Dutiful Daughter, in S. Altorki and C. El-Solh (eds.) *Studying Your Own Society: Arab Women in the Field*, Syracuse: Syracuse University Press.

Abu-Lughod, L. (1991). Writing Against Culture, in R. G. Fox (ed.) *Recapturing Anthropology: Working in the Present*, Santa Fe, NM: School of American Research Press, pp. 137–62.

Acker, J. (1988). Class, Gender, and the Relations of Distribution, *Signs: Journal of Women in Culture and Society* 13: 473–97.

Adler, F. (1975). *Sisters in Crime: The Rise of the New Female Criminal*, New York: McGraw-Hill.

Adler, P. A. (1985). *Wheeling and Dealing: An Ethnography of an Upper-Level Drug Dealing and Smuggling Community*, New York: Columbia University Press.

Agar, M. (1973). *Ripping and Running: A Formal Ethnography of Urban Heroin Addicts*, New York: Seminar Press.

Agar, M. (1977). Into That Whole Ritual Thing: Ritualistic Drug Use among Urban American Heroin Addicts, in B. du Toit (ed.) *Drugs, Rituals, and Altered States of Consciousness*, Rotterdam: A.A. Balkena.

Aguirre-Molina, M. (1991). Issues for Latinas, in P. Roth (ed.) *Alcohol and Drugs are Women's Issues*, Volume 1: A Review of the Issues, Metuchen, NJ: Women's Action Alliance and The Scarecrow Press Inc., pp. 93–100.

Alden, J. D. (1981). Holding Two Jobs: An Examination of Moonlighting, in S. Henry (ed.) *Informal Institutions*, New York: St. Martins Press, pp. 43–59.

Allen, H. (1987). Rendering Them Harmless: The Professional Portrayal of Women Charged with Serious Violent Crimes, in P. Carlen and A. Worrall (eds.) *Gender, Crime and Justice*, Milton Keynes: Open University Press, pp. 81–94.

Allen, J. (1990). *Sex and Secrets: Crimes Involving Australian Women Since 1880*, Melbourne: Oxford University Press.

Amott, T. L. and Matthaei, J. A. (1991). *Race, Gender and Work: A Multicultural Economic History of Women in the United States*, Boston: South End Press.

Anderson, E. (1990). *Streetwise: Race, Class and Change in an Urban Community*, Chicago: University of Chicago Press.

Anglin, M. D. and Hser, Y. (1987). Addicted Women and Crime, *Criminology* 25(2): 359–97.

Anglin, M. D., Hser, Y., and W. H. McGlothlin (1987). Sex Differences in Addict Careers, 2: Becoming Addicted, *American Journal of Drug and Alcohol Abuse* 13: 253–80.

Arnold, R. A. (1990). Processes of Victimization and Criminalization of Black Women, *Social Justice* 17(3): 153–66.

Auld, J., Dorn, N., and N. South (1986). Irregular Work, Irregular Pleasures: Heroin in the 1980s, in R. Matthews and J. Young (eds.) *Confronting Crime*, London: Sage, pp. 166–87.

Austin, R. (1992). 'The Black Community,' Its Lawbreakers, and a Politics of Identification, *Southern California Law Review* 65: 1769–817.

Ayres, I. and Braithwaite, J. (1992). *Responsive Regulation: Transcending the Deregulation Debate*, New York: Oxford University Press.

Babb, F. E. (1984). Women in the Marketplace: Petty Commerce in Peru, *Review of Radical Political Economics* 16(1): 45–59.

Babb, F. E. (1988). 'From the Field to the Cooking Pot': Economic Crisis and the Threat to Marketers in Peru, in G. Clark (ed.) *Traders Versus the State: Anthropological Approaches to Unofficial Economies*, Boulder, CO: Westview Press, pp. 17–40.

Bailey, V. T. and Waldinger, R. (1991). The Changing Ethnic/Racial Division of Labor, in J. H. Mollenkopf and M. Castells (eds.) *Dual City: Restructuring New York*, New York: Russell Sage Foundation, pp. 43–78.

Baskin, D., Sommers, I., and J. A. Fagan (1993). The Political Economy of Violent Female Street Crime, *Fordham Urban Law Journal* 20: 401–7.

Bearak, B. (1992). A Room for Heroin and HIV, *Los Angeles Times*, 27 September at A1.

Becker, H. (1963). *Outsiders: Studies in the Sociology of Deviance*, New York: Free Press.

Belenko, S. Fagan, J. and K. Chin (1989). Criminal Justice Responses to Crack, *Journal of Research in Crime and Delinquency* 28(1): 55–74.

Belenko, S., Nickerson, G., and T. Rubenstein (1990). *Crack and the New York Courts: A Study of Judicial Responses and Attitudes*, New York: Criminal Justice Agency.

Beller, A. (1984). Trends in Occupational Segregation by Sex and Race, 1960–1981, in B. F. Reskin (ed.) *Sex Segregation in the Workplace*, Washington, DC: National Academy Press.

Benton, L. (1994). Beyond Legal Pluralism: Towards a New Approach to Law in the Informal Sector, *Social and Legal Studies* 3(2): 223–42.

Biernacki, P. (1979). Junkie Work, 'Hustles' and Social Status Among Heroin Addicts, *Journal of Drug Issues* 9: 535–49.

Biernacki, P. and Waldorf, D. (1981). Snowball Sampling: Problems and Techniques of Chain Referral Sampling, *Sociological Methods and Research* 10(2): 141–63.

Binion, V. J. (1979). *Women's Drug Research Project, Addicted Women: Family Dynamics, Self-perceptions and Support Systems*, Rockville, MD: National Institute of Drug Abuse.

Blau, F. D. and Ferber, M. A. (1985). Women in the Labor Market: The Last Twenty Years, in L. Larwood, A. H. Stromberg and B. A. Gutek (eds.) *Women and Work: An Annual Review*, Volume 1, Beverly Hills, CA: Sage, pp. 19–49.

Blauner, R. (1987). Problems of Editing 'First Person' Sociology, *Qualitative Sociology* 10(1): 46–64.

Blauner, R. (1989). *Black Lives, White Lives: Three Decades of Race Relations in America*, Berkeley: University of California Press.

Block, A. A. (1977). Aw! Your Mother's in the Mafia: Women Criminals in Progressive New York, *Contemporary Crises* 1(1): 5–22.

Block, A. A. (1979). The Snowman Cometh: Coke in Progressive Era New York, *Criminology* 17(1): 75–99.

Block, A. A. and Chambliss, W. J. (1981). *Organizing Crime*, New York: Elsevier.

Blom, M. and van den Berg, T. (1989). A Typology of the Life and Work Styles of 'Heroin Prostitutes': From a Male Career Model to a Feminized Career Model, in M. Cain (ed.) *Growing up Good: Policing the Behaviour of Girls in Europe*, Newbury Park, CA: Sage. pp. 55–69.

Blume, S. (1990). Alcohol and Drug Problems in Women: Old Attitudes, New Knowledge, in L. Sederer (ed.) *Treatment Choices for Alcoholism and Substance Abuse*, Lexington, MA: Lexington Books.

Bohannon, P. (1955). Some Principles of Exchange and Investment Among the Tiv, *American Anthropologist* 57: 60–70.

Boissevain, J. (1972). *Network Analysis: Studies in Human Interaction*, The Hague: Mouton.

Boissevain, J. (1974). *Friends of Friends: Networks, Manipulators and Coalitions*, Oxford: Blackwell.

Borjas, G. and Tienda, M. (eds.) (1985). *Hispanics in the U.S. Economy*, New York: Academic Press.

Bourdieu, P. (1977). *Outline of a Theory of Practice*, Cambridge: Cambridge University Press.

Bourdieu, P. and Wacquant, L. J. D. (1992). *An Invitation to Reflexive Sociology*, Cambridge: Polity Press.

Bourgois, P. (1989). In search of Horatio Alger: Culture and Ideology in the Crack Economy, *Contemporary Drug Problems* 16(4): 619–49.

Bourgois, P. (1995). *In Search of Respect: Selling Crack in El Barrio*, New York: Cambridge University Press.

Bourgois, P. (1996). In Search of Masculinity: Violence, Respect and Sexuality among Puerto Rican Crack Dealers in East Harlem, *British Journal of Criminology* 36(3): 412–27.

Bourgois, P. and Dunlap, E. (1993). Exorcising Sex-for-Crack: An

Ethnographic Perspective from Harlem, in M. S. Ratner (ed.) *Crack Pipe as Pimp: An Ethnographic Investigation of Sex-for-Crack Exchanges*, New York: Lexington Books, pp. 97–132.

Bowen, E. S. (1954). *Return to Laughter*, London: Victor Gollancz.

Bowker, L. H. (1978). Women and Drugs—Beyond the Hippie Subculture, in L. H. Bowker (ed.) *Women, Crime and the Criminal Justice System*, Lexington, MA: Lexington Books, pp. 57–9.

Box, S. and Hale, C. (1983). Liberation and Female Criminality in England and Wales, *British Journal of Criminology* 23(1): 35–49.

Boyle, K. and Anglin, M. D. (1993). To the Curb: Sex Bartering and Drug Use Among Homeless Crack Users in Los Angeles, in M. S. Rather (ed.) *Crack Pipe as Pimp: An Ethnographic Investigation of Sex-for-Crack Exchanges*, New York: Lexington Books, pp. 159—86.

Braverman, H. (1974). *Labor and Monopoly Capital: The Degradation of Work in the 20th Century*, New York: Monthly Review Press.

Brodzki, B. and Schenck, C. (eds.) (1988). *Life/lines: Theorizing Women's Autobiography*, Ithaca, NY: Cornell University Press.

Brooklyn AIDS Task Force (1996). *1996 Brooklyn AIDS Fact Sheet*. New York: Brooklyn AIDS Task Force Technical Assistance Project.

Brownmiller, S. (1975). *Against Our Will: Men, Women and Rape*, Harmondsworth: Penguin.

Brunvand, J. H. (1983). *The Vanishing Hitchhiker: Urban Legends and Their Meanings*, London: Picador.

Bujra, J. (1975). Women Entrepreneurs of Early Nairobi, *Canadian Journal of African Studies* 9(2): 213–34.

Bureau of Justice Statistics (1991). *Special Report: Women in Prison*, Washington, DC: US Department of Justice, March.

Bureau of Justice Statistics (1992). *National Update*, Washington, DC: US Department of Justice, April.

Bureau of the Census (1980). *Current Population Reports*, Series P–23, No.107, Families Maintained by Female Householders, 1970–79, Washington DC: US Government Printing Office.

Bureau of the Census (1989a). *Current Population Reports*, Series P–20, No. 441, Households, Families, Marital Status and Living Arrangements, March, 1989. Washington, DC: US Government Printing Office.

Bureau of the Census (1989b). *Money Income of Households, Families, and Persons in the United States: 1987* Series P–60, No. 162, Washington DC: US Government Printing Office.

Bureau of the Census (1990). *Brooklyn in Touch*, Washington, DC: US Government Printing Office.

Burnham, L. (1985). Has Poverty been Feminized in Black America?, *Black Scholar* 16(2): 14–24.

Burt, M. (1991). *Over the Edge: The Growth of Homelessness in the 1980's*, Washington, DC: The Urban Institute.

Burton, L. (1990). Teenage Childbearing as an Alternative Life Course Strategy in Multigenerational Black Families, *Human Nature* 1: 1–37.

Cain, M. (1990). Towards Transgression: New Directions in Feminist Criminology, *International Journal of the Sociology of Law* 18: 1–18.

Campbell, A. (1990). The Invisibility of the Female Delinquent Peer Group, *Women and Criminal Justice* 2(1): 41–62.

Campbell, A. (1992). Untitled Panel Presentation on Girls, Gangs and Violence, paper presented at the Annual Meeting of the American Society of Criminology, New Orleans, November.

Campbell, A. (1993). *Out of Control: Men, Women and Aggression*, London: Pandora.

Campbell, K. E. (1988). Gender Differences in Job-Related Networks, *Work and Occupations* 15: 179–200.

Campbell, K. E., Marsden, P. V., and J. E. Hurlbert (1986). Social Resources and Socio-Economic Status, *Social Networks* 8: 97–117.

Caplan, P. (1988). Engendering Knowledge: The Politics of Ethnography, *Anthropology Today* 4(5): 8–12 and 4(6): 14–17.

Caplan, P. and Bujra, J. M. (eds.) (1978). *Women United, Women Divided: Cross-Cultural Perspectives on Female Solidarity*, London: Tavistock.

Carlen, P. (1988). *Women, Crime and Poverty*, Milton Keynes: Open University Press.

Carlen, P. (1992). Gender, Class, Racism and Criminal Justice: *Against* Global and Gender-Centric Theories; *For* Poststructuralist Perspectives, Paper Presented at the Conference on Inequality, Crime and Punishment, University of Georgia, April.

Carrithers, M. (1988). The Anthropologist as Author, *Anthropology Today* 4(4): 19–22.

Castells, M. and Portes, A. (1989). World Underneath: The Origins, Dynamics, and Effects of the Informal Economy, in A. Portes, M. Castells, and L. A. Benton (eds.) *The Informal Economy: Studies in Advanced and Less Developed Countries*, Baltimore, MD: The John Hopkins University Press, pp. 11–37.

Chambers, C. D. (1974). Narcotic Addiction and Crime: An Empirical Review, in J. A. Inciardi and C. D. Chambers (eds.) *Drugs and the Criminal Justice System*, Beverly Hills, CA: Sage.

Chambliss, W. J. (1978). *On the Take: From Petty Crooks to Presidents*, Bloomington: Indiana University Press.

Chapman, J. R. (1980). *Economic Realities and the Female Offender*, Lexington, MA: Lexington Books.

Chein, I., Gerard, D. L., Lee, R. S. and Rosenfeld E. (1964). *The Road to H: Narcotics, Juvenile Delinquency, and Social Policy*, New York: Basic Books.

Chesney-Lind, M. (1986). Women and Crime: The Female Offender, *Signs: Journal of Women in Culture and Society* 12(1): 78–96.

Chesney-Lind, M. (1995). Rethinking Women's Imprisonment: A Critical Examination of Trends in Female Incarceration, in B. Raffel-Price and N. J. Sokoloff (eds.) *The Criminal Justice System and Women: Offenders, Victims and Workers* (2nd edition), New York: McGraw-Hill, pp. 105–17.

Chesney-Lind, M. and Rodriguez, N. (1983). Women Under Lock and Key: A View From the Inside, *The Prison Journal* 63: 47–65.

Chesney-Lind, M. and Sheldon, R. (1992). *Girls, Delinquency and Juvenile Justice*, Pacific Grove, CA: Brooks/Cole Publishing.

Cheung, Y. W., Erickson, P. G., and T. C. Landau (1991). Experience of Crack Use: Findings from a Community-Based Sample in Toronto, *Journal of Drug Issues* 21(1): 121–40.

Clatts, M. C., Davis, W. R., Deren, S., and S. Tortu (1990). Sex for Crack: The Many Faces of Risk Within the Street Economy of Harlem, paper presented at the Second Annual AIDS Demonstration Conference, Bethesda, MD, November.

Claude, J. (1986). Poverty Patterns for Black Men and Women, *Black Scholar* 17(5): 20–3.

Clifford, J. (1986). On Ethnographic Allegory, in J. Clifford and G. E. Marcus (eds.) *Writing Culture: The Poetics and Politics of Ethnography*, Berkeley: University of California Press, pp. 98–121.

Clifford, J. (1988). *The Predicament of Culture: Twentieth-century Ethnography, Literature and Art*, Cambridge: Harvard University Press.

Clifford, J. and Marcus, G. E. (eds.) (1986). *Writing Culture: The Poetics and Politics of Ethnography*, Berkeley: University of California Press.

Cloward, R. A. and Ohlin, L. E. (1960). *Delinquency and Opportunity*, Glencoe, IL: The Free Press.

Cohen, A. K. (1955). *Delinquent Boys: The Culture of the Gang*, New York: Free Press.

Cohen, B. (1980). *Deviant Street Networks: Prostitution in New York*, Lexington, MA: Lexington Books.

Cohen, J. B., Hauer, L. B., and C. B. Wolfsy (1989). Women and IV Drugs: Parental and Heterosexual Transmission of Human Immunodeficiency Virus, *Journal of Drug Issues* 19(1): 39–56.

Colen, S. (1986). With Respect and Feelings, in J. Cole (ed.) *All American Women: Lines That Divide, Ties That Bind*, New York: Free Press, pp. 46–70.

Colen, S. (1989). Just A Little Respect: West Indian Domestic Workers in New York City, in E. Chaney and M. G. Castro (eds.) *Muchachas No More: Household Workers in Latin America and the Caribbean*, Philadelphia: Temple University Press, pp. 171–96.

Collins, P. Hill (1990). *Black Feminist Thought: Knowledge, Consciousness and the Politics of Empowerment*, Boston: Unwin Hyman.

Colson, E. and Scudder, T. (1988). *For Prayer and Profit: The Ritual,*

Economic and Social Importance of Beer in Gwembe District, Zambia, Stanford, CA: Stanford University Press.

Connell, R. W. (1987). *Gender and Power*, Stanford, CA: Stanford University Press.

Conrad, P. and Schneider, J. W. (1980). *Deviance and Medicalization: From Badness to Sickness*, St. Louis: Mosby.

Cook, D. (1987). Women on Welfare: In Crime or Injustice, in P. Carlen and A. Worrall (eds.) *Gender, Crime and Justice*, Milton Keynes: Open University Press.

Coombs, M. (1996). Interrogating Identity, *Berkeley Women's Law Journal and the African American Law and Policy Report* (Joint Issue), pp. 222–49.

Cooper, H. (1979). Woman as Terrorist, in F. Adler and R. Simon (eds.) *The Criminology of Deviant Women*, Boston: Houghton Mifflin Co.

Corcoran, M. and Parrott, S. (1992). Black Women's Economic Progress, paper presented at Social Science Research Council Conference, Ann Arbor, MI, June.

Correctional Association Reporter, (1991). New York, April.

Courtwright, D., Joseph, H., and D. DesJarlais (1989). *Addicts who Survived: An Oral History of Narcotic Use in America*, Knoxville: University of Tennessee Press.

Covington, J. (1985). Gender Differences in Criminality Among Heroin Users, *Journal of Research in Crime and Delinquency* 22(4): 329–54.

Covington, J. (1988). Crime and Heroin: The Effects of Race and Gender, *Journal of Black Studies* 18: 486–506.

Crenshaw, K. (1989). Demarginalizing the Intersection of Race and Sex: A Black Feminist Critique of Antidiscrimination Doctrine, Feminist Theory, and Antiracist Politics, *University of Chicago Legal Forum*, pp. 139–67.

Crenshaw, K. (1991). Mapping the Margins: Intersectionality, Identity Politics, and Violence Against Women of Color, *Stanford Law Review* 43: 1241–99.

Crites, L. (ed.) (1976). *The Female Offender*, Lexington, MA: Lexington Books.

Curtis, R. (1990). An Ethnographic Study of the Impact of TNT Interventions in Flatbush, unpublished report, New York: Vera Institute of Justice.

Curtis, R. (1993). Drug Distribution in Bushwick, Brooklyn: 1991–2, unpublished manuscript.

Curtis, R. (1996). *An Ethnographic Study of the Effects of the Tactical Narcotics Team on Street-level Drug Markets in Three Police Precincts in Brooklyn*, (Doctoral dissertation, Columbia University), MI: University Microfilms International.

Curtis, R. and Hamid, A. (1997). State-sponsored Violence in New York City and Indigenous Attempts to Contain it: The Mediating Role of the Third Crown (Sgt. at Arms) of the Latin Kings, manuscript submitted for publication.

Curtis, R. and Maher, L. (1993). Highly Structured Crack Markets in the Southside of Williamsburg, Brooklyn, in J. Fagan (ed.) *The Ecology of Crime and Drug Use in Inner Cities*, New York: Social Science Research Council.

Curtis, R. and Sviridoff, M. (1994). The Social Organization of Street-level Drug Markets and its Impact on the Displacement Effect, in R. P. McNamara (ed.) *Crime Displacement: The Other Side of Prevention*, New York: Cummings and Hathaway, pp. 155–71.

Curtis, R., Friedman, S. R., Neaigus, A., Jose, B., Goldstein, M., and G. Ildefonso (1995), Street-level Drug Markets: Network Structure and HIV Risk, *Social Networks* 17: 229–49.

Dai, B. (1937). *Opium Addiction in Chicago*, Montclair, NJ: Patterson Smith.

Daly, K. (1992). Women's Pathways to Felony Court: Feminist Theories of Lawbreaking and Problems of Representation, *Southern California Review of Law and Women's Studies* 2(1): 11–52.

Daly, K. (1993). Class-Race-Gender: Sloganeering in Search of Meaning, *Social Justice* 20(1–2): 56–71.

Daly, K. (1994). Criminal Law and Justice System Practices as Racist, White and Racialized, *Washington and Lee Law Review*, 51(2): 431–64.

Datesman, S. K. (1981). Women, Crime and Drugs, in J. A. Inciardi (ed.) *The Drugs-Crime Connection*, Beverly Hills, CA: Sage.

Davis, A. Y. (1981). *Women, Race and Class*, New York: Random House.

Denzin, N. (1970). *The Research Act*, Chicago: Aldine.

Des Jarlais, D. C., Friedman, S., and D. Strug (1986). AIDS and Needle Sharing Within the IV Drug Use Subculture, in D. Feldman and T. Johnson (eds.) *The Social Dimensions of AIDS: Methods and Theory*, New York: Praeger, pp. 141–60.

Devault, M. L. (1990). Talking and Listening from Women's Standpoint: Feminist Strategies for Interviewing and Analysis, *Social Problems* 37(1): 96–116.

Dex, S. (1987). *Women's Occupational Mobility: A Lifetime Perspective*, London: Macmillan.

di Leonardo, M. (ed.) (1991). *Gender at the Crossroads of Knowledge: Feminist Anthropology in the Postmodern Era*, Berkeley: University of California Press.

Dixon, D. (1991). *From Prohibition to Regulation: Bookmaking, Anti-Gambling and the Law*, Oxford: Clarendon Press.

Dorienger, P. and Piore, M. (1975). *Internal Labor Markets and Manpower Analysis*, Lexington, MA: D.C. Heath.

Douglas, M. (1966). *Purity and Danger*, London: Routledge and Kegan Paul.

Dow, L. M. (1977). High Weeds in Detroit, *Urban Anthropology* 6(2): 111–28.

Drennan, M. (1991). The Decline and Rise of the New York Economy, in

J. H. Mollenkopf and M. Castells (eds.) *Dual City: Restructuring New York*, New York: Russell Sage Foundation, pp. 25–41.

Drug Use Forecasting (1990). *Drugs and Crime in America*, Washington, DC: National Institute of Justice.

Drug Use Forecasting (1991). *Drugs and Crime, 1990: Annual Report*, Washington, DC: National Institute of Justice.

Duelli-Klein, R. (1983). How to Do What We Want to Do: Thoughts About Feminist Methodology, in G. Bowles and R. Duelli-Klein (eds.) *Theories of Women's Studies*, London: Routledge and Kegan Paul.

Duncan, G. D. and Hoffman, S. D. (1989). Teenage Underclass Behavior and Subsequent Poverty: Have the Rules Changed?, paper presented at the Conference on 'The Truly Disadvantaged', Chicago, September.

Dunlap, E. (1991). Shifts and Changes in Drug Subculture Norms and Interaction Patterns, paper presented at the Annual Meeting of the American Society of Criminology, San Francisco, November.

Dunlap, E., Johnson, B. D., Manwar, A., and L. Maher (in press), Who They Are and What They Do: Female Crack Sellers in New York City, *Women and Criminal Justice*.

Easteal, P. (1994). Don't Talk, Don't Touch, Don't Feel: The Dysfunctional Culture of Women's Prisons, *Alternative Law Journal* 19(2): 53–7.

Edlin, B. R., Irwin, K. L., Ludwig, D. D., McCoy, H. V., Serrano, Y., Word, C., Bowser, B. P., Faruque, S., McCoy, C. B., Schilling, R. F., and S. D. Holmberg (1992), High-Risk Sex Behavior Among Young Street-Recruited Crack Cocaine Smokers in Three American Cities: An Interim Report, *Journal of Psychoactive Drugs* 24(4): 363–71.

Edwards, R. (1979). *Contested Terrain: The Transformation of the Workplace in the Twentieth Century*, New York: Basic Books.

Edwards, R., Reich, M., and D. Gordon (eds.) (1975). *Labor Market Segmentation*, Lexington, MA: D.C. Heath.

Eldred, C. A. and Washington, M. M. (1976). Interpersonal Relationships in Heroin Use by Men and Women and their Role in Treatment Outcome, *International Journal of the Addictions* 11: 117–30.

Erickson, P. G. and Murray, G. F. (1989a). Sex Differences in Cocaine Use and Experiences: A Double Standard Revived?, *American Journal of Drug and Alcohol Abuse* 15(2): 135–52.

Erickson, P. G. and Murray, G. F. (1989b). The Undeterred Cocaine User: Intention to Quit and its Relationship to Perceived Legal and Health Threats, *Contemporary Drug Problems* 16(2): 141–56.

Erickson, P. G. and Watson, V. A. (1990). Women, Illicit Drugs and Crime, *Research Advances in Alcohol and Drug Problems*, 10: 251–72.

Etter-Lewis, G. (1991). Black Women's Life Stories: Reclaiming Self in Narrative Texts, in S. B. Gluck and D. Patai (eds.) *Women's Words: The Feminist Practice of Oral History*, New York: Routledge, pp. 43–58.

Ettore, E. (1992). *Women and Substance Abuse*, London: Macmillan

Fagan, J. A. (1989). Editor's Introduction: Myths and Realities About Crack, *Contemporary Drug Problems* 16(4): 527–33.

Fagan, J. A. (1992). Drug Selling and Licit Income in Distressed Neighborhoods: The Economic Lives of Street-level Drug Users and Dealers, in A. Harrell and G. Petersen (eds.) *Drugs, Crime and Social Isolation: Barriers to Urban Opportunity*, Washington DC: Urban Institute Press.

Fagan, J. A. (ed.) (1993). *The Ecology of Crime and Drug Use in Inner Cities*, New York: Social Science Research Council.

Fagan, J. A. (1994). Women and Drugs Revisited: Female Participation in the Cocaine Economy, *Journal of Drug Issues* 24(2): 179–225.

Fagan, J. A. (1995). Women's Careers in Drug Use and Drug Selling, *Current Perspectives on Aging and the Life Cycle* 4: 155–90.

Fagan, J. A. and Chin, K. (1989). Initiation into Crack and Cocaine: A Tale of Two Epidemics, *Journal of Contemporary Drug Problems* 16(4): 579–617.

Fagan, J. A. and Chin, K. (1991). Social Processes of Initiation into Crack, *Journal of Drug Issues* 21(2): 313–43.

Fahim, H. (ed.) (1982). *Indigenous Anthropology in Non-Western Countries*, Durham, NC: Carolina Academic Press.

Fardon, R. (ed.) (1990). *Localising Strategies*, Edinburgh, Scottish Academy Press, cited in J. Okely (1992), Participatory Experience and Embodied Knowledge, in J. Okely and H. Calloway (eds.) *Anthropology as Autobiography*, New York: Routledge, pp. 1–28.

Farley, J. E. (1987). Disproportionate Black and Hispanic Unemployment in US Metropolitan Areas, *American Journal of Economics and Sociology* 46(2): 129–50.

Faupel, C. E. (1991). *Shooting Dope: Career Patterns of Hard-Core Heroin Users*, Gainesville, FL: University of Florida Press.

Feldman, H. W., Agar, M. H., and G. Beschner (1979). *Angel Dust: An Ethnographic Study of PCP Users*, Lexington, MA: Lexington Books.

Feldman, H. W., Espada, F., Penn, S., and S. Byrd (1993). Street Status and the Sex-for-Crack Scene in San Francisco, in M. S. Ratner (ed.) *Crack Pipe as Pimp: An Ethnographic Investigation of Sex-for-Crack Exchanges*, New York: Lexington Books, pp. 133–58.

Ferman, L. A. (1985). The Role of the Informal Economy in the Economic Development of Low Income Neighborhoods, Ann Arbor MI: The Institute of Labor and Industrial Relations, The University of Michigan, unpublished paper.

Ferman, L. A. and Berndt, L. E. (1981). The Irregular Economy, in S. Henry (ed.) *Informal Institutions*, New York: St. Martin's Press, pp. 26–42.

Fiddle, S. (1967). *Portraits From a Shooting Gallery*, New York: Harper and Row.

Fiddle, S. (1976). Sequences in Addiction, *Addictive Diseases: An International Journal* 2(4): 553–68.

Fiege, E. L. (1979). *The Irregular Economy: Its Size and Macro-Economic Implications*, Madison: Social Systems Research Institute, University of Wisconsin.

File, K. N. (1976). Sex Role and Street Roles, *International Journal of the Addictions* 11(2): 263–8.

File, K. N., McCahill, T. W., and L. D. Savitz (1974). Narcotics Involvement and Female Criminality, *Addictive Diseases: An International Journal* 1(2): 177–88.

Finestone, H. (1957). Cats, Kicks and Color, *Social Problems* 5(7): 3–13.

Finkelhor, D. and Baron, L. (1986). Risk Factors for Child Sexual Abuse, *Journal of Interpersonal Violence* 1: 43–71.

Fischer, C. and Oliker, S. (1983). A Research Note on Friendship, Gender, and the Life Cycle, *Social Forces* 62: 124–32.

Fischer, H. C. and Dubois, E. X. (1937). *Sexual Life During the World War*, London: Francis Aldor.

Fitzpatrick, J. P. (1990). Drugs and Puerto Ricans in New York City, in R. Glick and J. Moore (eds.) *Drugs in Hispanic Communities.* New Brunswick, NJ: Rutgers University Press, pp. 103–26.

Fitzpatrick, J. P. and Martin, J. M. (1978). Puerto Rican Addicts and Non-Addicts: A Comparison, New York: Institute for Social Research, Fordham University, unpublished report.

Folb, E. A. (1980). *Runnin' Down Some Lines*, Cambridge: Harvard MA: University Press.

Foucault, M. (1985). *The History of Sexuality, ii. The Use of Pleasure*, New York: Vintage.

Fox, R. G. (ed.) (1991). *Recapturing Anthropology: Working in the Present*, Santa Fe, NM: School of American Research Press.

Frank, A. W. (1990). Bringing Bodies Back In: A Decade in Review, *Theory, Culture and Society* 7: 131–62.

Frank, B. (1987). *Current Drug Use Trends in New York City: December 1987*, New York: New York State Department of Substance Abuse Services.

Frank, B. and Hopkins, W. (1989). Current Drug Use Trends in New York City: June 1989, in Community Epidemiology Work Group, *Epidemiologic Trends in Drug Abuse: Proceedings*, Rockville, MD: National Institute of Drug Abuse.

Frank, G. (1979). Finding the Common Denominator: A Phenomenological Critique of the Life History Method, *Ethos* 7(1): 68–94.

Freeland, J. B. and Campbell, R. S. (1973). The Social Context of First Marijuana Use, *International Journal of the Addictions* 8(2): 317–24.

Friedman, S. R. (1995). Promising Social Network Research Results and Suggestions for a Research Agenda, in R. H. Needle, S. G. Genser and R. T. Trotter (eds.) *Social Networks, Drug Abuse, and HIV Transmission*, NIDA Research Monograph No. 151, Rockville, MD: National Institute on Drug Abuse, pp. 196–215.

Fullilove, M. T. and Fullilove, R. E. (1989). Intersecting Epidemics: Black Teen Crack Use and Sexually Transmitted Diseases, *JAMA* 44(5): 146–53.

Fuss, D. (1989). *Essentially Speaking: Feminism, Nature and Difference*, New York: Routledge.

Gabriel, A. and McAnarney, E. R. (1983). Parenthood in Two Subcultures: White Middle Class Couples and Black Low Income Adolescents in Rochester, New York, *Adolescence* 71: 679–94.

Game, A. and Pringle, R. (1983). *Gender At Work*, Sydney: George Allen and Unwin.

Gaughan, J. P. and Ferman, L. A. (1987). Towards an Understanding of the Informal Economy, *The Annals of the American Academy of Political and Social Sciences* (Special Issue on the Informal Economy) 493: 15–25.

Geertz, C. (1973). *The Interpretation of Cultures*, New York: Basic Books.

Geertz, C. (1988). *Works and Lives: The Anthropologist as Author*, Stanford, CA: Stanford University Press.

Gerstein, D. R., Judd, L. L., and Rovner S. A. (1979). Career Dynamics of Female Heroin Addicts, *American Journal of Drug and Alcohol Abuse* 6(1): 1–23.

Geter, R.S. (1994). Drug User Settings: A Crack House Typology, *The International Journal of the Addictions* 29(8): 1015–27.

Giddens, A. (1984). *The Constitution of Society*, Berkeley: University of California Press.

Gilfus, M. E. (1992). From Victims to Survivors to Offenders: Women's Routes of Entry and Immersion into Street Crime, *Women and Criminal Justice* 4(1): 63–88.

Gilligan, C. (1982). *In a Different Voice: Psychological Theory and Women's Development*, Cambridge: Harvard University Press.

Glaser, B. and Strauss, A. (1970). *The Discovery of Grounded Theory*, Chicago: Aldine.

Glick, R. (1990). Survival, Income and Status: Drug Dealing in the Chicago Puerto Rican Community, in R. Glick and J. Moore (eds.) *Drugs in Hispanic Communities*, New Brunswick, NJ: Rutgers University Press, pp. 77–101.

Glick, R. and Moore, J. (eds.) (1990). *Drugs in Hispanic Communities*, New Brunswick, NJ: Rutgers University Press.

Gluck, S. B. and Patai, D. (eds.) (1991). *Women's Words: The Feminist Practice of Oral History*, New York: Routledge.

Glueck, S. and Glueck, E. (1934). *Five Hundred Delinquent Women*, New York: Alfred Knopf.

Goldberg, G. S. and Kremen, E. (1987). The Feminization of Poverty: Only in America?, *Social Policy* 17: 3–14.

Goldstein, P. J. (1979). *Prostitution and Drugs*, Lexington, MA: Lexington Books.

Goldstein, P. J. (1985). The Drugs/Violence Nexus: A Tripartite Conceptual Framework, *Journal of Drug Issues* 15: 493–506.

Goldstein, P. J. (1990). Female Substance Abusers and Violence, in B. Forster and J. Colman Salloway (eds.) *The Socio-Cultural Matrix of Alcohol and Drug Use: A Sourcebook of Patterns and Factors*, Lewiston, NY: Edwin Meller Press.

Goldstein, P. J., Ouellet, L. J., and Fendrich M. (1992). From Bag Brides to Skeezers: A Historical Perspective on Sex-for-Drugs Behavior, *Journal of Psychoactive Drugs* 24(4): 349–61.

Goldstein P. J., Spunt, B., Belluci, P., and T. Miller (1991a). Frequency of Cocaine Use and Violence: A Comparison Between Men and Women, in S. Schuber and C. Schade (eds.) *The Epidemiology of Cocaine Use and Abuse*, NIDA Research Monograph No. 110, Rockville, MD: National Institute on Drug Abuse, pp. 113–38.

Goldstein, P. J., Spunt, B., Belluci, P., and T. Miller (1991b). Volume of Cocaine Use and Violence: A Comparison Between Men and Women, *Journal of Drug Issues* 21(2): 345–67.

Gomberg, E. S. (1982). Historical and Political Perspective: Women and Drug Use, *Journal of Social Issues* 38: 9–23.

Goode, E. (1970). *The Marijuana Smokers*, New York: Basic Books.

Goode, E. (1984). *Deviant Behavior*, Englewood Cliffs, NJ: Prentice Hall.

Gordon, D. M. (ed.) (1977). *Problems in Political Economy: An Urban Perspective*, Lexington, MA: D.C. Heath.

Gordon, D. M., Edwards, R., and M. Reich (1982). *Segmented Work: Divided Workers.*, New York: Cambridge University Press.

Gramsci, A. (1971). *Selections From the Prison Notebooks*, London: Lawrence and Wishart.

Greenleaf, V. (1989). *Women and Cocaine: Personal Stories of Addiction and Recovery*, Los Angeles: Lowell House.

Grimshaw, J. (1986). *Philosophy and Feminist Thinking*, Minneapolis: University of Minnesota Press.

Grund, J.-P. C. (1993). *Drug Use as a Social Ritual: Functionality, Symbolism and Determinants of Self-Regulation*, Rotterdam: Erasmus University, Instituut voor Verslavingsonderzoek (IVO) Series 4.

Gutmann, P. (1977). The Subterranean Economy, *Financial Analyst's Journal* pp. 26, 27, 34.

Guttmann, P. (1979). The Subterranean Economy, *Tax and Spending* April: 4–11.

Hagan, T. (1988). A Retrospective Search for the Etiology of Drug Abuse: A Background Comparison of a Drug-Addicted Population of Women and a Control Group of Non-Addicted Women, in L. S. Harris (ed.) *Problems of Drug Dependence 1987*, Proceedings of the 49th Annual Scientific Meeting, The Committee on Problems of Drug Dependence, NIDA Research

Monograph No. 81, Rockville, MD: National Institute on Drug Abuse, pp. 254–61.

Hagedorn, J. M. (1988). *People and Folks: Gangs, Crime and the Underclass in a Rustbelt City*, Chicago: Lakeview Press.

Hagedorn, J. M. (1994). Homeboys, Dope Fiends, Legits and New Jacks, *Criminology* 32(2): 197—219.

Hale, S. (1991). Feminist Method, Process, and Self-Criticism: Interviewing Sudanese Women, in S. B. Gluck and D. Patai (eds.) *Women's Words: The Feminist Practice of Oral History*, New York: Routledge, pp. 121–36.

Hamburg, B. A. (1986). Subsets of Adolescent Mothers: Developmental, Biomedical and Psychosocial Issues, in J. Lancaster and B. Hamburg (eds.) *School-Age Pregnancy and Parenthood*, New York: Aldine De Gruyter.

Hamid, A. (1989). Incubation Times and Subsequent Use, paper presented at the Annual Meeting of the American Ethnological Society, Sante Fe, NM, May.

Hamid, A. (1990). The Political Economy of Crack-Related Violence, *Contemporary Drug Problems* 17(1): 31–78.

Hamid, A. (1991a). From Ganja to Crack: Caribbean Participation in the Underground Economy in Brooklyn, 1976–1986, Part 1, Establishment of the Marijuana Economy, *International Journal of the Addictions* 26(6): 615–28.

Hamid, A. (1991b). From Ganja to Crack: Caribbean Participation in the Underground Economy in Brooklyn, 1976–1986, Part 2, Establishment of the Cocaine (and Crack) Economy, *International Journal of the Addictions* 26(7): 729–38.

Hamid, A. (1991c). Crack: New Directions in Drug Research, Part 1, Differences Between the Marijuana Economy and the Cocaine/Crack Economy, *International Journal of the Addictions* 26(8): 825–36.

Hamid, A. (1991d). Crack: New Directions in Drug Research, Part 2, Factors Determining the Current Functioning of the Crack Economy—A Program for Ethnographic Research, *International Journal of the Addictions* 26(9): 913–22.

Hamid, A. (1992a). The Developmental Cycle of a Drug Epidemic: The Cocaine Smoking Epidemic of 1981–1991, *Journal of Psychoactive Drugs* 24(4): 337–48.

Hamid, A. (1992b). Drugs and Patterns of Opportunity in the Inner City, in A. Harrell and G. Peterson (eds.) *Drugs, Crime and Social Isolation: Barriers to Urban Opportunity*. Washington, DC: Urban Institute Press, pp. 209–39.

Hamid, A. (1993). Nickels Markets in Flatbush, in J. Fagan (ed.) *The Ecology of Crime and Drug Use in Inner Cities*, New York: Social Science Research Council.

Hamid, A. (forthcoming). *The Political Economy of Drugs*, New York: Guilford Press.

Hamilton, M. (1993). Sociology—The Poor Relation in Alcohol and Drug Research? *Drug and Alcohol Review* 12: 359–67.

Hammersley, M. and Atkinson, P. (1983). *Ethnography: Principles in Practice,* London: Tavistock.

Harrell, A. and Peterson, G. (eds.) (1992). *Drugs, Crime and Social Isolation: Barriers to Urban Opportunity,* Washington, DC: Urban Institute Press.

Harris, A. R. (1977). Sex and Theories of Deviance, *American Sociological Review* 42: 3–16.

Harrison, B. (1974). *Urban Economic Development,* Washington, DC: The Urban Institute.

Harrison, B. (1977). Institutions on the Periphery, in D. M. Gordon (ed.) *Problems in Political Economy: An Urban Perspective,* Lexington, MA.: D.C. Heath.

Harrison, P. A. (1989). Women In Treatment: Changing Over Time, *International Journal of the Addictions,* 24: 655–73.

Hart, K. (1973). Informal Income Opportunities and Urban Employment in Ghana, *Journal of Modern African Studies* 11: 61–89.

Hart, K. (1987). The State and the Informal Economy, paper presented at the Annual Conference of the Caribbean Studies Association, Belize, May.

Hartmann, H. I. (1979). The Unhappy Marriage of Marxism and Feminism, in L. Sargent (ed.) *Women and Revolution,* New York: Monthly Review Press.

Hartmann, H. I. and Markusen, A. (1980). Contemporary Marxist Theory and Practice: A Feminist Critique, *Review of Radical Political Economics* 12: 87–94.

Hartmann, H. I., Roos, P. A., and D. J. Treiman (1985). An Agenda for Basic Research on Comparable Worth, in H. I. Hartmann (ed.) *Comparable Worth: New Directions for Research,* Washington, DC: National Academy Press.

Hastrup, K. (1992). Writing Ethnography: State of the Art, in J. Okely and H. Callaway (eds.) *Anthropology and Autobiography,* New York: Routledge, pp. 116–33.

Hawkins, J. D. and Fraser, M. W. (1985). The Social Networks of Street Drug Users: A Comparison of Descriptive Propositions from Control and Differential Association Theories, *Social Work Research and Abstracts* 21: 2–43.

Hay, D. (1975). Property, Authority and the Criminal Law, in D. Hay, P. Linebaugh, J. G. Rule, E. P. Thompson and C. Winslow, *Albion's Fatal Tree,* London: Allen Lane, pp. 17–63.

Henry, S. (ed.) (1981). *Can I Have it in Cash?,* London: Astragal Books.

Henry, S. (ed.) (1981). *Informal Institutions,* New York: St. Martin's Press.

Henry, S. (1982). The Working Unemployed: Perspectives on the Informal Economy and Unemployment, *Sociological Review* 30: 460–77.

Henry, S. (1988). Can the Hidden Economy be Revolutionary? Towards a Dialectical Analysis of the Relations between Formal and Informal Economies, *Social Justice* 15(3–4): 29–59.

Hillsman, S. (1992). *The Community Effects of Street Level Narcotics Enforcement: A Study of the New York City Police Department's Tactical Narcotics Teams*, Interim Report, New York: Vera Institute of Justice.

Hobbs, D. (1993). Peers, Careers, and Academic Fears: Writing As Field-Work, in D. Hobbs and T. May (eds.) *Interpreting the Field: Accounts of Ethnography*, Oxford: Clarendon Press, pp. 45–64.

Hoffman, L. and Culley, M. (eds.) (1985). *Women's Personal Narratives: Essays in Criticism and Pedagogy*, New York: Modern Language Association.

Hoigard, C. and Finstad, L. (1992), (trans. K. Hanson, N. Sipe and B. Wilson). *Backstreets: Prostitution, Money and Love*, Oxford: Polity Press.

hooks, b. (1984). *Black Feminist Theory: From Margin to Center*, Boston: South End Press.

hooks, b. (1989). *Talking Back: Thinking Feminist, Thinking Black*, Boston: South End Press.

hooks, b. (1990). *Yearning: Race, Gender and Cultural Politics*, Boston: South End Press.

Hoyman, M. (1987). Female Participation in the Informal Economy: A Neglected Issue, *The Annals of the American Academy of Political and Social Science* (Special Issue on the Informal Economy) 493: 64–82.

Hser, Y., Anglin, M. D., and M. W. Booth (1987). Sex Differences in Addict Careers, 3: Addiction, *American Journal of Drug and Alcohol Abuse* 13(3): 231–51.

Hser, Y., Anglin, M. D., and W. H. McGlothlin (1987). Sex Differences in Addict Careers, 1: Initiation of Use, *American Journal of Drug and Alcohol Abuse* 13(1): 33–57.

Hunt, D. (1990). Drugs and Consensual Crimes: Drug Dealing and Prostitution, in J. Q. Wilson and M. Tonry (eds.) *Drugs and Crime*, (Crime and Justice, Volume 13), Chicago: University of Chicago Press.

Hurley, D. (1991). Women, Alcohol and Incest: An Analytical Review, *Journal of Studies on Alcohol* 52(3): 253–62.

Hussey, M. and Petchers, M. (1989). The Relationship between Sexual Abuse and Substance Abuse among Psychiatrically Hospitalized Adolescents, *Child Abuse and Neglect* 13: 319–25.

Ianni, F. A. J. (1974). New Mafia: Black, Hispanic and Italian Styles, *Social Science and Modern Society* March/April: 26–39.

Ianni, F. A. J. and Ianni, E. R. (1972). *A Family Business*, London: Routledge and Kegan Paul.

Iglehart, A. S. (1985). Brickin' It and Going to the Pan: Vernacular in the Black Inner-City Heroin Lifestyle, in B. Hanson, G. Beschner, J. M. Walters, and E. Bovelle (eds.) *Life with Heroin: Voices from the Inner City*, Lexington MA: D.C. Heath.

Inciardi, J. A. (1972). The Poly-Drug Abuser: A New Situational Offender, in F. Adler and G. O. W. Mueller (eds.) *Politics, Crime and the*

International Scene: An Inter-American Focus. San Juan, Puerto Rico: North-South Center for Technical and Cultural Exchange, pp. 60–8.

Inciardi, J. A. (1986). *The War on Drugs: Heroin, Cocaine and Public Policy*, Palo Alto, CA: Mayfield.

Inciardi, J. A. (1987). Beyond Cocaine: Basuo, Crack and Other Coca Products, *Contemporary Drug Problems* 14: 461–92.

Inciardi, J. A. (1989). Trading Sex for Crack among Juvenile Crack Users: A Research Note, *Contemporary Drug Problems* 16(4): 689–700.

Inciardi, J. A. and Pottieger, A. E. (1986). Drug Use and Crime Among Two Cohorts of Women Narcotics Users: An Empirical Assessment, *Journal of Drug Issues* 16: 91–106.

Inciardi, J. A., Lockwood, D., and A. E. Pottieger (1993). *Women and Crack Cocaine*, New York: Macmillan.

Inciardi, J. A., Pottieger, A. E., and C. E. Faupel (1982). Black Women, Heroin and Crime: Some Empirical Notes, *Journal of Drug Issues* 14: 91–106.

Inciardi, J. A., Pottieger, A. E., Forney, M. A., Chitwood, D. D., and D. C. McBride (1990). Prostitution, IV Drug Use, and Sex-for-Crack Exchanges Among Serious Delinquents: Risks for HIV Infection, *Criminology* 29(2): 221–35.

James, J. (1976). Prostitution and Addiction: An Interdisciplinary Approach. *Addictive Diseases: An International Journal* 2(4): 601–18.

James, J., Gosho, C., and R. W. Wohl (1979). The Relationship Between Female Criminality and Drug Use, *International Journal of the Addictions* 14(2): 215–19.

Jensen, G. and Tienda, M. (eds.) (1988). *Divided Opportunities: Minorities, Poverty and Social Policy,* New York: Plenum Press.

Jewell, K. S. (1988). *Survival of the Black Family: The Institutional Impact of US Social Policy*, New York: Praeger.

Jiminez, J. B. (1989). Cocaine, Informality, and the Urban Economy in La Paz, Bolivia, in A. Portes, M. Castells, and L. A. Benton (eds.) *The Informal Economy: Studies in Advanced and Less Developed Countries*, Baltimore, MD: The Johns Hopkins University Press, pp. 135–48.

Johnson, B. D. (1991). The Crack Era in New York City, *Addiction and Recovery*, May/June: 24–7.

Johnson, B. D., Goldstein, P. J., Preble, E., Schmeidler, J., Lipton, D. S., Spunt, B., and T. Miller (1985). *Taking Care of Business: The Economics of Crime by Heroin Abusers*, Lexington, MA: Lexington Books.

Johnson, B. D., Hamid, A., and E. Morales (1987). Critical Dimensions of Crack Distribution, paper presented at the Annual Meeting of the American Society of Criminology, Montreal, November.

Johnson, B. D., Hamid, A., and H. Sanabria (1992). Emerging Models of Crack Distribution, in T. M. Mieczkowski (ed.) *Drugs and Crime: A Reader*, Boston: Allyn and Bacon, pp. 56–78.

Johnson, B. D., Natarajan, M., Dunlap, E., and E. Elmoghazy (1994). Crack Abusers and Noncrack Abusers: Profiles of Drug Use, Drug Sales and Nondrug Criminality, *Journal of Drug Issues* 24(1): 117–41.

Johnson, B. D., Williams, T., Dei, K., and H. Sanabria (1990). Drug Abuse and the Inner City: Impact on Hard Drug Users and the Community, in M. Tonry and J. Q. Wilson (eds.) *Drugs and Crime*, (Crime and Justice, Volume 13), Chicago: University of Chicago Press, pp. 9–67.

Kalant, O. J. (translator) (1987). *Maier's Cocaine Addiction [Der Kokainismus 1926]*, Toronto: Addiction Research Foundation.

Kandel, D. B. and Davies, M. (1991). Friendship Networks, Intimacy and Illicit Drug Use in Young Adulthood: A Comparison of Two Competing Theories, *Criminology* 29(3): 441–67.

Kane, H. H. (1881). *Opium Smoking in America and China*, New York: G. P. Putnam's.

Kanter, R. M. (1977). *Men and Women of the Corporation*, New York: Basic Books.

Kanter, R. M. (1981). Women and the Structure of Organizations: Explorations in Theory and Behavior, in O. Grusky and G. A. Miller (eds.) *The Sociology of Organizations: Basic Studies*, New York: Free Press.

Kasarda, J. E. (1992). The Severely Distressed in Economically Transforming Cities, in A. Harrell and G. Petersen (eds.) *Drugs, Crime and Social Isolation: Barriers to Urban Opportunity*, Washington, DC: Urban Institute Press.

Kasinitz, P. (1992). *Caribbean New York: Black Immigrants and the Politics of Race*, Ithaca, NY: Cornell University Press.

Katz, J. (1988). *Seductions of Crime*, New York: Basic Books.

Katz, J. (1991). The Motivation of the Persistent Robber, in M. Tonry (ed.) *Crime and Justice: A Review of Research*, (*Crime and Justice* Volume 14), Chicago: University of Chicago Press, pp. 277–306.

Kenna, M. E. (1992). Changing Places and Altered Perspectives: Research on a Greek Island in the 1960s and in the 1980s, in J. Okely and H. Callaway (eds.) *Anthropology and Autobiography*, New York: Routledge, pp. 147–62.

King, D. K. (1988). Multiple Jeopardy, Multiple Consciousness: The Context of a Black Feminist Ideology, *Signs: Journal of Women in Culture and Society*, 14(1): 42–72.

Kirschenman, J. (1991). Gender within Race in the Labor Market, paper presented at the Urban Poverty and Family Life Conference, Chicago October.

Kleiman, M. R. (1992). *Against Excess: Drug Policy for Results*, New York: Basic Books.

Klein, D. and Kress, J. (1976). Any Woman's Blues: A Critical Overview of Women, Crime and the Criminal Justice System, *Crime and Social Justice* 5: 34–49.

Klovdahl, A. S., Potterat, J. J., Woodhouse, D. E., Muth, J. B., Muth, S. Q., and W. W. Darrow (1994). Social Networks and Infectious Disease: The Colorado Springs Study, *Social Science and Medicine* 38: 79–88.

Kochman, T. (1972). The Kinetic Element in Black Idiom, in T. Kochman (ed.) *Rappin' and Stylin' Out*, Urbana: University of Illinois Press.

Koester, S. and Schwartz, J. (1993). Crack, Gangs, Sex and Powerlessness: A View from Denver, in M. S. Ratner (ed.) *Crack Pipe as Pimp: An Ethnographic Investigation of Sex-for-Crack Exchanges*, New York: Lexington Books, pp. 187–203.

Kohn, M. (1992). *Dope Girls: The Birth of the British Drug Underground*, London: Lawrence and Wishart.

Kolata, G. (1989). Despite its Promise of Riches, the Crack Trade Seldom Pays, *New York Times*, 26 November at A1.

Krohn, M. and Thornberry, T. (1991). Network Theory: A Model for Understanding Drug Abuse Among African-American and Hispanic Youth, Working Paper Number 10, Albany, New York, Hindelang Criminal Justice Research Center.

Ladner, J. A. (1971). *Tomorrow's Tomorrow: The Black Woman*, Garden City, NY: Doubleday and Company.

Lapham, L. H. (1989). A Political Opiate: The War on Drugs is a Folly and a Menace, *Harpers*, December.

Lee, F. R. (1991). For Gold Earrings and Protection, More Girls Take Road to Violence, *New York Times*, 25 November at A1.

Lemert, E. M. (1951). *Social Pathology*, New York: McGraw-Hill.

Liebow, E. (1967). *Tally's Corner: A Study of Negro Streetcorner Men*, Boston: Little Brown and Company.

Limon, J. E. (1991). Representation, Ethnicity, and the Precursory Ethnography: Notes of a Native Anthropologist, in R. G. Fox (ed.) *Recapturing Anthropology: Working in the Present*. Santa Fe, NM: School of American Research Press, pp. 115–35.

Lindesmith, A. R. (1967). *The Addict and the Law*, Bloomington: Indiana University Press.

Logio-Rau, K. A. (1994). Women, Drugs and Prostitution: The Impact of Race and Ethnicity, paper presented at the 64th Annual Meeting of the Eastern Sociological Society, Baltimore, March.

Long, J. (1990). Drug Use Patterns in Two Los Angeles Barrio Gangs, in R. Glick and J. Moore (eds.) *Drugs in Hispanic Communities*, New Brunswick, NJ: Rutgers University Press.

Lorde, A. (1984). *Sister Outsider*, Freedom, CA: The Crossing Press.

Lowenthal, M. D. (1975). The Social Economy in Urban Working-Class Communities, in G. Gappert and H. M. Rose (eds.) *The Social Economy of Cities*, Beverly Hills, CA: Sage.

Lowenthal, M. D. (1981). Non-market Transactions in an Urban Community, in S. Henry (ed.) *Can I Have it in Cash?*, London: Astragal Books.

Lubiano, W. (1993). Black Ladies, Welfare Queens and State Minstrels: Ideological Warfare by Narrative Means, in T. Morrison (ed.) *Race-ing*

Justice, En-Gendering Power: Essays on Anita Hill, Clarence Thomas and the Construction of Social Reality, London: Chatto and Windus, pp. 323–63.

Lundgren-Gaveras, L. (1991). Informal Network Support, Public Welfare Support and the Labor Force Activity of Urban Low-Income Single Mothers, paper presented at the Chicago Urban Poverty and Family Life Conference, Chicago October.

McCall, G. J. (1978). *Observing the Law: Field Methods in the Study of Crime and the Criminal Justice System,* New York: Free Press.

McClintock, A. (1993). Sex Workers and Sex Work: Introduction, *Social Text*, 37: 1–10.

McCrohan, K. F. and Smith, J. D. (1986). A Consumer Expenditure Approach to Estimating the Size of the Underground Economy, *Journal of Marketing* 50: 48–60.

McLanahan, S. S., Sorensen, A., and D. Watson (1989). Sex Differences in Poverty 1950–1980, *Signs: Journal of Women in Culture and Society* 15(1): 102–22.

McRobbie, A. (1982). The Politics of Feminist Research: Between Talk, Text and Action, *Feminist Review* 12: 46–57.

MacGaffey, J. (1987). *Entrepreneurs and Parasites: The Struggle for Indigenous Capitalism in Zaire*, New York: Cambridge University Press.

Madonna (1990). *Vogue*, Warner Bros. Records.

Maher, L. (1990). Criminalizing Pregnancy: The Downside of A Kinder Gentler Nation, *Social Justice* 17(3): 111–35.

Maher, L. (1992a) Punishment and Welfare: Crack Cocaine and the Regulation of Mothering, *Women and Criminal Justice* 3(2): 35–70.

Maher, L. (1992b). Reconstructing the Female Criminal: Women and Crack Cocaine, *Southern California Review of Law and Women's Studies* 2(1): 131–54.

Maher, L. (1995a). In the Name of Love: Women and Initiation to Illicit Drugs, in R. Dobash, R. Dobash and L. Noaks (eds.) *Gender and Crime*, Cardiff: University of Wales Press, pp. 132–66.

Maher, L. (1995b). Dope Girls: Gender, Race and Class in the Drug Economy, (Doctoral dissertation, Rutgers University), Ann Arbour, MI: University Microfilms International.

Maher, L. (1996). Hidden in the Light: Discrimination and Occupational Norms Among Crack Using Street-level Sexworkers, *Journal of Drug Issues* 26(1): 145–75.

Maher, L. and Curtis, R. (1992). Women on the Edge of Crime: Crack Cocaine and the Changing Contexts of Street-level Sex Work in New York City, *Crime, Law and Social Change* 18(3): 221–58.

Maher, L. and Curtis, R. (1995). In Search of the Female Urban Gangsta: Change, Culture and Crack Cocaine, in B. Raffel-Price and N. J. Sokoloff (eds.) *The Criminal Justice System and Women: Offenders, Victims and Workers* (2nd edition), New York: McGraw-Hill, pp.147–66.

Maher, L. and Daly, K. (1996). Women in the Street-level Drug Economy: Continuity or Change?, *Criminology* 34(4): 465–91.

Maher, L. and Waring, E. J. (1990). Beyond Simple Differences: White Collar Crime, Gender and Workforce Position, *Phoebe: An Interdisciplinary Journal of Feminist Scholarship, Theory and Aesthetics* 2(1): 44–54.

Maher, L., Dunlap, E., and Johnson, B. D. (1997). Black Women's Pathways to Involvement in Illicit Drug Distribution and Sales: An Ethnographic Analysis, manuscript submitted for publication.

Maher, L., Dunlap, E., Johnson, B. D., and Hamid, A.(1996). Gender, Power, and Alternative Living Arrangements in the Inner-City Crack Culture, *Journal of Research on Crime and Delinquency* 33(2): 181–205.

Mahood, L. (1990). *The Magdalenes: Prostitution in the Nineteenth Century*, New York: Routledge.

Malahleha, G. M. (1984). An Ethnographic Study of Shebeens in Lesotho, Unpublished Ph.D. Thesis, Department of Sociology, University of Surrey.

Maloff, D., Becker, H. S., Fonaroff, P. and J. Rodin (1979). Informal Social Controls and Their Influence on Substance Use, *Journal of Drug Issues* 9: 161–84.

Malveaux, J. (1990). Gender Difference and Beyond: An Economic Perspective on Diversity and Commonality Among Women, in D. L. Rhode (ed.) *Theoretical Perspectives on Sexual Difference*. New Haven: Yale University Press.

Mann, C. R. (1987). Black Women who Kill, in R. L. Hampton (ed.) *Violence in the Black Family*, Lexington, MA: Lexington Books..

Mare, R. and Winship, C. (1988). Ethnic and Racial Patterns of Educational Attainment and School Enrollment, in G. Jensen and M. Tienda (eds.) *Divided Opportunities: Minorities, Poverty and Social Policy*, New York: Plenum Press.

Marsden, P. V. (1987). Core Discussion Networks of Americans, *American Sociological Review* 52: 122–31.

Mattera, P. (1985). *Off the Books: The Rise of the Underground Economy*, London: Pluto Press.

Messerschmidt, J. W. (1986). *Capitalism, Patriarchy and Crime*, Totawa, NJ: Rowan and Littlefield.

Messerschmidt, J. W. (1993). *Masculinities and Crime*, Lanham, MD: Rowan and Littlefield.

Mieczkowski, T. (1986). Geeking Up and Throwing Down: Heroin Street Life in Detroit, *Criminology* 24(4): 645–66.

Mieczkowski, T. (1990). Crack Dealing on the Street: An Exploration of the YBI Hypothesis and the Detroit Crack Trade, paper presented at the Annual Meeting of the American Society of Criminology, Baltimore, November.

Mieczkowski, T. (1994). The Experiences of Women Who Sell Crack: Some Descriptive Data from the Detroit Crack Ethnography Project, *Journal of Drug Issues* 24(2): 227–48.

Mieczkowski, T. M. (ed.) (1991). *Drugs and Crime: A Reader*, Boston: Allyn and Bacon.

Miller, B. A., Downs, W. R., Gondoli, D. M, and A. Keil (1987). The Role of Childhood Sexual Abuse in the Development of Alcoholism in Women, *Violence and Victims* 2(3): 157–72.

Miller, E. (1986). *Street Woman*, Philadelphia: Temple University Press.

Miller, J. (1993). Gender and Power on the Streets: The Ecology of Street Prostitution in an Era of Crack Cocaine, unpublished paper.

Miller, W. B. (1958). Lower Class Culture as a Generating Milieu of Gang Delinquency, *Journal of Social Issues* 14: 5–19.

Millman, M. (1975). She Did it All for Love: A Feminist View of the Sociology of Deviance, in M. Millman and R. Moss Kanter (eds.) *Another Voice: Feminist Perspectives on Social Life and Social Science*, New York: Anchor Books, pp. 251–79.

Mingione, E. (1985). Social Reproduction of the Surplus Labour Force: The Case of 'Southern Italy', in N. Redclift and E. Mingione (eds.) *Beyond Employment*, Oxford: Blackwell.

Mintz, S. (1971). Men, Women and Trade, *Comparative Studies in Society and History* 13: 247–68.

Mitchell, J. C. (1969). *Social Networks and Urban Situations*, Manchester: Manchester University Press.

Mitchell-Kernan, C. (1972). Signifying and Macking: Two Afro-American Speech Acts, in J. Gumperz and D. Hymes (eds.) *Directions in Socio-Linguistics: The Ethnography of Communication*, New York: Holt, Rhinehart and Winston, pp. 161–79.

Mollenkopf, J. H. and Castells, M. (eds.) (1991). *Dual City: Restructuring New York*, New York: Russell Sage Foundation.

Mondanaro, J. (1989). *Chemically Dependent Women: Assessment and Treatment*, Lexington, MA: Lexington Books.

Moore, D. (1992). Deconstructing 'Dependence': An Ethnographic Critique of an Influential Concept, *Contemporary Drug Problems* 19: 459–90.

Moore, G. (1990). Structural Determinants of Men's and Women's Personal Networks, *American Sociological Review* 55: 726–35.

Moore, J. W. (1990). Mexican American Women Addicts: The Influence of Family Background, in R. Glick and J. Moore (eds.) *Drugs in Hispanic Communities*, New Brunswick, NJ: Rutgers University Press, pp. 127–53.

Moore, J. W. (1991). *Going Down to the Barrio: Homeboys and Homegirls in Change*, Philadelphia: Temple University Press.

Moore, J. W. and Devitt, M. (1989) Addicted Mexican-American Mothers, *Gender & Society*, 3: 53–78.

Moore, K. A. and Waite, L. J. (1977). Early Childbearing and Educational Attainment, *Family Planning Perspectives* 9: 220–5.

Morningstar, P. J. and Chitwood, D. D. (1987). How Women and Men Get

Cocaine: Sex-Role Stereotypes and Acquisition Patterns, *Journal of Psychoactive Drugs* 19(2): 135–42.

Morris, A. (1987). *Women, Crime and Criminal Justice*, Oxford: Basil Blackwell.

Mort, F. (1987). *Dangerous Sexualities: Medico-Moral Panics in England Since 1830*, London: Routledge.

Mott, F. L. and Maxwell, N. L. (1981). School-Age Mothers: 1968 and 1979, *Family Planning Perspectives* 13: 287–92.

Murphy, S. (1991). Maternal Crack/Cocaine Use: Ethnographic Reports, paper presented at the Annual Meetings, American Society of Criminology, San Francisco, November.

Murphy, S. and Rosenbaum, M. (1992). Women Who Use Cocaine Too Much: Smoking Crack vs. Snorting Cocaine, *Journal of Psychoactive Drugs* 24(4): 381–8.

Murphy, S. and Waldorf, D. (1991). Kickin' Down to the Street Doc: Shooting Galleries in the San Francisco Bay Area, *Contemporary Drug Problems* 18(1): 9–29.

Musto, D. F. (1973). *The American Disease: Origins of Narcotic Control*, New Haven: Yale University Press.

Naffine, N. (1985). The Masculinity-Femininity Hypothesis: A Consideration of Gender-based Personality Theories of Female Crime, *British Journal of Criminology* 25(4): 365–81.

Naffine, N. (1986). Women and Crime, in D. Chappell and P. Wilson (eds.) *The Australian Criminal Justice System*, Sydney: Butterworths.

Naffine, N. (1987). *Female Crime: The Construction of Women in Criminology*, Sydney: Allen and Unwin.

Neaigus, A., Friedman, S. R., Curtis, R., Des Jarlais, D. C., Furst, R. T., Jose, B., Mota, P., Stepherson, B., Sufian, M., Ward, T., and J. W. Wright (1994). The Relevance of Drug Injectors' Social Networks and Risk Networks for Understanding and Preventing HIV Infection, *Social Science and Medicine* 38: 67–78.

Needle, R. H., Genser, S. G., and R. T. Trotter (eds.) (1995) *Social Networks, Drug Abuse, and HIV Transmission*, NIDA Research Monograph No. 151, Rockville, MD: National Institute on Drug Abuse.

Nelli, H. S. (1976). *The Business of Crime: Italians and Syndicate Crime in the United States*, New York: Oxford University Press.

Nelson, N. (1978). 'Women Must Help Each Other': The Operation of Personal Networks Among Buzaa Beer Brewers in Mathare Valley, Kenya, in P. Caplan and J. M. Bujra (eds.) *Women United, Women Divided: Cross-Cultural Perspectives on Female Solidarity*, London: Tavistock, pp. 77–98.

New York City Department of Planning (1993) *Community District Needs Fiscal Year, 1993*, New York: Department of City Planning.

New York State Department of Correctional Services (1988). *Female New*

Court Commitments 1976–1987. Albany NY: Division of Program Planning, Research and Evaluation.

New York State Department of Correctional Services (1990a). *Female Drug Commitment Population 1987–1989*, Albany NY: Division of Program Planning, Research and Evaluation.

New York State Department of Correctional Services (1990b). *Identified Substance Abusers*, Albany NY: Division of Program Planning, Research and Evaluation.

O'Donnell, J. A. (1969). *Narcotic Addicts in Kentucky*. Washington, DC: US Government Printing Office.

O'Neill, J. (1985). Role Differentiation and the Gender Gap in Wage Rates, in L. Larwood, A. H. Stromberg, and B. A. Gutek (eds.) *Women and Work: An Annual Review*, Volume 1. Beverly Hills, CA: Sage, pp. 50–75.

Oakley, A. (1981). Interviewing Women: A Contradiction in Terms, in H. Roberts (ed.) *Doing Feminist Research*, London: Routledge and Kegan Paul, pp. 30–61.

Ohnuki-Tierney, E. (1984). Native Anthropologists, *American Ethnologist* 11(3): 584–6.

Okely, J. (1992). Anthropolgy and Autobiography: Participatory Experience and Embodied Knowledge. In J. Okely and H. Callaway (eds.) *Anthroplogy & Autobiography*, New York: Routledge, pp. 1–28.

Okely, J. (1996). *Own or Other Culture*, London: Routledge.

Okely, J. and Callaway, H. (eds.) (1992). *Anthropology and Autobiography*, New York: Routledge.

Oppenheimer, E. (1989). Young Female Drug Misusers: Towards an Appropriate Policy, in M. Cain (ed.) *Growing up Good: Policing the Behaviour of Girls in Europe*, Newbury Park, CA: Sage, pp. 177–96.

Ouellet, L. J., Wiebel, W. W., Jiminez, A. D., and W. A. Johnson (1993). Crack Cocaine and the Transformation of Prostitution in Three Chicago Neighborhoods, in M. S. Ratner (ed.) *Crack Pipe as Pimp: An Ethnographic Investigation of Sex-for-Crack Exchanges*, New York: Lexington Books, pp. 69–96.

Padilla, F. (1992). *The Gang as an American Enterprise*, New Brunswick, NJ: Rutgers University Press.

Pahl, R. E. (1980). Employment, Work and the Domestic Division of Labour, *International Journal of Urban and Regional Research* 4: 1–20.

Pahl, R. E. (1984). *Divisions of Labour*, New York: Basil Blackwell.

Pahl, R. E. (1988). Some Remarks on Informal Work, Social Polarization and the Social Structure, *International Journal of Urban and Regional Research* 12: 247–67.

Painter, N. I. (1979). *The Narrative of Hosea Hudson*, Cambridge MA: Harvard University Press.

Parker, H., Bakx, K., and R. Newcombe (1988). *Living With Heroin*, Milton Keynes: Open University Press.

Patai, D. (1991). US Academics and Third World Women: Is Ethical Research Possible?, in S. B. Gluck and D. Patai (eds.) *Women's Words: The Feminist Practice of Oral History*, New York: Routledge, pp. 137–53.

Pearson, G. (1987). *The New Heroin Users*, Oxford: Basil Blackwell.

Perlman, J. E. (1976). *The Myth of Marginality: Urban Poverty and Politics in Rio de Janeiro*, Berkeley: University of California Press.

Perry, L. (1979). *Women and Drug Use: An Unfeminine Dependancy*. London: Institute for the Study of Drug Dependancy.

Perry, L. (1987). Fit to be Parents? *Druglink*, Jan/Feb: 6.

Pettiway, L. E. (1987). Participation in Crime Partnerships by Female Drug Users: The Effects of Domestic Arrangements, Drug Use, and Criminal Involvement, *Criminology* 25(3): 741–66.

Phoenix, A. (1988). Narrow Definitions of Culture: The Case of Early Motherhood, in S. Westwood and P. Bhachu (eds.) *Enterprising Women: Ethnicity, Economy and Gender Relations*, London: Routledge.

Pinkney, A. (1984). *The Myth of Black Progress*, New York: Cambridge University Press.

Piore, M. J. (1977). The Dual Labor Market: Theory and Implications, in D. M. Gordon (ed.) *Problems in Political Economy: An Urban Perspective*, Lexington, MA: D.C. Heath.

Polanyi, K. (1957). The Economy As Instituted Process, in K. Polanyi, C. M. Arensberg, and H. W. Pearson (eds.) *Trade and Market in Early Empires*, Glencoe, IL: Free Press.

Polanyi, K., Arensberg, C. M., and H. W. Pearson (eds.) (1957). *Trade and Market in Early Empires*, Glencoe, IL: Free Press.

Portes, A. and Borocz, J. (1988). The Informal Sector under Capitalism and State Socialism: A Preliminary Comparison, *Social Justice* 15(3–4): 17–28.

Portes, A., Castells, M., and L. A. Benton (eds.) (1989). *The Informal Economy: Studies in Advanced and Less Developed Countries*, Baltimore: The Johns Hopkins University Press.

Portes, A., Castells, M., and L. A. Benton (1989). Conclusion: The Policy Implications of Informality, in A. Portes, M. Castells, and L. A. Benton (eds.) *The Informal Economy: Studies in Advanced and Less Developed Countries*, Baltimore: The Johns Hopkins University Press, pp. 298–311.

Portes, A. and Sassen-Koob, S. (1987). Making It Underground: Comparative Material on the Informal Sector in Western Market Economies, *American Journal of Sociology* 93: 30–61.

Powell, D. (1993). *Out West: Perceptions of Sydney's Western Suburbs*, Sydney: Allen and Unwin.

Preble, E. and Casey, J. (1969). Taking Care of Business: The Heroin User's Life on the Street, *International Journal of the Addictions* 4: 1–24.

Puyo, A. M. (1979). Family Headship and Drug Addiction Among Male Puerto Rican Youths: An Investigation of Quality of Family Life,

(Doctoral dissertation, Fordham University), Ann Arbour, MI: University Microfilms International.

Rabinow, P. (1977). *Reflections on Fieldwork in Morocco*, Berkeley: University of California Press.

Rainwater, L. (1966). Crucible of Identity: The Negro Lower-class Family, in T. Parsons and K. Clark (eds.) *The Negro American*, Boston: Houghton Mifflin Company.

Ratner, M. S. (ed.) (1993a). *Crack Pipe as Pimp: An Ethnographic Investigation of Sex-for-Crack Exchanges*, New York: Lexington Books.

Ratner, M. S. (1993b). Sex, Drugs and Public Policy: Studying and Understanding the Sex-for-Crack Phenomenon, in M. S. Ratner (ed.) *Crack Pipe as Pimp: An Ethnographic Investigation of Sex-for-Crack Exchanges*, New York: Lexington Books, pp. 1–36.

Reed, B. G. (1991). Linkages: Battering, Sexual Assault, Incest, Child Sexual Abuse, Teen Pregnancy, Dropping out of School and the Alcohol and Drug Connection, in P. Roth (ed.) *Alcohol and Drugs Are Women's Issues*, Volume 1: A Review of the Issues, Metuchen, NJ: Women's Action Alliance and The Scarecrow Press Inc. pp. 130–49.

Reinarman, C. R. and Levine, H. G. (1989). Crack in Context: Politics and Media in the Making of a Drug Scare, *Contemporary Drug Problems*, 16(4): 535–77.

Reskin, B. and Hartman, H. (1986). *Women's Work, Men's Work*. Washington, DC: National Academy Press.

Reskin, B. F. and Roos, P. A. (1990). *Job Queues, Gender Queues: Explaining Women's Inroads in Male Occupations*, Philadelphia: Temple University Press.

Reuter, P., MacCoun, R., and P. Murphy (1990). *Money from Crime: A Study of the Economics of Drug Dealing in Washington, DC*, Santa Monica, CA: The Rand Corporation, Drug Policy Research Center.

Robbins, C. (1989). Sex Differences in Psychosocial Consequences of Alcohol and Drug Abuse, *Journal of Health and Social Behavior* 30: 117–30.

Roberts, D. E. (1991). Punishing Drug Addicts who Have Babies: Women of Color, Equality and the Right of Privacy, *Harvard Law Review*, 104(7): 1419–82.

Rock, P. (1977). Review of Smart's 'Women, Crime and Criminology', *British Journal of Criminology* 17: 392–95.

Rodriguez, C. E. (1989). *Puerto Ricans: Born in the USA*, Boston: Unwin Hyman.

Rogler, L. and Santana-Cooney, R. (1984). *Puerto Rican Families in New York City: Intergenerational Processes*, Maplewood, NJ: Waterfront.

Rosenbaum, M. (1979). Difficulties in Taking Care of Business: Women Addicts as Mothers, *American Journal of Drug and Alcohol Abuse* 6(4): 431–46.

Rosenbaum, M. (1981a). Sex Roles Among Deviants: The Woman Addict, *International Journal of the Addictions* 16(5): 859–77.

Rosenbaum, M. (1981b). When Drugs Come into the Picture, Love Flies out the Window: Love Relationships Among Women Addicts, *International Journal of the Addictions* 16(7): 1197–206.

Rosenbaum, M. (1981c). *Women on Heroin*, New Brunswick, NJ: Rutgers University Press.

Rosenbaum, M., Murphy, S., Irwin, J., and L. Watson (1990). Women and Crack: What's the Real Story, unpublished paper.

Rossi, P. H. (1989). *Down and Out in America: The Origins of Homelessness*, Chicago: University of Chicago Press.

Roth, P. (ed.) (1991a). *Alcohol and Drugs are Women's Issues*, Volume 1: A Review of the Issues, Metuchen, NJ: Women's Action Alliance and The Scarecrow Press Inc.

Roth, P. (ed.) (1991b). *Alcohol and Drugs are Women's Issues*, Volume 2: The Model Program Guide, Metuchen, NJ: Women's Action Alliance and The Scarecrow Press Inc.

Russell, D. E. H. (1983). The Incidence and Prevalence of Intrafamilial and Extrafamilial Sexual Abuse of Female Children, *Child Abuse and Neglect: The International Journal* 7(2): 133–46.

Russell, D. E. H. (1986). *The Secret Trauma: Incest in the Lives of Girls and Women*, New York: Basic Books.

Russell, S. A. and Wilsnack, S. (1991). Adult Survivors of Child Sexual Abuse: Substance Abuse and Other Consequences, in P. Roth (ed.) *Alcohol and Drugs Are Women's Issues*, Volume 1: A Review of the Issues, Metuchen, NJ: Women's Action Alliance and The Scarecrow Press Inc, pp. 61–70.

Russell, S. A., Wilsnack, S. C., Klassen, A. D., and Deitz, S. R. (1988). Consequences of Childhood Sexual Abuse among Problem Drinking and Nonproblem Drinking Women in a US National Survey, paper presented at the Annual Meeting, American Society of Criminology, Chicago, November.

Said, E. W. (1979). *Orientalism*, New York: Vintage Books.

Said, E. W. (1989). Representing the Colonized: Anthropology's Interlocutors, *Critical Inquiry* 15 (Winter): 205–25.

Sassen-Koob, S. (1983). Labor Migration and the New Industrial Division of Labor, in J. Nash and M. P. Fernandez-Kelly (eds.) *Women, Men and the International Division of Labour*, New York: SUNY Press.

Sassen-Koob, S. (1985). Changing Composition and Labor Market Location of Hispanic Immigrants in New York City, in G. Borjas and M. Tienda (eds.) *Hispanics in the US Economy*, New York: Academic Press, pp. 299–322.

Sassen-Koob, S. (1986). New York City Economic Restructuring and Immigration, *Development and Change* 17: 85–119.

Sassen-Koob, S. (1987). Growth and Informalization at the Core, in M. P. Smith and J. R. Feagin (eds.) *The Capitalist City*, New York: Blackwell.

Sassen-Koob, S. (1988). *The Mobility of Labor and Capital*. New York: Cambridge University Press.

Sassen-Koob, S. (1989). New York City's Informal Economy, in A. Portes, M. Castells, and L. A. Benton (eds.) *The Informal Economy: Studies in Advanced and Less Developed Countries*, Baltimore, MD: The Johns Hopkins University Press, pp. 60–77.

Sassen-Koob, S. (1991). The Informal Economy, in J. H. Mollenkopf and M. Castells (eds.) *Dual City: Restructuring New York*, New York: Russell Sage Foundation, pp. 79–101.

Scheper-Huges, N. (1992). *Death without Weeping: The Violence of Everyday Life in Brazil*, Berkeley: University of California Press.

Schur, E. (1969). *Our Criminal Society: The Social and Legal Sources of Crime*, Englewood Cliffs, NJ: Prentice Hall.

Scott, J. C. (1985). *Weapons of the Weak: Everyday Forms of Peasant Resistance*, New Haven: Yale University Press.

Sears, K. B. (1989). The Significance of Relationships with Important Male 'Others' in the First Conviction of Female Offenders, (Doctoral dissertation), The Fielding Institute, Ann Arbor, MI: University Microfilms International.

Sedlak, A. J. (1991a). *National Incidence and Prevalence of Child Abuse and Neglect: 1988*. Washington, DC: Westat Inc.

Sedlak, A. J. (1991b). *Supplementary Analyses of Data on the National Incidence of Child Abuse and Neglect: 1988*, Washington, DC: Westat Inc.

Sharff, J. W. (1987). The Underground Economy of a Poor Neighborhood, in L. Mullings (ed.) *Cities of the United States: Studies in Urban Anthropology*, New York: Columbia University Press, pp. 19–50.

Shaw, C. R. (1930). *The Jack Roller*, Chicago: University of Chicago Press.

Shostak, M. (1981). *Nisa: The Life and Words of a !Kung Woman*, Cambridge MA: Harvard University Press.

Shostak, M. (1989). What the Wind Won't Take Away: The Genesis of Nisa—the Life and Words of a !Kung Woman, in The Personal Narratives Group (eds.) *Interpreting Women's Lives: Feminist Theory and Personal Narratives*, Bloomington: Indiana University Press.

Shover, N. (1991). Burglary, in M. Tonry (ed.) *Crime and Justice: A Review of Research*, (*Crime and Justice* Volume 14), Chicago: University of Chicago Press, pp. 73–113.

Silbert, M. H. and Pines, A. M. (1984). Occupational Hazards of Street Prostitutes, *Criminal Justice and Behavior* 8(4): 395–9.

Simms, M. C. (1988). *The Choices that Young Black Women Make: Education, Employment and Family Formation*, Wellesley College Center for Research on Women, Working Paper No. 190.

Simms, M. C. and J. Malveaux (eds.) (1989). *Slipping Through the Cracks: The Status of Black Women*, New Brunswick, NJ: Transaction Books.

Simon, R. (1975). *Women and Crime*. Lexington, MA: Lexington Books.

Simone, T. M. (1989). *About Face: Race in Postmodern America*, NY: Automedia.

Smart, C. (1976). *Women, Crime and Criminology: A Feminist Critique*, London: Routledge and Kegan Paul.

Smart, C. (1977). Reply to Paul Rock, *British Journal of Criminology* 17: 397–9.

Smart, C. (1979). The New Female Criminal: Reality or Myth?, *British Journal of Criminology* 19: 50–9.

Smart, C. (1989). *Feminism and the Power of Law*, New York: Routledge.

Smithberg, N. and Westermeyer, J. (1985). White Dragon Pearl Syndrome: A Female Pattern of Drug Dependence, *American Journal of Drug and Alcohol Abuse* 11: 199–207.

Sokoloff, N. J. (1992). *Black Women and White Women in the Professions: Occupational Segregation by Race and Gender, 1960–1980*, New York: Routledge.

Solomon, F. (1988). *1987 Narcotics Division Arrests: Arrestee Characteristics and Criminal Court Case Processing*, New York: New York City Criminal Justice Agency.

Sommers, I. and Baskin, D. (1991). The Situational Context of Violent Female Offending, paper presented at the Annual Meetings of the American Society of Criminology, San Francisco, November.

Sommers, I. and Baskin, D. (1992). Sex, Race, Age, and Violent Offending, *Violence and Victims* 7(3): 191–201.

Soto, E. (1983). Sex Role Traditionalism and Assertiveness in Puerto Rican Women Living in the United States, *Journal of Community Psychology* 11: 346–54.

Sowder, B. and Weissman, G. (1989). NADR Project Revealing New Data on High-risk Behavior among Women, *NADR Network* 1(2).

Spalter-Roth, R. M. (1988). The Sexual Political Economy of Street Vending in Washington, DC, in G. Clark (ed.) *Traders Versus the State: Anthropological Approaches to Unofficial Economies*, Boulder, CO: Westview Press, pp. 165–87.

Spiller, H. (1987). Mama's Baby, Papa's Maybe: An American Grammar Book, *Diacritics* 17(2): 65–81.

Spivak, G. C. (1986). Imperialism and Sexual Difference, *Oxford Literary Review* 8(1&2): 225–40.

Spradley, J. P. (1979). *The Ethnographic Interview*, New York: Holt, Rinehart and Winston.

Spunt, B., Goldstein, P. J., Belluci, P., and T. Miller (1990). Race, Ethnicity and Gender Differences in the Drugs-Violence Relationship, *Journal of Psychoactive Drugs* 22(3): 293–303.

Stacey, J. (1988). Can There be a Feminist Ethnography?, *Women's Studies International Forum* 11(1): 21–7.

Stacey, J. (1991). Can There be a Feminist Ethnography?, in S. B. Gluck and

D. Patai (eds.) *Women's Words: The Feminist Practice of Oral History*, New York: Routledge, pp. 111–19.

Stack, C. B. (1974a). *All Our Kin: Strategies for Survival in a Black Community*, New York: Harper and Row.

Stack, C. B. (1974b). Sex Roles and Survival Strategies in an Urban Black Community, in M. Zimbalist Rosaldo and L. Lamphere (eds.) *Woman, Culture and Society*, Stanford: Stanford University Press, pp. 113–28.

Stanley, L. L. (1918). Morphinism and Crime, reprinted in H. W. Morgan (1974), *Yesterday's Addicts: American Society and Drug Abuse, 1865–1920*, Norman: University of Oklahoma Press, pp. 80–5.

Stansell, C. (1982). Women, Children, and the Uses of the Streets: Class and Gender Conflict in New York City, 1850–1860, *Feminist Studies* 2: 309–35.

Steffensmeier, D. (1980). Sex Differences in Patterns of Adult Crime 1965–1977: A Review and Assessment, *Social Forces* 58: 1080–108.

Steffensmeier, D. (1983). Organization Properties and Sex-Segregation in the Underworld: Building a Sociological Theory of Sex Differences in Crime, *Social Forces* 61(4): 1010–32.

Steffensmeier, D. and Streifel, C. (1993). Trends in Female Crime 1960–1990, in C. C. Culliver (ed.) *Female Criminality: The State of the Art*, New York: Garland Publishing, pp. 63–101.

Steffensmeier, D., Steffensmeier, R. H., and Rosenthal, A. L. (1979). Trends in Female Violence 1970–1977, *Sociological Focus* 12(3): 217–27.

Sterk, C. E. and Elifson, K. W. (1990). Drug-Related Violence and Street Prostitution, in M. de La Rosa, E. Y. Lambert, and B. Gropper, (eds.) *Drugs and Violence: Causes, Correlates, and Consequences*, NIDA Research Monograph 103, Rockville, MD: National Institute on Drug Abuse.

Strang, J., Griffiths, P., and M. Gossop. (1990) Crack and Cocaine Use in South London Drug Addicts: 1987–1989, *British Journal of Addiction* 85(2): 193–6.

Suffet, F. and Brotman, R. (1976). Female Drug Use: Some Observations, *International Journal of the Addictions* 11: 19–23.

Sullivan, M. L. (1986). Getting Over: Economy, Culture and Youth Crime in Three Urban Neighbourhoods, (Doctoral dissertation, Columbia University), Ann Arbor MI: University Microfilms International.

Sullivan, M. L. (1989). *Getting Paid: Youth Crime and Work in the Inner City*, Ithaca, NY: Cornell University Press.

Sum, A., Fogg, N., and R. Taggart (1988). Whithered Dreams: The Decline in the Economic Fortunes of Young, Non-College Educated Male Adults and Their Families, unpublished paper prepared for the William T. Grant Foundation Commission on Family, Work, and Citizenship.

Susser, I. (1982). *Norman Street: Poverty and Politics in an Urban Neighborhood*, New York: Oxford University Press.

Sutter, A. G. (1966). The World of the Righteous Dope Fiend, *Issues in Criminology* 2(2): 177–222.

Suttles, G. (1968). *The Social Order of the Slum*, Chicago: University of Chicago Press.

Sutton, C. R. (1987). The Caribbeanization of New York City and the Emergence of a Transnational Socio-Cultural System, in C. R. Sutton and E. M. Chaney (eds.) *Caribbean Life in New York City: Sociocultural Dimensions*, New York: Center for Migration Studies, pp. 15–30.

Taylor, A. (1993). *Women Drug Users: An Ethnography of a Female Injecting Community*, Oxford: Clarendon Press.

Taylor, C. S. (1990). *Dangerous Society*, East Lansing: Michigan State University Press.

Taylor, C. S. (1993). *Girls, Gangs, Women and Drugs*, East Lansing: Michigan State University Press.

Tedlock, D. (1983). *The Spoken Word and the Work of Interpretation*, Philadelphia: University of Pennsylvania Press.

Terry, C. E. and Pellens, M. (1928). *The Opium Problem*, New York: Bureau of Social Hygiene.

Thrasher, F. M. (1926). *The Gang*, Chicago: University of Chicago Press.

Tonry, M. and Wilson, J. Q. (eds.) (1990) *Drugs and Crime*, (Crime and Justice, Volume 13), Chicago: University of Chicago Press.

Treiman, D. and Hartman, H. (1981). *Women, Work and Wages*, Washington, DC: National Academy Press.

US Commission on Civil Rights (1972). *Demographic, Social, and Economic Characteristics of New York City and the New York Metropolitan Area* (Hearings on the Civil Rights of Puerto Ricans, Staff Report, February), Washington, DC: US Government Printer.

US Department of Labor, Bureau of Labor Statistics (1987). *Area Manpower Survey: New York Regional Office*, Washington DC: US Government Printing Office.

Valentine, B. (1978). *Hustling and Other Hard Work: Life Styles in the Ghetto*, New York: Free Press.

Vanderstaay, S. (1992). *Street Lives: An Oral History of Homeless Americans*, Philadelphia: New Society Publishers.

Vandor, M., Juliana, P. and R. Leone (1991). Women and Illegal Drugs, in P. Roth (ed.) *Alcohol and Drugs are Women's Issues*, Volume 1: A Review of the Issues, Metuchen, NJ: Women's Action Alliance and The Scarecrow Press Inc., pp. 155–60.

Vigil, D. (1988). *Barrio Gangs*, Austin: University of Texas Press.

Wacquant, L. J. D. (1992). Toward a Social Praxeology: The Structure and Logic of Bourdieu's Sociology, in P. Bourdieu and L. Wacquant, *An Invitation to Reflexive Sociology*, Cambridge: Polity Press.

Waldinger, R. (1985). Immigration and Industrial Change in the New York City Apparel Industry, in G. J. Borjas and M. Tienda (eds.) *Hispanics in the U. S. Economy*, New York: Academic Press.

Waldorf, D. (1973). *Careers in Dope*, Englewood Cliffs, NJ: Prentice Hall.

Waldorf, D., Reinarman, C., and S. Murphy (1991). *Cocaine Changes: The Experience of Using and Quitting*, Philadelphia: Temple University Press.

Walkowitz, J. R. (1980). *Prostitution and Victorian Society: Women, Class and the State*, Cambridge: Cambridge University Press.

Wallace, R. (1985). *Shock Waves of Community Disintegration in New York: Public Policy and the Burning of the Bronx*, New York: PISCS Inc.

Wallace, R. and Wallace, D. (1986). *Origins of Public Health Collapse in New York City: The Dynamics of Planned Shrinkage, Contagious Urban Decay and Social Disintegration*, New York: PISCS Inc.

Waterston, A. (1993). *Street Addicts in the Political Economy*, Philadelphia: Temple University Press.

Weatherby, N. L., Schultz, J. M., Chitwood, D. D., McCoy, H. V., McCoy, C. B., Ludwig, D. D., and B. R. Edlin (1992). Crack Cocaine Use and Sexual Activity in Miami, Florida, *Journal of Psychoactive Drugs* 24(4): 373–80.

Weeks, J. (1981). *Sex, Politics and Society: The Regulation of Modern Sexuality Since 1800*, London: Longman.

Weeks, J. (1985). *Sexuality and its Discontents: Meanings, Myths and Modern Sexualities*, London: Routledge and Kegan Paul.

Weiner, N. A. and M. E. Wolfgang, (1985). The Extent and Character of Violent Crime in America, in L. A. Curtis (ed.) *American Violence and Public Policy*, New Haven: Yale University Press.

Wellman, B. (1985). Domestic Work, Paid Work and Net Work, in S. Duck and D. Perlman (eds.) *Understanding Personal Relationships*, London: Sage.

Weppner, R. S. (ed.) (1977). *Street Ethnography: Selected Studies of Crime and Drug Use in Natural Settings*, Beverly Hills, CA: Sage.

White, R. (1990). *No Space of Their Own: Young People and Social Control in Australia*, Melbourne: Cambridge University Press.

Whyte, W. F. (1943). *Street Corner Society*, Chicago: University of Chicago Press.

Widom, C. S. (1989). Child Abuse, Neglect and Violent Criminal Behavior, *Criminology* 27: 251–71.

Widom, C. S. (1990). *The Cycle of Violence*, National Institute of Justice Research in Brief, Washington, DC: US Department of Justice.

Williams, G. (1967). Control by Licensing, *Current Legal Problems* 20: 81–103.

Williams, R. (1976). *Keywords: A Vocabulary of Culture and Society*, London: Fontana.

Williams, R. (1988). *Beyond Human Capital: Black Women, Work and Wages*, Wellesley College Center for Research on Women, Working Paper No. 183.

Williams, T. (1989). *The Cocaine Kids*, Reading, MA: Addison-Wesley.

Williams, T. (1992). *Crackhouse: Notes From the End of the Line*, New York: Addison-Wesley.

Williams, T., Dunlap, E., Johnson, B. D., and A. Hamid (1992). Personal Safety in Dangerous Places, *Journal of Contemporary Ethnography* 21(3): 343–74.

Willis, P. (1977). *Learning to Labour*, Farnborough, UK: Saxon House.

Wilson, N. K. (1993). Stealing and Dealing: The Drug War and Gendered Criminal Opportunity, in C. C. Culliver (ed.) *Female Criminality: The State of the Art*, New York: Garland Publishing, pp. 169–94.

Wilson, W. J. (1987). *The Truly Disadvantaged: The Inner City, the Underclass, and Public Policy*, Chicago: University of Chicago Press.

Wolfson, N. (1976). Speech Events and Natural Speech: Some Implications for Sociolinguistic Methodology, *Language and Society* 5(2): 189–209.

Woodiwiss, M. (1988). *Crime, Crusades and Corruption: Prohibitions in the United States 1900–1987*, London: Pinter Publishers.

Worth, D. (1990). Minority Women and AIDS; Culture, Race and Gender, in D. Feldman (ed.) *Culture and AIDS*, New York: Praeger.

Wyatt, G. E. (1985). The Sexual Abuse of Afro-American Women and White Women in Childhood, *Child Abuse and Neglect: The International Journal* 9: 507–19.

Young, E. (1990). The Role of Incest Issues in Relapse, *Journal of Psychoactive Drugs* 22(2): 249–58.

Young, L. (1954). *Out of Wedlock*, New York: McGraw-Hill.

Young, M. and Willmott, P. (1957). *Family and Kinship in East London*, London: Routledge and Kegan Paul.

Zedner, L. (1991). Women, Crime, and Penal Responses: A Historical Account, in M. Tonry (ed.) *Crime and Justice: A Review of Research*, (*Crime and Justice* Volume 14), Chicago: University of Chicago Press, pp. 307–62.

Zinberg, N. E. (1984). *Drug, Set and Setting: The Basis for Controlled Intoxicant Use*, New Haven: Yale University Press.

Index